BULLYING

LAURA MARTOCCI

BULLYING

The Social Destruction of Self

TEMPLE UNIVERSITY PRESS
Philadelphia   Rome   Tokyo

TEMPLE UNIVERSITY PRESS
Philadelphia, Pennsylvania 19122
www.temple.edu/tempress

Library of Congress Cataloging-in-Publication Data

Martocci, Laura.
  Bullying : the social destruction of self / Laura Martocci.
    pages cm
  Includes bibliographical references and index.
  ISBN 978-1-4399-1072-6 (hardback : alk. paper) —
ISBN 978-1-4399-1073-3 (paper : alk. paper) — ISBN 978-1-4399-
1074-0 (e-book) 1. Bullying. 2. Social psychology. I. Title.
  BF637.B85.M268 2014
  302.34'3—dc23

                                             2014018162

♾ The paper used in this publication meets the requirements of the
American National Standard for Information Sciences—Permanence
of Paper for Printed Library Materials, ANSI Z39.48-1992

Printed in the United States of America

   6 8 9 7 5

For Jonathan, Noa, and Quin,

my supportive bystanders

You know, I think of loss in terms of myself—you know, I changed my name, I changed my name, I changed who I was. At least once I turned down being in a smarter class than I could have been because I just didn't want to be like [*pauses*] you know.
—Dan

I didn't cry. I didn't lash out. I just withdrew. It didn't give me any satisfaction. I mean, you want to strike back with a vengeance. [*Pauses*] And as old as I am now, if I see someone walking down the hallway who looks beefy or muscular, I have to consciously tell myself that I am not in a position of subservience to that person. I am not secondary to that person, not inferior. I actually have to tell myself that because I [*pauses*] just instinctively defer to that person as a superior, as an alpha dog.
—Ken

Even today I hide out because I think if I get too big, too visible, I feel unsafe. At the same time I want [to be visible].
—Anonymous

One thing after another in seventh grade and I stopped trying to excel—at anything—for fear of public humiliation.
—Laurie

CONTENTS

Preface   xi

Acknowledgments   xiii

Introduction   1

1 The Cultural-Historical Foundations of Bullying Culture   8

   A Brief Synopsis of Cultural Change   8
   Religion and Shame: The Historical Possibility of Redemption   15
   The Socialization of Children and the Root of Contemporary Shame   19
   Constructing a Social Problem: Bullying and the Double-Edged
   Sword of the Media   22

2 Social Forces and Bullying   27

   Gossip   28
   Laughter   35
   Stereotypes and Categories   40
   Competition   45

3 Shame and Identity   55

   Shame: The Social Mechanics of a Social Emotion   57
   Shame and Anger   64
   The Psychodynamics of Anger and the Neurodynamics of Pain   70
   Guilt   79
   Re-visioning Shame: The Strengths and Weaknesses
   of a New Paradigm   81
   Summary   87

4 Grieving and Grief Work: Negotiating Social Pain and Personal Loss   89

   Traditional Conceptualizations of Grief   96
   New Models of Grieving and Grief Work   100
   Bullying: A Special Case of Loss and the Pitfall of Rumination   103
   Rumination and Depression: Social-Psychological-Neurological
   Interface   106
   A Final Note   113

5 Narrative Writing and the Reconstruction of Self   116

   Overview   116
   Storying the Brain   117
   Expressive Writing: Integrating the Neural, the Social, and
   the Psychological   120
   Storying Experiences: Writing Chaos and the Reclamation of Voice   127
   Memory   133
   Narrating an Audience and Defining a Victim: The Paradox
   of Social Stories   138
   A Final Note   140

6 Tying Up Loose Ends: Challenges *to* Bystanders, Challenges
   of Cyberspace   142

   Everyone Else: A Breakdown of Bystander Responsibility   144
   Cyberspace: New Dynamics, New Challenges, New Potentials   148

   Postscript: Practical Suggestions   154

   Appendix A: The Uniqueness of Self and Personal Biography   157

   Appendix B: The Re-visioning of Liberation and Womanist
   Theologies   158

   Appendix C: Scheff and Retzinger: The Redemptive Role of
   Communication   160

   Appendix D: Lyn Lofland's "Threads of Social Connectedness"   162

   Appendix E: The Dynamics Underlying Expressive Writing:
   Why Does It Work?   163

   Appendix F: Traumarama!, *Seventeen* Magazine, and
   Prepackaged Shame   164

   Notes   167

   References   191

   Index   207

PREFACE

I was bullied.

Like many others, I have a story to tell.

A story to fashion and refashion, depending on the reason it comes to mind and to whom I am recounting it.

Unlike many others, I have no horrific incident to narrate, no turning point in middle or high school for which I am still seeking closure. Although I sat at a distance from the popular lunch table and was rarely invited to parties, I had a coterie of close friends. While I might have felt pangs of exclusion and can still name classmates who found something about me they could snicker at, I don't really remember their words. My few, close friendships insulated me, and luckily, none of those friends betrayed my trust.

Instead, my traumatic experience of bullying occurred after the tumultuous school years, when I was an adult. And it is more than likely that this book was prompted by my need to make sense of that experience.

Yet even now, as I sit in front of my computer and contemplate sharing this story, I feel a faint inner quaking. I imagine *her* reading the words and reviving her campaigns of subversion. I can *feel* the exaggerated eye roll that curdled my confidence, the one that preceded a contemptuous "*Ohhhh pleeeeeeassse*" (followed by a condescending commentary on my choices or a twisted re-visioning of my actions and intentions, all rounded off with the names of everyone who agreed). At the same time I imagine my friends today, shaking their heads and sighing, "Ugh, why do you still let her bother you? *Who cares* what she might say? Really, what *can* she do at this point?" (And I know what they aren't saying—get over it!)

And they are right. So how do I explain my distinct, ongoing unease?

Mostly I don't. I pour another glass of wine and change the subject, because it is embarrassing to admit that my heart still pounds at the thought of running into her; that she still, somehow, provokes anxiety in me; and that, like someone with post-traumatic stress disorder, I only manage the distress I feel, no longer expecting equanimity.

Undeniably, any lingering stress is compounded by its own illegitimacy. Like many victims, I learned not only that the psychic devastation I experienced was invalid but that ongoing reverberations reflect my own inadequacy. Owing to this, my experiences remain shadowed by shame. Troublesome memories of my own complicity in victimization feed the recurring echoes of trauma. How did it all get so out of hand? How did a relationship become so toxic as to reduce a promising doctoral candidate (who had lived and lectured internationally) to a depressed, inadequate shell of her—of my—former self? What could have caused me to view accomplishments as inconsequential and self-image as fraudulent? How did I come to believe that the angry, insecure woman I was reduced to was my true self, unmasked at last? What were the weapons that destroyed confidence in my intelligence and professionalism and the hopes and aspirations that fed them?

In exploring my own story, I have come to write a social story of bullying—an academic narrative to be sure, yet one informed by incessant poking and probing at psychic wounds and by scrutiny of the grounds for their healing.

ACKNOWLEDGMENTS

This book took shape with the support and input of a diverse, unrelated cohort of individuals. First and foremost, I am deeply indebted to all the victims who offered to revisit their pain and share their memories. Many of the interviews I conducted do not appear in these pages, but the voices of everyone I spoke with enriched my understanding of both victimization and support, as well as the cost of survival. I am particularly grateful to Ken, Dan, Laurie, Caroline, and an anonymous participant, all of whom allowed me to transcribe their shame.

I am also indebted to the Interlibrary Loan staff of Wagner College, who made it their personal business to track down every request I sent their way.

My students, especially Alexandra Mallilo, Chris Fourman, Samantha Siegel, and Danielle Lucchese, committed many personal hours to the SARA Project, expanding and adapting the intervention (in elementary school classrooms), bringing back stories, spurring insights, and training new students. My debt to them is enormous.

My family, including my parents, Mary and Tony, and my dear palooza friends all supported this project over the past months, in tangible and intangible ways. I am deeply grateful for their encouragement, love, and forbearance.

Finally, my editors, Micah Kleit at Temple and Rebecca Logan and Mary Ann Short at Newgen, supported this project with patience, grace, and insight. Lucia Stern and Jonathan Bricklin also offered invaluable feedback, and I am profoundly appreciative of their gentle candor.

BULLYING

INTRODUCTION

In the late 1990s a rash of shootings—eight separate incidents occurring between October 1997 and May 1999—stunned the nation. Beginning on October 1, 1997, when Luke Woodham killed his mother and then went to school, where he gunned down nine classmates (killing two), the tragedies continued with Michael Carneal's rampage in Paducah, Kentucky, where, on December 1, 1997, he killed three and wounded five; Joseph Todd's killing of two in Stamps, Arkansas, two weeks later; Mitchell Johnson and Andrew Golden's March 1998 shooting spree, which killed five and wounded ten in Westside, Arkansas; Andrew Wurst's April 25 killing of a teacher and wounding of three students at a dinner-dance in Edinboro, Pennsylvania; Kip Kinkel's murder of his parents and subsequent school cafeteria rampage, during which he killed two and wounded twenty-five in May 1998; Dylan Klebold and Eric Harris's horrific April 1999 carnage at Columbine High School, which killed thirteen and injured twenty-four; and T. J. Solomon's May 20, 1999, shooting and injuring of six at Heritage High School in Conyers, Georgia.[1] The epidemic appeared to have run its course—for the moment. But what had caused it? What should and could we do to prevent another tragedy?

This series of school shootings woke us up to the paucity of cultural narratives that speak to violence, youth culture, and, as I argue in this book, *shame*. School shootings functioned as a prism, exposing and focusing attention on the nasty underbelly of social interaction. Early assessment of these tragedies made it clear that the usual suspects, with profiles grounded in class or race, were not responsible for the rampages. The shooters were not angry young men with histories of run-ins with authorities. Most did not lack material assets, come from broken families, or strike those around them as degenerate. None abused drugs or were characterized by their peers as mentally unstable (e.g., a loose cannon that had finally gone off).[2] And perhaps most surprisingly, none appeared to be looking to exact revenge. Often, in fact, the shooters were unaware of whom they hit—nearly all witnesses described the killings as random (Newman et al. 2004; Cullen 2009; Langman 2009).[3] If stereotypes linked to deviance (economic or racial motivations), mental instability, and revenge are sidelined, how are we to make sense of these atrocities? What could possibly have motivated this level of violence, seemingly perpetrated by the kids next door? Behind the question *why* stood gunmen we *all* knew. Every school has Klebolds, Carneals, and Johnsons. Their very familiarity was—is—deeply disturbing and precludes formulaic answers. It precludes, even, a determination of whether they were acting, as both deviance and mental instability narratives would argue, or *reacting*, as revenge narratives would contend.

The day after Columbine, speculation by an ad hoc group of news personalities and psychologists identified the shooters as cultural deviants (emos,* hipsters, Marilyn Manson fans, and other assorted pathetic, antiestablishment wannabes) but soon moved to portraying the young gunmen as driven to extremes by humiliation, marginalization, and social disgrace. The killers were social outcasts, bullied and provoked beyond tolerable limits and goaded by violent movies and video games, lax parenting (and laxer-still gun laws), and Satan. By and large white, middle class, and unremarkable, all the young shooters committed unthinkable atrocities. But were *they* responsible? Or were they victims?[4] Could the Sturm und Drang of adolescent culture in the late twentieth century produce a pain capable of provoking these rampages? Of motivating suicides?

Bullying narratives, which shifted responsibility from deviant subcultures (with inordinate influence over young white males) to normative behaviors within adolescent culture, made sense of the shootings and were quickly embraced and endorsed by the public. Numerous books (*Lost Boys*, 2000; *Odd Girl Out*, 2002; *Queen Bees and Wannabes*, 2002; *Rampage*, 2004) and movies (*Mean Girls*, 2004) delved deep into the violence at the heart of (male and female) adolescent culture. These early offerings and countless other books, movies, podcasts, TED talks, conferences, and symposia over the years have attempted to color in our (minimal, outdated) sketches of the social forces buffeting our youth.

Whether these analyses, in their detailed constructions of adolescent economies, have correctly assessed the motives underlying the school tragedies is,

---

* *Emos*, as it is used here, refers to shy, sensitive, angst-ridden teens. Clad primarily in T-shirts and jeans, they are critical of mainstream culture, even antiestablishment, and are often linked to a depressed or angry affect.

at this point, a moot question. The fact is society has bought into the notion of bully cultures (despite lone voices that question the accuracy of the bullying rationale, with its simplistic good-versus-evil characterizations of behavior).[5] Whether it is *the* driving force behind school rampages and teen suicides or simply links the horrific and inexplicable to familiar—and thus comfortable—cultural narratives (such as victimization or injustice corrected by a mythic lone rebel taking matters into his own hands) is no longer relevant. Bullying has become the cause du jour, linking shooters to an extant dynamic in need of reappraisal. The identification of common social markers (peripheral social status, effeminate behavior) coupled with individual personality traits (low self-esteem, depression, anger) placed emphasis on psychological factors (as opposed to economic, racial, or evil forces). This psychodynamic starting point, which called for elaborations to well-worn narratives, could account for the *recurrence* of rampages, as well as the similarities and differences in both shooters and communities. Psychologistic rationales framed the tragedies in a way that offered the possibility of control while leaving the cultural world and our beliefs about its dynamics intact.[6]

Causal or not, bullying has been correlated with recent tragedies, drawing attention to the cruelties of adolescent culture and prompting the realization that social discourse has broken down around the commonplace experience of peer-related emotional violence. School rampages and teen suicides have become a gateway into the heart of adolescent—and cultural?—darkness.

If bullying was a problem at any of these now-infamous schools, as it is at tens of thousands of schools across the nation, why was it never addressed?

Discouraged? Censured? Reprimanded?

The easy answer to this question is that it was never identified as an issue, let alone constructed as a *social* problem. No cultural claims were made about the deleterious effects of bullying (or the deviancy of bullies), and no contributing causal factors were identified. We had yet to acknowledge the full, devastating potential that psychological cruelty could tap and had yet to link legitimate *social forces* (including gossip, stigmatization, Othering, public shaming, and ostracization) to extreme, desperate responses. Even now, having determined (correctly or incorrectly) that bullying has consequences beyond individual well-being, we remain at a loss when challenged to address it—a difficulty that is, in no small part, linked to the inability to isolate behaviors and label them deviant.[7]

The complexities surrounding any attempt to define and address bullying, as well as respond to its victims, are rooted in much larger cultural shifts and the new social issues they trailed. Changes that long ago eroded homogeneous cultural authority, fragmenting morality, muddled the lines between right

and wrong. Religious mandates and the unambiguous moral behavior and social responsibility they orchestrated were interrupted, their god weakened by
growing diversity and overrun by the (secular) engine of progress. What did it
now mean to transgress, and what would it take to atone and be forgiven? How
and in what principles were morality, justice, and redemption now grounded?
Progress signaled the twilight of traditional moral discourse. Redemption fell
by the wayside, as justice came to be increasingly oriented around respect for
the freedom and rights of the individual (see Sandel 2009).

Chapter 1 offers a cultural-historical overview of how we got here. It
frames the emergence of bullying in a brief history of culture, emphasizing
the underlying social forces and their relation to personal crises of meaning.
Mobility, rapidly changing demographics, and industrialization converged,
upending the transcendent religious authority that moored moral codes and
oriented an individual's choices, actions, and sense of purpose and identity.
Secular legal codes were concerned with protecting the right of the individual
to assert personal tastes, preferences, and points of view, while public opinion (grounded in the import accorded to others' attitudes and sentiments)
assumed responsibility for curbing preferences and dictating the *right* point
of view. With greater and greater frequency, the vacillating court of public
opinion (others) handed down judgments, meted out sentences, and oversaw
compliance. Their opinions, no less than any religious branding of the flesh,
inscribed inadequacies, reputations, and identity on the body, asserting dominion over minds and souls. To the extent that individuals were invested
in others, moored to and contingent on their gaze, identity was tethered to
their capricious impressions, assumptions, and speculations. And these were
no longer guided by shared, overarching values.

Yet as David Riesman points out in *The Lonely Crowd* (1950), others came
to afford the individual a sense of belonging and identity, providing a refuge
from the psychological and ontological insecurity that followed the decenter-
ing of God and the moral universe. They safeguarded her from the meaningless and ennui that accompanied this displacement, which was compounded
by abundance and the lessening of struggles for survival. Plenty and an ethos
of consumption had further loosened her tether to a known world, one oriented by the necessity of production. The disequilibrium wrought by these
radical economic and cultural changes was stabilized by others, but at what
cost?*

---

* Michel Foucault considered "gaze" to be integral to surveillance and the regulation of
power in society. For Foucault (who focused on the institutionalization of gaze and its
articulation in systems of surveillance in his seminal *Discipline and Punish* [1975]), gaze
is a relationship. It speaks to the distribution of power, self-regulation, and beliefs about
knowledge (who gazes, and who is gazed upon?).

Through an elaboration of the construction of self and the role of others in the search for meaning (on a cultural as well as a personal level), the problem of bullying is lent depth and perspective. In the wake of cultural upheaval, a waning of the possibility of redemption becomes singularly significant. The secular ramifications of this forfeiture, a consideration that emerges from the overview sketched in Chapter 1, orient the remainder of the book. As the chapters unfold, detailing the social forces that situate and maintain bullying, this potential—or its loss—looms large. In the absence of religious certainty, the crimes for which one is branded are shifting and unclear, and the possibility for expiation, reparation, and salvation, vague (who will redeem social sinners and on what grounds?). Yet it is precisely the promise of readmittance to the fold, the belief that belonging is once again possible—*hope* itself—that is missing from contemporary experiences of rejection, inadequacy, and shame.

Chapter 1 outlines social theory that may be familiar to many readers, who may prefer to start with Chapter 2, which begins to discuss the social forces that sustain bullying. Chapter 2 opens with an analysis of the dynamics of sociation* that are simultaneously engaged (or co-opted) in support of bullying: gossip, laughter, stereotyping, and competition. These legitimate forms of social discourse have the capacity to marshal social power in the policing of group norms. They function in ways that construct social bonds and create solidarity, uniting even as they divide, signaling belonging even as they reject, and absolving even while threatening condemnation. Within this dual nature lie the seeds of hope. A full grasp of this potential will enable society to (re)employ forces of destruction in the (re)construction of self and relationship. This power—the ability to turn these discourses back on themselves—must be reclaimed.

Chapter 3 explores the destructive consequence of gossip, laughter, and stereotyping: shame. Shame is a social as well as a moral emotion whose power stems from the psychological and physiological need to belong. Through shaming, society censors its members, denying relationship and rejecting claims of belonging. The chaos and pain occasioned by public humiliation is often managed by anger or violence, oriented externally or internally. Aggression denies the break that is threatened by shame, while defending the coherence of the assumptive world, by *blaming* (other or self). Reactive, it responds to the anguish of social rejection with passionate attempts at damage control—or control by damage—aimed at the (internal) source or (external) cause of pain. Disruptive, even offensive, behavior is tolerated and perhaps promoted by a culture that denies shame and is thus incapable of holding out hope for its resolution. Awareness of the complexities that intertwine shame and rage did

---

* *Sociation*, according to *Merriam-Webster*'s online dictionary, is a mode or process of social interaction, whether associative or dissociative.

in fact surface in many analyses that attempted to make sense of school rampages. Despite this connection, response to these tragedies (extensive, costly school interventions) has not privileged shame. Shame remains hidden. It is an illegitimate, shameful emotion. And as long as it remains unacknowledged, bullying and victimization cannot be effectively addressed.

Chapters 4 and 5 respond to the social significances of shame and the rupture of connection outlined in Chapter 3. Recognition of the nature of the damage done by bullying—the disorientation caused by the severance of self-sustaining bonds to community—positions victims and orients attempts to redress their plight. If society truly grasps and acknowledges the pain and confusion caused by emotional violence and psychological abuse, it will quickly come to provide victims the space they require for mourning their loss of connection. In this model, *recognition* of a victim's need is itself inclusive, and its accommodation goes far toward supporting her attempts to renegotiate her relationship to the world. Social space given over to grieving in addition to sympathy protocols, including allowances made for grief work, are integral to her process and are discussed at length. In addition, the neuropsychological consequences of social rejection are considered: if factored into her overall state, as well as her capacity for response, what we now know about brain-firing *requires* grief paradigms.

Ultimately, her processing of social pain (grief work) affords her the possibility to *construct different self-narratives*—ones that, in repositioning Others, reposition self. Chapter 5 explores means by which she can find and (re)claim her voice, embracing her lack, her pain, her truth. In renarrating self, she begets significances for (and redeems) her pain, transforming the wreckage of shame into a story that connects past, present, and future (Martocci 2013). The potential for transformation—the promise reflected in caterpillars becoming butterflies, ugly ducklings becoming swans, a phoenix rising from the ashes—already exists in stories that circulate within culture. They can be readily appropriated by bullying-victim narratives to highlight and reinforce latent, imaginable, dormant, future possibilities.

In this re-visioning, both the community and bystanders are key. Chapter 6 attempts to tie up loose ends with regard to bystander responsiveness and begins to address the novel exigencies that attend the dynamics of sociation in cyberspace. Throughout these considerations it becomes clear that, despite the breakdown of cultural and moral authority, the preoccupation with self, and the legal enshrinement of individual freedoms, there remains an ongoing longing for community (see, for example, John Hewitt's *Dilemmas of the American Self* [1989], Robert Putnam's *Bowling Alone* [2000], Robert Bellah and colleagues' "lifestyle enclaves" [1985], Benedict Anderson's "imagined communities" [(1983) 1991], and Anthony Cohen's "communities of meaning" [1985]).[8] This desire may have roots in our evolutionary history and be hardwired into our brains (a possibility explored in Chapter 3). Community, however vaguely it is constructed and defined, retains an ability to motivate personal behavior and coordinate civic action. *We*, as a community, have identified bullying as a social problem, and we, as a community and as bystanders, must learn *how* to become a condition of possibility for victims. What exactly is needed from us, as culture begins to script hope, redemption, empathy, and transformation into emerging narratives?

1

THE CULTURAL-HISTORICAL
FOUNDATIONS OF
BULLYING CULTURE

There was something particularly American about it—
blaming yourself for bad luck—*that resistance to seeing our
life as affected by social forces*, a tendency to attribute larger
problems to individual behavior.
    —PHILIPP MEYER, *American Rust* (emphasis added)

Social cruelty, public humiliation, bullying: aggressions identified in all
societies throughout history (think of the rampant gossip of European
courts—so well illustrated in movies like *Dangerous Liaisons*—or Edith
Wharton's characters, clawing their way toward a better life). Yet today, these
aggressions are implicated in suicides and rampage killings. Why? Why now
and not two centuries ago? Half a century ago? If the behaviors themselves
have not changed, what has?

One way to understand bullying in the twenty-first century is to contrast
the forces at play in contemporary society with those that prevailed in older,
more religious communities. Loss of traditional values and infrastructures
dovetailed with the unchecked expansion of competition. Identity became
linked to success—or failure. More importantly, unscrupulous means of
advancement no longer threatened damnation; nor did resisting such temp-
tations promise salvation. While the fading prospect of eternal hellfire was
significant, it was the loss of salvation—a possibility available to saints and
sinners alike—that gave rise to many of the issues and difficulties that beset
modernity. Although the new economic order opened possibilities, horizons
expanded on the backs of failures and losers. And losers, with only themselves
to blame, *had little chance of atonement or redemption.*

A Brief Synopsis of Cultural Change

It is the impotence of the cultural super-ego rather than
the potency of the id that is the crucial fact of our time.
    —PHILIP RIEFF, *The Triumph of the Therapeutic*

As is well known, Enlightenment thinking, in its quest for knowledge and a better society, overran religious authority. In debunking beliefs with facts, it sidelined transcendent moral truths with information and (amoral) laws of nature. As belief systems gave way, the security that had characterized an individual's tether to larger value structures was replaced by doubt and uncertainty. Clear knowledge of right and wrong disintegrated, and the possibility of salvation—of knowing, even, how to live a good life—was lost. With this profound shift in American culture, the self was no longer situated by a tangible set of beliefs detailing *what it meant to be human.*

A common thread running through historical analyses of this shift is the import, and increasing centrality, of the psychotherapeutic outlook. Belief in an omnipotent, omniscient god rapidly gave way to a belief in autonomous selves (and the immanent identity attached to them).[1] Individualism reclaimed (wo)man from God, helping her (re)gain possession of a self, which it positioned as central. "Psychology ha[d] an explanation for everything because it locate[d] the sources of everything within the self" (Carrette and King 2005, 64).[2] It ordered and oriented life, not unlike the religious ideologies it superseded, systematizing unbelief. The body, which traditional religions had identified as the battleground for good and evil, fell before the mind, in which rational thought waged war with the human condition itself: the instincts.[3]

Even individuals only vaguely aware of the emerging psychologistic worldview embraced the new opportunities that were linked to it. Prosperity, growth, and an increasing division of labor disbanded communities that were integrated through deprivation and restrictive moralities. The ethos of otherworldly salvation through self-denial increasingly gave way to this-worldly self-fulfillment. Cultural anxiety followed upon this shift, which privileged a secular, progressive version of free will (a core tenet of Christianity). All manner of possibilities were annexed to this pivotal doctrine.[4] Unshackled from its religious context, free will broadened the possibilities for self-determination while simultaneously eroding restraint and self-control. Ultimately, however, this new expansiveness, which positioned self at center, offered no basis on which to orient choice or identity. The absence of any indication of *what* an individual should choose—or even aspire to, beyond satisfaction of individual needs and the avoidance of suffering—tainted this freedom, quickly leading to existential despair.[5]

Suffering, in this new paradigm, became aligned with the new significance accorded the self. No longer understood in terms of Christ's sacrifice, or as a test of faith, suffering was instead linked to *desire.* Desire—the needing, craving, and wanting of objects or others that were no longer (or never had been) attainable—was not to be denied; nor was the suffering it caused to be borne. Rather, it was to be remediated—by letting go. Moving on and expanding into the world facilitated the discovery of alternative self-fulfillments. Their possibility made the individual responsible for her own pain and misery. Choice (not unlike salvation) afforded individuals the opportunity to discover happiness. Unlike salvation, it freed them to explore the external and internal worlds while emerging norms emboldened, even pressed, them to do so.

The right to ongoing, open-ended self-determination fit hand in glove with the aggrandizing norms of a nation colonizing a new continent. In much the same way that America believed itself to be determining its own destiny, its citizens became responsible for determining their own fate (Emerson's *Self-reliance*, Thoreau's *Civil Disobedience*, and Whitman's *Song of Myself* stand as testimonials to this belief). National goals gradually became ideologies; their means of realization became ends in themselves. No longer simply children of God or curators of biblical laws on earth, individuals instead had dominion over the land and were masters of their own fortune.

———

Rapidly changing material, social, and demographic conditions required a host of new—and daily—psychological adaptations. Identity, detached from small, traditional communities (where it was ordered by clear moral struggles), began to locate and establish itself in new roles and opportunities. Having to impress their worth on strangers (and, at the same time, rely on impressions of them), individuals increasingly focused on the construction of a social self. This carefully crafted identity was oriented toward bridging and connecting with others. (Public face, front-stage performances, and social identity were hardly new modalities. However, swelling cities, new technologies, and un-expected prosperity ushered in new terms of interaction and forced greater reliance on a self who traded on the attributes of public identity.) Personality (whose root is the Greek word for *mask*) soon emerged as *the* guiding principle of identity construction, the basis on which individuals could draw others to themselves and make claims on them. "Personality meant the ability to be attractive to others, to stand out in a crowd.... Poise and charm, rather than adherence to a moral code; personal grooming and health, rather than hard work and self-sacrifice, were the important behaviors to learn" (Cushman 1995, 64).

New techniques of self-presentation placed unfamiliar strains on the in-dividual. Composing and managing a lucid, even appealing, public persona, while negotiating underlying uncertainties, stressed (and often fractured) a coherent sense of identity. One's inner true self, however that was conceived, came to be seen as the puppeteer responsible for orchestrating fluid and varied enactments of identity. But what values guided presentations of self, and on what were they based? Doubt and uncertainty destabilized self as a referent, paradoxically causing independent social actors to turn to and vest increasing authority in others.[6]

David Riesman's seminal work *The Lonely Crowd* (1950) charts the increasing importance—and influence—of others.[7] He argues that throughout the early stages of expansion, even as individuals began cultivating personality and the opinions of peers, they retained the psychological imprint of traditional norms and mores. These values continued to inform and organize their orientation toward the world, producing what Riesman calls the "inner-directed character type."[8] Inner-directed individuals possessed an "internal gyroscope," a mobile morality steeped in holdover values, including integrity and discipline, self-sacrifice, hard work, and a drive to improve themselves. On a day-to-day basis, no less than in times of crisis, these men and women fell back on the ethics of an earlier era, which they had internalized. On the frontiers of social life, they found resources within themselves, capacities that translated as self-reliance.[9] This is not to suggest that a comprehensive measure of self was unaffected by the opinions of peers, customers, and colleagues. Inner-directed individuals relied on others and were significantly influenced by their judgments. Nonetheless, deeply habituated values maintained their self-coherence, manifesting as personal character traits that lent them social distinction and identity (honest, hardworking, thrifty), while giving rise to the mythos of rugged individualism that was the hallmark of this culture in transition.[10]

Yet next generations, at an increasing distance from the ethos of traditional culture, as well as from the scarcity and frugality that often informed it, struggled anew to negotiate meaning in their lives. As wealth increased and culture oriented itself around consumption, inner gyroscopes became antiquated and increasingly obsolete, once again problematizing personal identity and relationship to the world. Rudderlessness, anomie, and an overwhelming, morbid introspection returned to threaten the American Dream (see Durkheim's [(1897) 1997] classic treatise on suicide). The self had expanded into seemingly exciting, uncharted territories, only to find that psychological liberation often led to a vast wilderness of nothing. As in the American West, building and construction were needed—but along what blueprints and with what materials?

Changing demographics, increases in prosperity, and the dying off of an inner-directed generation only increased the import of making and maintaining a favorable impression, of constructing social identities that would, through patterns of acting endorsed by others, deepen into modes of being and becoming. The opinion of others superseded rusting inner gyroscopes, orienting the individual's connection to the world, offering guidance and even meaning. Man (woman) remained the measure of all things, but, as Whellis put it, it was no longer the *inner* man who measured; it was the *other* man (1958, 18).

Or more correctly, other *men* (and *women*). Interacting with an increasing variety of people, each embodying a different social relationship, other-directed individuals came to rely on fluidity in social role playing. Attunement and flexibility allowed for great adaptation in response. Riesman argues that sensitivity to the gaze of the other replaced inner gyroscopes with radar. This mental equipment, which detected subtleties of style and nuances in response, homed in on clues for processing experience:

> The inner-directed person, though he often sought and sometimes achieved a relative independence of public opinion and of what the neighbors thought of him, was in most cases very much concerned with his good repute and, at least in America, with "keeping up with the Joneses." These conformities, however, were primarily external, typified in such details as clothes, curtains, and bank credit. . . . In contrast with this pattern, the other-directed person, though he has his eye very much on the Joneses, aims to keep up with them not so much in external details as in the quality of his inner experience. That is, his great sensitivity keeps him in touch with others on many more levels than the externals of appearance and propriety . . . for guidance in what experiences to seek and in how to interpret them. (Riesman 1961, 23–24)

With self increasingly grounded in others, the threat of disappointing them and being rejected gained significance.[11] Riesman notes that "the other-directed person wants to be loved rather than esteemed; he wants not to impress . . . others, but in the current phrase, to relate to them; he seeks less a snobbish status in the eyes of others, more an assurance of being emotionally in tune with them" (1961, 431). Simply put, she or he wants to belong, wants to be characterized as like-minded and worthy of inclusion. Looking to tether self relationally, individuals became other-directed virtuosos, packaging and peddling a self attuned to the subtle cues given off by others.[12] Yet despite the cultivation and refinement of social radar, certainty remained just out of reach.

Riesman's sweeping social analysis and its simplified character types spoke to postwar nostalgia for a moral past and articulated concerns about institutionalization, standardization, and conformity. Becoming adept at rapid accommodation and superficial intimacies raised the question of *who* was fitting in. Tethering self to shifting opinions and cultural changes grounded identity in little more than conformism, increasing certainty at the expense of individuality. Self-determination and authenticity, traded for security and a feeling of belonging, now seemed too great a cost.[13] For better or worse, however, Riesman's all-but-ontological analysis of other-orientedness sets the stage for personal turmoil in the face of social humiliation, rejection, and bullying.[14]

Subsequent social analyses, which used Riesman's book as a springboard for the exploration of evolving social dynamics, came to posit a new character type—one that fits well in bullying narratives: the narcissist. Self-absorbed yet insecure, narcissists are defined by increasing emotional and psychological neediness and a preoccupation with individual self-gratification.[15] Denizens of the late twentieth and early twenty-first centuries, they are awash in a sea of simulations and competing social voices, disoriented by the cacophony of others clamoring for attention in a world of manipulated surfaces. Left to manufacture an identity from "materials furnished by advertising and mass culture, themes of popular film and fiction, and fragments torn from a vast range of cultural traditions" (Lasch 1979, 91), they cling to their *desire*, allowing *its* authenticity to orient choices and navigate the promises of meaning contained in ever-new pastiches and recycled images.

Narcissistic strategies of being (forged in the malls of America and the playground of cyberspace) have become survival tactics in this world. Caught up in the gratification of manufactured appetites (needs) yet paradoxically dependent on others to filter desire, construct leisure, and interpret experiences, narcissists are preoccupied with the spectacle of *stylized* consumption (of symbols, objects, and others, no less than self-image). *Correct desiring* guarantees multiple levels of satisfaction, including the hunger to be noticed, allowing prestige and distinction to accrue to individuals who accurately articulate it.[16] Reliance on others to code the styles of appropriate desiring (in order to communicate belonging and success) and on peers to decode (and affirm) an individual's correct packaging of self makes narcissistic consumption continuous with ongoing, other-oriented identity construction:

> Notwithstanding his occasional illusions of omnipotence, the narcissist depends on others to validate his self-esteem. He cannot live without an admiring audience. His apparent freedom from family ties and institutional constraints does not free him to stand alone or to glory in his individuality. On the contrary, it contributes to his insecurity, which he can overcome only by seeing his "grandiose self" reflected in the attentions of others, or by attaching himself to those who radiate celebrity, power, charisma. For the narcissist, the world is a mirror, whereas the rugged individualist saw it as an empty wilderness to be shaped to his own design. (Lasch 1979, 10)[17]

Grounded in *gaze*, in looking and being looked at, consumers are primed to both judge and be victimized.[18] (As Heidi Klum so tersely warns on *Project Runway*, "One day you're in, and the next day, you're out.") An urgency to be seen and to be affirmed, to *be*, promotes social aggression, locking bullies and their targets in a dynamic of need fostered by culture itself.

Where is the fracture point in this cycle?

Although socially defined by the opinions of others, individual identity coheres around *experiences*. Even needy, narcissistic selves are *autobiographical*, constructed in terms of accumulated personal history (including instances of approval or rejection, articulations of desire, and the opportunities open to the individual). Understood this way, the shifting kaleidoscope of self, as a whole, is only *obliquely* determined by the gaze of others (see Appendix A). However, during adolescence, experience is limited, making each autobiographical fragment appear large and weighted with significance. The foundations of identity are under construction, as are the skill sets needed to balance emerging (autobiographical) self with the views of others. As experience multiplies and broadens its base, the influence of any single incident or the gaze of any particular individual or group is likely to lessen. Yet even with an expansion of interpersonal knowledge, which tempers the influence of one or another event or individual, the felt experience of shame and humiliation does not change.

Not only does it not change, but the number of opportunities to experience shame increases. Though each experience might be less and less weighted, the increasing number of claims on the individual multiply the opportunity for social failure. Young people are expected to submit to progressively complex, even contradictory social demands that involve a fluctuating set of expectations (made by a heterogeneous group of others whose agendas are often in conflict). Failure to meet them, or to prioritize claims along any accepted moral code, threatens social stigmatization. Even attuned, well-intended individuals fall short and inevitably need to negotiate inadequacy (and humiliation). These are inescapable autobiographical experiences.

This is the heart of the problem. Failure is unavoidable, but shame, along with salvation and damnation, was relegated to the rubble heap of religiosity, displaced and denied admittance to the new cultural order. What, then, is to be made of deficient performance? How is a person to process the feelings of disgrace and inadequacy associated with it and redeem herself? Shame itself has become shameful. Michael Lewis (2003) likens it to a subatomic particle, known only by the trace it leaves—downcast eyes and crumpled spines (as well as rampages and suicides?). How can we even think about shame in a culture that not only has sanitized the concept from its discourses but appears to endorse "traits that would have been cause for shame in former times," as personified in its "pop cultural heroes . . . mostly noteworthy for their pride in their aggressiveness, crudity, narcissism, and general boorishness" (Broucek 1991, 135)?[19]

Despite cultural silence around shame or even the shameless public posturings that attempt to defy, banish, or delegitimate its felt experience, shame continues to colonize *being* in the world. Every one of us makes choices that (implicitly) reference this moral emotion, even allowing its specter to organize our lives. Nonetheless, culture continues to resist exploring its social and psychological characteristics, creating a blind spot that now threatens the health of society. As long as its use and abuse as a force of social control remains unacknowledged, its nature and consequences become invisible. And what we *will not* see can hurt us.

Religion and Shame: The Historical Possibility of Redemption

Often overlooked, it was the *possibility of redemption* within moral communities that helped negotiate failure and regulated a sense of shame. Loss of face, often associated with the public practice of shaming, was a familiar, known experience in traditional societies. Humiliation and humility were sponsored by, and overtly embedded in, a religious worldview that foregrounded atonement, forgiveness, and salvation. This potential and the hope it nurtured are pivotal. Modeled on the possibility of absolution and salvation that Jesus Christ bought back through his shameful death on the cross, redemption *is* Christianity's founding gesture. Those who transgressed were able to repent, suffer penances, and be purified, redeemed, and reconciled with God.[20] Atonement, and the promise it held, became paradigmatic: *the* dynamic around which culture, society, and individual relationships were structured. Its ideology no less than its ethos shaped the norms and infrastructure of community. Confession of wrongdoing, admission of unworthiness, and penance willingly suffered (in the hopes of forestalling both eternal damnation and social excommunication) was a known, expected social sequence. The act of *public* allocution (within orchestrated spectacles of shaming) affirmed the moral codes that bound community while trading on this hope. Forgiveness and salvation were contingent on owning one's inadequacies and *assuming responsibility for their cost to society*. Only by relinquishing pride, enduring public disgrace, and suffering the loss of social capital could an individual be purified and readmitted to the fold. Hester Prynne's *A* articulates the terms of her continued connection to society. In fact, for the community to "offer forgiveness before the requisite hard work of self-examination, *public confession*, and *shame* [was] equally wrong" (Newman et al. 2004, 189).

Scrutiny and vigilant personal and social monitoring were mandated of every member of this society. Transgressions not only risked calling down God's wrath on the community but posed a tangible threat to the social order that ensured the group's survival. Elders, congregation leaders, magistrates, and *bystanders* (the gatekeepers of society) oversaw the process of remediation and purification. Their gaze had the power to censure, to humiliate, and/or to punish, as well as to forgive, holding the potential for social salvation in its sight.[21] Plainly put, the gaze of others had—and continues to have—the power to morally and socially indict members of the community, as well as the capacity to *ratify* (formal) judgments or to *mitigate* them in minor yet all-important ways. Although wrongdoing was assessed in terms of God's laws, sinners were accountable, in a much more direct fashion, to the community.

It was the social body that actively watched, reported, policed, bore witness, and endorsed (or undermined) behaviors and penances, *administrating* judgments and justice (although those of pure heart—or the truly repentant—had transcendent means by which to withstand the trials, tribulations, and even wrongful judgments of this world).

Reflecting on the importance of atonement dynamics for the stability of the group, it becomes clear that confession and apology spoke (and continue to speak) to the willingness of the individual to recognize and submit to the moral authority of the social body. Both also testify to her character, and

> one's moral character is considered to be the trait that is indicative of one's likelihood of following the rules of society. . . . Thus a sincere confession (i.e., a confession with remorse) connotes that an immoral deed has been done, but by a person who has recovered morality and will not behave this way in the future. . . . [Put differently,] someone within the group who refuses to play by the rules can be a danger to the very integrity and safety of the group. But by voluntarily confessing and showing remorse, a transgressor can demonstrate that the codes of the group have been internalized and are still important. (Gold and Davis 2005, 125–126)

While sincere remorse and admission of culpability are still active elements of social intercourse, tempting a simple turn from the protocols of disgrace in traditional society to more recent configurations, such a move is premature. Even if the possibility of redemption was acknowledged as *pivotal* for the remediation of social transgressions, its appropriation (to a multicultural, secular society) would be challenging. Although similarities abound— the accused are still publicly humiliated, frequently apologize, and routinely go to great lengths to assure the group that their transgressions will not be repeated—the differences are crucial. Many mistakes and missteps in the school yard (or corporate office or PTA) are *relative* and the possibility of shame free floating. The basis for judgment is unstable, even unspecified, the judges themselves transient, and the possibility of absolution uncertain. (Moreover, bullies are not often interested in forgiveness or in readmitting penitents to the fold. Nor are those found lacking able to acknowledge and negotiate their shame, *because they have no means to process it.*)

This was not the case in small, traditional communities, where shame functioned in a rarified atmosphere: culture was homogeneous, and members of society had no real option but to submit to the authority of the group (relocating to a new community was often not possible). Right and wrong were unambiguous, and hiding one's transgressions was difficult. More than this, religious communities "*valorized suffering as redemptive and modeled 'unconditional obedience'*

as the way of salvation" (Kotsko 2010, 27; emphasis added). These core principles and the metaphysical system to which they belonged devalued human
agency, requiring "a passive rather than an active stance, while the notions of
obedience . . . undercut self-determination" (29). Such underlying values were
increasingly at odds with the ideologies that fostered the taming of the West
and are in distinct opposition to the norms regulating secular, narcissistic
cultures. Given these differences, it is hardly feasible to lop off the religious
aspects of the atonement paradigm and attempt to appropriate it to contemporary culture. However, it stands to reason that there are points at which
underlying dynamics themselves can be refitted to a secular tradition.

Looking closer at the process of secularization, it appears that obedience
to the opinion of others replaced obedience to God's commands. Although
the residents of Mayberry and River City never talked much about it, they
depended on the threat of shame to maintain social order.[22] (While con man
Harold Hill epitomized shameless agency and self-determination, he lived
in a world where atonement rituals continued to implicitly orchestrate sociation.[23] The politics of forgiveness—confession, penance, restitution and
redemption—remained pivotal to relationships, and the opinions of others
needed to be weighed against the cost of independence and worldly success.)
Spiritual damnation may have fallen by the wayside, but public humiliation
and social branding remained a force to be reckoned with. The threat of ac-
quiring a reputation—what neighbors might think—remained prohibitive,
despite the efforts of therapists or the loosening of social norms.[24]

While looking to others for affirmation was expected, even normative, this
mental orientation (which became increasingly comprehensive) did not reflect
the ideals or principles of psychologistic culture. The individual, in claiming power, was expected to break free from the shackles of religion, parental
authority, and others' determinations. The conflict that this gave rise to is
especially apparent around the experience of shame. Even though the esteem
of others was of increasing psychological import, therapists (the authorities
or high priests of culture) railed against the shame that others had the power
to wield (and the suffering identified with it). Shame had no place in the new
paradigm. It was the root of much misery, conflict, and habituated self-efface-
ment, which was *no longer valorized*. It was thus incumbent on the individual
to deny shame power, which to many translated as deny shame. The individual needed to reclaim sovereignty and remain free of such moral claims and
shackles on the self. Failure to renounce shame left individuals vulnerable to
psychic malaise, which came to be viewed as an illness to be treated and overcome.[25] Authority, now vested in the individual, was at odds with the authority
given over to others, and the tension between these two has yet to be resolved
(as is evident in responses to bullying: "She *should* be able to ignore them and
not let what they said bother her"). Whether an individual acknowledges the

experience of shame or not, she is expected to pull herself up by the bootstraps and overcome—that is, redeem herself—yet there is no clear template for accomplishing this.[26] (Financial success is the most reliable redemption strategy. For young people, access to resources helps cultivate friendships and affirmation while smoothing over transgressions and brokering forgiveness.)

Importantly, even if an individual is successful in securing forgiveness on an interpersonal level, she may, as a member of a disenfranchised group, be subject to ongoing social shame. Many have been—and continue to be—denied admittance to the culture of plenty, denied the opportunity to assert independence and self-determination. Deficient by nature, inadequate, or not fully human, women, blacks, and a majority of the poor (especially immigrants) were not enfranchised in this cultural system (nor are overweight individuals, gender-benders, and Muslims enfranchised in school and work communities today). How did these individuals, categorically incapable of social success, negotiate their ongoing shame, which was a condition of their existence? How have they managed it? How have they overcome the degradation of their very *being*, when they saw (and continue to see) themselves as others see them? When they collude in their own oppression and self-negation? Inferior, inadequate, and deserving of rejection, these invisible populations affirm the limited and limiting identities conferred on them, entrenched in both conscious and subliminal self-loathing. Fundamentally flawed, no less than their ancestors born into original sin, their coherent conceptions of self are predicated on ceding self-determination, even agency, and accepting a mantle of shame, of which they have been long-suffering curators.

Oppressed groups, it turns out, have not ceded the possibility of redemption to secular authorities. Religion remains a deep underground reservoir in American culture, a resource for those who were or are unstoried and invisible in the American Dream narrative.[27] By retaining hope in otherworldly salvation and coming to reinterpret obedience, suffering, and submission in this world, these groups have retained and realigned core religious tenets. Put differently, the principles derived from the Christian foundation myth, around which life is oriented, have been re-visioned. This Christ has come to tell a different story, a tale that *valorizes resistance* to the rich and the powerful, renarrating the place and the role of the disenfranchised in society (see Appendix B). Caesar must be given his due, but this due does not coincide with the oppressive claims of white patriarchial society. Subjugation and inequality will no longer be suffered as the price of redemption. Those who are bullied, ridiculed, and rejected may have much to learn from these populations, who have negotiated oppression and marginalization by a dominant culture, especially women and blacks, who allied themselves with liberation and womanist theologies. They came to reject foundational myths that required them to relinquish agency, restored their shame, and allowed oppression itself to become a condition of transformation. Such renarrating, and the cognitive reorganization it may yield, is precisely what is called for by the most recently identified disenfranchised group: victims of bullying.[28] The possibility of redemption for those who remain social pariahs requires nothing less and is explored in Chapter 5.

The Socialization of Children and the Root of Contemporary Shame

The remainder of this book addresses the potential for redemption in contemporary society: the terms and conditions of shame. Denial of clear opportunities for remediation was and is in keeping with shame's delegitimated status. Independent, self-determined individuals should have little need of redemption and belonging. Yet they remain uncertain of their own authority, unsure whether they are the legitimate seat of judgment or public opinion is. Either way, they continue to experience shame, falling into crises colored by self-doubt, loathing, and self-blame—damned if they do and damned if they don't. How does one live up to contradictory expectations of self? What does one do about failures? (Is forgiveness something offenders are entitled to? Something the offended are obligated to offer? On what basis are its terms negotiated?) Worse yet, individuals lack the ability to even articulate this predicament, because admitting one feels shame (i.e., has reason to be ashamed) is a second order of failure.

The key (yet often overlooked) reason for this dilemma, as well as for society's failure to eliminate shame, lies in the origin and nature of the authority invested in the gaze of others. The opinions of others resonate on deep psychological levels, ones integral to the individual's construction of self, because they are *patterned during early childhood socialization*. During these years, parents or guardians have a moral authority over children, who are invested in pleasing them. Dependents rely on guardians to frame, format, and organize their daily lives, if not their very being in the world, and to that extent are invested in others' configuration of their identity. Regardless of the model of childhood socialization that is privileged (cognitive, developmental, behavioral, social, or child-centered; determinist, functional, or constructionist), children rely on caregivers for survival and early on adjust their actions to adult rules, expectations, dictates, and anticipated reactions. As agents of socialization, caregivers and educators model, evaluate, and respond to behaviors. They may critique a child by parodying her actions or teasing her or otherwise measure her performance against standards they have set. A caregiver may use humor to illustrate how a behavior is inappropriate or rely on reason to explain why it is improper or unacceptable. Alternatively, they may yell, punish, or simply turn a look of disgust or contempt on a child. *Any* of these responses is capable of eliciting shame, guilt, and a sense of failure, though some are more likely to do so than others. "The task of parents is to teach their children to internalize values and to motivate their children, in the absence of the parents, not to violate these standards, rules, and goals. What better way to prevent the child from doing this than by producing a strong emotion? The production of shame, even at normal levels, is an ideal device for instilling internalized values" (Lewis 1992, 112). Clearly, in this context, shame has an *ongoing, adaptive, regulatory function* and can be *employed in ways that do not demand repression or preclude reintegration.* The mistakes or failures that evoke it can usually be addressed and negative self-feelings overcome by an acknowledgment of wrongdoing, a willingness to take responsibility, a display of remorse, and a correcting of behaviors. *Children routinely redeem themselves* in such a manner. Dances of atonement are a shame-management skill set, one employed early on in the negotiation of social humiliation and feelings of inadequacy.[29] Despite changes to content and mode over the past decades and centuries, shaming and atonement rituals continue to be normative practices in the socialization of children, developing their ability to reconcile criticism, disapprobation, and the emotions they arouse *if these emotions are acknowledged.*

Once children leave home to attend school, primary relationships to authority are attenuated. Peers begin vying for influence, challenging young people to expand their circle of significant others and broaden their base of identity. As emotional and psychological investments shift to peers, young people take significant steps in *discovering their own agency,* their own voice, and the ability to, themselves, gaze. As new intimacies begin to hold sway, young people must figure out boundaries and negotiate their violation—whether they are the offenders or the offended. *Throughout this period of learning, bullying appears most virulent.* Habituated to a concern with the gaze and pronouncements of another—and response to it, whether passive compliance, grudging behavioral adjustment, or risky defiance—young people have internalized processes for atonement, remediation, and the reconciliation of bonds. The nature of infractions and who is transgressed against change, but the dynamics surrounding wrongdoing, restitution, and forgiveness are *assumed* to remain intact.

This expectation has, with increasing frequency, left young people unprepared for the responses of their peers or the social consequences of failure. Compliance and dances of atonement may not only fail to result in reparation to social bonds but instead call out further degradation. Ironically, the adjustment involved in the transition from parental to peer authority may be especially problematic for children raised in nurturing, child-centered homes, where the response of authority figures has been guided by respect for choices and a concern with imparting self-confidence. Acceptance and unconditional love do not prepare these children for unfavorable rejoinders couched in ridicule, humiliation, and rejection. Having been weaned on a sense of their own uniqueness and importance, reinforced by attention, praise, reasoning, kind criticism, fair rebukes, gentle laughter, and reintegrative shaming, they find it difficult to negotiate the tearing down of self and the less forgiving practices that reign in the school yard. Consequently, these children may be more likely to be confounded by social disapproval and respond inappropriately, puzzled, devastated, and/or angered by their voice not being privileged, their feelings not being relevant.[30]

With formerly effective dances of atonement often viewed as feeble, inadequate, or even ridiculed on playgrounds and buses, in school hallways and cafeterias, young people are given pause. Psychological violence and emotional cruelty violate expectations. They mock the belief that appropriate propitiation and efforts to change will absolve culprits (of perhaps unknown trespasses) while serving as a condition of reinstatement into relationship. The *incomprehensibility of the failure* of well-known patterns for absolution and the restitution of bonds is perhaps why we see, over and over again, victims of bullying trying—sometimes desperately—to appease, atone, be forgiven, and be readmitted to the group. Their understanding of relationship has been stamped with this social motif, and they are often not yet in a position, developmentally, socially, or autobiographically, to counter the social authority and moral superiority asserted by peers.

How, then, are they to negotiate wrongdoing or troublesome relationships outside the home; how do they work? How are expectations communicated and failures addressed and overcome? Do young people have options when familiar formulas do not result in reconciliation?

Social conflict, and the various discourses of domination it may lead to, usually unfolds and plays out in the relatively closed community of schools, which are not unlike traditional small towns. Mobility is limited, and public identity, which informs private conceptions of self, is derived from the same cross-referencing sources.[31] Known by, or at least known to, most members of these institutions, young people are limited by the social status conferred on them. Escaping a reputation may prove difficult once identity is spoiled. Trying too hard may backfire and become a new stigmatized identity: "pathetic," "wannabe," "sad," or just "sorry." A paucity of reference groups and limited opportunity make it difficult to forge new connections and construct alternative selves. Even schools that claim diversity in student populations have a narrowly defined internal economy* that often privileges assets beyond an individual's

---

* John Fiske notes that "in a consumer society, all commodities have cultural as well as functional values. To model this we need to extend the idea of an economy to include a cultural economy where the circulation is not one of money, but of meanings and pleasures. Here the audience, from being a commodity, now becomes a producer, a producer of meanings and pleasures" (1989, 27).

control (appearance, athletic prowess, accessories of style, unchaperoned space for entertaining, and ability to obtain controlled substances), setting the stage for crisis.[32] (On the other hand, a spoiled identity is at least visible, and some may consider it preferable to the rejection implied by social invisibility. Alone and unsecured by relationship, young people may find in abuse a connection, even if the cost is self.)

What is to be done for undesirables, for hopeless social lepers? Penances are unspecified, insufficient, or simply mocked, and social salvation is not in the offing. What recourse is left to such a person?[33] What further ransom can be offered? What options does she have? *She has conceded (to peers or society at large) the authority to judge,* whether willingly or unwillingly, and stands in need of redemption, but by whom?[34]

At this point it is impossible not to rush in and say, "Bystanders!" Who else? And if their capacity to redeem (defined in the next chapters) is combined with resistance to oppression modeled by liberation and womanist theologies (Appendix B), the outlines of a coherent social response to bullying seem likely to emerge.

Constructing a Social Problem: Bullying and the Double-Edged Sword of the Media

Much about a society can be learned by examining its social problems, analyzing how it languages and formulates issues, identifying the norms and values that underlie the claims being made, probing the extent to which problems go hand in hand with its definition of deviance, and noting the individuals to whom the label is applied (and conversely, those who apply it). Power structures of a society are revealed through such questioning, which unpacks how and why society transforms conditions into social problems, no less than when, where, and who will be found in violation of new norms. (Bullying was problematized in response to white male rampages, which, it has been argued, deflects responsibility from perpetrators.)[35]

As discussed previously, values of independence and self-sufficiency carry a moral force in American culture—one that has readily translated into a belief that targets should handle whatever is thrown at them, rise to the occasion, find their backbone, stop being a crybaby, and deal with it. In this view, social aggression is a bump in the road, a test of character or the stuff one is made of. Social humiliation and rejection are the individual's problem to negotiate and overcome. In fact, should a target not be able to overcome them or successfully override bullies' agendas, she is the one who deviates from norms. Looked at this way, bullying is part of the socialization process, the negotiation of boundaries, transgressions, and identity in an interplay that establishes a social pecking order. As in the past, personality (the ability to attract others and make claims on them) is key. Developing personality builds a platform for connection and is especially important for marginalized individuals trying to compensate for their differences (i.e., "deficiencies"—shortness, heaviness, asymmetrical or disproportionate facial features, etc.). The expectation that individuals should and will learn to negotiate social hardships, including broken relationships and social aggression, by toughing it out is not unfounded or without merit. But it is limited and allows social Darwinism to preclude the construction of bullying as a social problem. Unkind behavior is found in all walks of life; what is important is how the *individual* copes with it.

Bullying overcame the strong cultural objections to its formulation as a problem when Columbine unfolded, live, on national television. As soon as rejection and humiliation were linked to the atrocities that flooded our living rooms, social aggression, shame, and ostracization became clear threats to the social fabric. Collective horror, grief, and pain quickly gave rise to fear, galvanizing social action. The identification of a causal factor—bullying—allowed society to begin managing the helplessness, anxiety, and sadness precipitated by unthinkable, unpredictable rampages and to believe it possible to gain some semblance of control over such occurrences in the future (a belief that has not been supported by the increase in shooting sprees over the past decade and a half). In demanding that we "Stop bullying now!" society has come together and is coping through proactive attempts to curtail social Darwinism.[36]

The process of transforming existing conditions into social problems, as is in progress with bullying, has been variously configured by functional, normative, labeling, value-conflict, and interactionist schools of thought. Each perspective defines society—its conditions, dynamics, values, and conflicts—from a differing vantage point. The clearest, most comprehensive operationalization of this process, set forth by Kent Sandstrom, Daniel Martin, and Gary Fine (2009), offers insight into additional aspects of, and obstacles to, problematizing social aggression. Following *banning* (raising social outcry), the authors identify *detection, attribution*, and *reaction* as integral, interrelated aspects of the process by which conditions are translated into problems. Detection, the second step, is, not surprisingly, the sticking point for bullying. Social aggression must somehow be separated from adolescent posturing, from trash-talking, teenage dramas, and normal situational experiences that will resolve themselves. These challenges, which preclude self-identification as a victim, suggest a need to position bullying as social terrorism, as a threat to community that requires, normalizes, and supports the (active) input of *all* group members. Disrupting psychological abuse and emotional violence relies on informants, and who better able to identify social torment than peers, who are on the ground and in the trenches?[37] The grapevine, enhanced by social media, instantly spreads word of public spectacles: face-offs, humiliations, cruelties, and reactions are instantly tweeted, posted, and dissected by the school or work community. Victims and victimizers are known to their peer cohort.

In addition to detection is the difficulty in determining *attribution*. Attribution is the ability to assign a reason to behavior—what was the *intent* behind it? Was it unknowing ("I didn't mean for her to get so upset about it"); did those involved feel coerced to participate ("It was Bella's idea. We just kind of went along."); or was it deliberate ("So? It was funny.")? Teen dramas often collapse these distinctions in the process of exploring boundaries, making attribution a slippery slope. Even those close to the situation may have difficulty determining whether and to what extent the escalation is mere posturing by both parties. Precisely for this reason, policies and behavior codes often bypass intent. In so doing they become behaviorally oriented caricatures, dragnets readily eluded by instigators and aggressors.

Finally, any behavior that is defined as a social problem must clearly articulate appropriate reaction to its transgression. (Note that indications of an issue's severity, as well as requirements for reparation, are implicit in the framing of the issue itself.) Reaction not only specifies who is to be sanctioned, when, by whom, and how but cues social response to those who have suffered. Formal responses—conduct codes, bylaws, and legal recourse—change weekly, on a state-by-state, school-by-school, company-by-company basis, making it futile to outline them here. (They can be found on innumerable websites and are detailed in school and workplace policies.) Laws and policies are intended to go hand in hand with informal support for those who are targeted. This informal aspect, as it relates to victims as well as bystanders, orients the remaining chapters of this book.[38]

In so many ways, bystanders are the linchpin underlying the success of this new social initiative, but actively engaging them poses significant challenges. For example, mixed messages from victims themselves, who may accept and endorse some degree of abuse (believing themselves responsible), let bystanders off the hook. What are *they* to do if even the victim agrees that she is queer, fat, or a loser? A related issue involves culpability. Are bystanders expected to intervene when there is truth to the character indictments? (She did steal from *x*, lie to *y*, or hook up with *z*'s boyfriend.) Victims are often not blameless; otherwise, they are likely invisible and ignored. How or why intervene when judgments are passed for legitimate reason, elicited by transgressions that *should* call out disapprobation? At what point does negative feedback become abuse? Should appropriate sanctions be determined case by case and in light of their anticipated effect on the culprit-victim or by the nature of the infraction itself?[39] Last, the elusive basis on which judgments are passed (the opinions of others) make them difficult to counter, further deterring bystander involvement.

As the voice of the public, the media are positioned to help negotiate these challenges, to spearhead change by modeling new normative expectations (how often do main characters—other than in period pieces like *Mad Men*—smoke?). Yet media involvement with, and relationship to, bullying is complex. Consider, for example, the inconsistent, even contradictory values informing one evening of broadcast: the nightly news covers a local incident of harassment, allegations of bullying, and official responses to the incident. Social cruelties, including persecution, public humiliation, and inflammatory gossip, are decried, and respect for dignity of each individual and tolerance of differences is advocated. Members of the community are interviewed, all lament what has happened, and several share their own stories. This programming is followed by entertainment news, which showcases the latest Hollywood scandals, seizing on and embellishing instances of degradation and creating public spectacle over another's indiscretions. Prurient interest in exposing the suffering and shame of others stands in sharp contrast to the compassionate antibullying values promoted in the preceding newscast. This voyeuristic entertainment news is followed by a reality-TV show, with judges renowned for their scathing, belittling remarks or casts who stir drama and create conflict by mocking, berating, and excoriating fellow cast members, even backstabbing co-competitors for our entertainment.[40] Series that are successful fan daily stresses and instigate tensions (between ax-men, fishermen, ice-road truckers, housewives of [insert place], Cajun swamp dwellers, or families who outdegrade each other), building toward nasty climaxes that are highly rated and eagerly anticipated. Thus, even while the media keeps attention focused on bullying, keeps social abuse in the public eye, and constructs bullying as a social problem, it endorses mockery, rejection, and abusive interactions in its programming.

Reality TV has created a fan base (bystanders) eager to be entertained by public disgrace, hungry for compelling dramas that are at odds with the principles of antibullying advocated on the evening news. Mob mentalities and social scapegoating bond communities of viewers over the very behaviors we decry in our school yards. Not even lip service is paid to rejecting these spectacles, and no cultural narratives promote empathy for the losers. (What norms encourage bystanders to text and tweet their chagrin over scathing humiliations to sponsors, talk show hosts, and media personalities?) No cultural story balances celebration of winning with respect for trying, encouraging audience members to feel admiration for those willing to risk public judgment only to be voted off the island, the catwalk, or the stage; banished from the kitchen; or not handed a rose.[41] How, then, are losers to be redeemed? Why would failure in any arena be experienced as anything other than humiliating inadequacy and loss of connection?

2

SOCIAL FORCES AND BULLYING

If evil begins when someone crosses a line, then it may be
promoted by anything that tends to make the line fuzzy or
unclear, including ambiguity and misinformation.
  —ROY BAUMEISTER, *Evil*

S ocial aggression and bullying became the focus of the nation's attention
on April 20, 1999, as the rampage at Columbine unfolded live on national
television. Tragically, it took this unthinkable atrocity to put emotional
violence and psychological cruelty on the cultural radar. And what surprised
us most was their apparent ubiquity. Taunting, exclusion, and other cruelties
that have always been a part of growing up were suddenly understood to be *key
constitutive elements* of adolescent culture. Young people were (and continue
to be) prevailed on to take it (i.e., swallow the humiliation and pain) on a daily
basis. There are no boundaries circumscribing social persecution, few sanctions against it, and no way to avoid it.

The prevalence of psychological violence may be related to the fact that
much of what we loosely call bullying has roots in healthy impulses and normative styles of interacting. Information gathering about others is a survival
tactic, assisting in the navigation of social currents, helping to position individuals in relation to people, events, and exchanges. And it is the nuances
within interactions—tonal inflections, laughter, eye rolling, sighing, shrugging, nervous tapping, or avoiding eye contact—that provide as much and
potentially more *significant* information than the exchange itself.[1] Physical
expressions complement interactions, situating content, communicating additional information about relationships, and signaling appropriate response.
Bullying comes alive in these nuances and thrives in the spaces where coded
exchanges occur. Innuendos, allusions, and oblique dissembling offer interpretations of social information that may or may not be motivated by malice, may or may not seek to manipulate others, may or may not segue into

divisive them (or her) versus us positions. Even something as straightforward as spending time with people who share views, tastes, or sexual preferences creates boundaries, identifying individuals who *do not* hold them. When do discussions affirming one's own position become gossip *about* those affirming alternative views? When do preferences regarding one's company begin to pointedly *exclude* others?

To better understand the complexities of bullying behaviors and the normative interactive dynamics in which they are embedded, this chapter explores the *social* forces relevant to creating and maintaining the language games of bullying within culture. What ways do the dynamics of social interaction, notably gossip, laughter, and stereotyping, coupled with the cultural ethos of competition, support and enable emotional violence? What is the *nature* of gossip, laughter, stereotyping, and competition? What properties are intrinsic to the *forms* themselves, and how have they been *transformed* through culture's appropriation of them? Laying bare these dynamics, all of which are caught up in bullying, allows the identification of points at which these interactions are subverted, as well as windows for intervention. That is, a fuller understanding of these social forces may suggest whether, where, and how their ability to harm may be modified or whether, where, and how they themselves might be marshaled to counter social aggression.

Gossip

Perhaps the cruelest punishment for slanderers, nags, and gossips, when simple gagging wasn't enough, was the brank, sometimes called the "gossip's bridle" or "scold's helm." This was a sort of heavy iron cage, that covered the head; a flat tongue of iron, sometimes spiked, was thrust into the mouth over the criminal's tongue. Less sophisticated areas made do with a "simpler machine—a cleft stick pinched on the tongue." Either system pretty much insured silence.
—JAMES A. COX, "Bilboes, Brands, and Branks"

Ella: You know the ChicBoutique? I saw Sara in there—and I'm pretty sure she was buying the blue dress in the window for prom.
Aaliyah: Are you serious? Wasn't Jacqui looking at that dress?
Lexi: Ewww. Who cares. That dress is *soooo* ugly!
Keisha: What "dress"? It's barely a shirt—one she is *way* too fat to even think about wearing.
[*Hoots of laughter*]
Lexi: How can she afford it anyway? Isn't she always wearing the same sorry boots and jeans? And her hair . . .

Jayde: I don't know—if she accessorizes it right, I think it could look okay.

Keisha: Maybe—but it's so obvious she's only buying it because she wants to hook up with Devon. How sad is that?

This fictional exchange is a classic example of gossip. The topic being discussed is trivial and likely of little consequence to the participants themselves. Therefore, toward what end does it occur? What function does it serve? The negative speculation around Sara's purchase may be the beginnings of a bullying campaign, but that is not its clear aim. So what is the point of this disparaging discussion?

Some would say none, seeing in gossip nothing more than a preoccupation with superficial aspects of day-to-day affairs. As Nicholas Emler notes, it is often "regarded as the province of idle minds; only people who have nothing better to do stand around gossiping. It is unreliable and inaccurate, an entirely fallible source of information about other people. Its motivations are disreputable; tellers are motivated by mischief, rancor, or spite; listeners by a prurient and improper interest in matters that are none of their business" (1994, 117–118). In this view, gossip has no (social) function, and engaging in it rightfully elicits contempt.

Social interactionists reject this trivialization, instead configuring gossip as a form of social bonding, through which identities, both self and other, are negotiated. Social exchange theorists would add that a cost-benefit analysis goes into this negotiation. Feminists view the whole through a very different social lens, construing the exchange as a form of subversive discourse, one that flies in the face of masculine, goal-oriented rhetoric. And finally, postmodernists would add a coda elaborating Michel Foucault's understanding of power.[2]

Gossip has the potential to be all these things, many of them simultaneously. On what grounds, though, can any of them be privileged over the commonsensical dismissal of gossip as meaningless, trifling chatter?

To begin, researchers exploring the origins of human intelligence have noted the significance of gossip in a social evolutionary scheme. The social brain theory, or Machiavellian intelligence hypothesis, which contends that the evolution of primate intelligence is predicated on the need to negotiate complex social problems, explores the idea that exploitative behavior, deception, betrayal, and infidelity might have been of particular relevance to our ancestors. When survival relied heavily on relationships, this type of knowledge would have been crucial. Other sorts of information (nonsocial, nonnarrative facts) were not as relevant to the maintenance of social bonds integral to self-preservation. Research suggests that today, with physical survival guaranteed, the maintenance of these bonds remains crucial. *Social* preservation is integral to survival, and the tending of relationships is no less important. As the term *social media* suggests, communication remains

> biased toward social over non-social information. This was tested by passing social and non-social information along multiple chains of participants. Experiment 1 found that gossip, defined as information about intense third-party social relationships, was transmitted with significantly greater accuracy and in significantly greater quantity than equivalent non-social information concerning individual behavior or the physical environment. . . . It was therefore concluded that human cultural transmission is biased toward information concerning social interactions over equivalent non-social information. (Mesoudi, Whiten, and Dunbar 2006, 405)

Understood thus, seemingly inconsequential small talk—the informal whisperings, chit-chat, and sharing of social information—emerges from the sidelines of triviality and begins to assume place, significance, and meaning. Although casual, this diffuse, ambiguous, and nonpurposeful wordplay functions as more than idle chatter. "By talking to one person, we can find out a great deal about how others are likely to behave, how we should react to them when we actually meet them and what kinds of relationships they have with third parties. All these things allow us to coordinate our social relationships within a group more effectively" (Dunbar 1992, 31).

Gossip's nonlinear narrative structure and its seemingly meaningless verbal meandering also factor into its reputation for being little more than trivial, irresponsible hearsay. Feminists, developmental psychologists, and artists of all genres have allied themselves against this dismissive interpretation of small talk, exposing cultural biases that privilege goal-oriented dialogues. Despite their resistance, discrimination against gestures and speech acts that do not conform to rational, linear protocols is culturally entrenched and difficult to change. Gossip flies in the face of these sensible orderings. It flaunts a structure that parallels the seemingly nonpurposeful movement of many creative activities that are engaged in the logic of their own unfolding. Embracing such aimless, even illogical, rambling is not as meaningless as it might seem. The flow of gossip mimics the organic imaginativeness of play, which, developmental psychologists assert, is one of (if not *the*) single most significant things a child can do.[3] Play is interaction with, and negotiation of, the external world *in terms of* the internal world, as in its own way is gossip. Through ostensibly pointless exchanges (at times characterized by sophisticated, creative repartee) individuals gather social information, deconstruct it, appropriate it, and integrate it into their own alternative narratives. Through this process they develop opinions, perspectives, and values that are reflected in their negotiation of relationships in their life world.

In this, gossip, like improv, follows where it leads, which differs on the basis of who is present and the status and nature of their relationship to each other. People relate differently to each member of their social circle, and unique, intersubjective connections shape and mold exchanges. Although a person may feel that she is only passing on what she heard, the information is filtered, consciously or subconsciously. Some aspects are highlighted, others downplayed. That Sara's purchase was selected as a topic for discussion lends it significance, suggesting a social investment in the action. Subtleties and innuendos embedded in the telling further position the gossiper in relation to her audience, giving those privy to her gossiping access to her private thoughts, feelings, and motivations. Even seemingly factual, ends-directed communications are conveyed with a tone, body language, or emoticons standing in for them. What was Ella's tone in sharing her initial piece of information? Did it emerge as a tangent to other discussions, enriching them, or was sharing it an event in itself? Offerings of information invite responses that position each gossiper to the inside story, exposing opinions, feelings, and values.[4] Rejoinders such as "How can she afford it?" or "That dress is *soooo* ugly!" or even "What 'dress'? It's barely a shirt—one she is *way* too fat to even think about wearing" situate individuals *to each other* in terms of Sara's purchase. And this information is of much greater significance than Sara buying a particular dress. Values, petty annoyances, biases, and dispositions are shared in these comments (read, "*I* would never wear that"); meanings are negotiated ("You're being too hard on her. If she accessorizes it right, it could look okay."); and the self-revelations crucial to cementing relationships, as well as identity within those relationships, are fostered in these exchanges.

In trusting others with their opinions (speculative, value-laden communications that fall outside linear, rational male models), gossipers engage in behavior that *creates, and maintains, intersubjective social bonds.* By sharing prejudices and predilections, a gossiper exposes herself to the gaze of others, believing they will respect, if not affirm, her point of view. Self-exposure challenges others to reveal *their* opinions, judgments, and assessment of the situation ("How can she afford it?" or "She wants to hook up with Devon"). These are not careful, guarded, sensible comments but offers and counteroffers of trust and vulnerability, the orchestration of belonging. While the topic (Sara's purchase) provides a common ground, friendships are built, managed, and cultivated around the risk and trust involved in each girl's response to, and analysis of, this piece of information. We might then speculate about whether Jayde is playing it safe with a neutral comment or, conversely, trusts these girls enough to safely disagree. Give-and-take is full of subtexts and connotations, weaving rapport and understanding, *creating* relationship. The dance of reciprocal sharing builds bridges of intimacy over vast chasms of vulnerability and insecurity, cementing friendships in the routine affirmation of shared values. Spanning subjectivities and sustaining interdependencies, gossip is central to the organization of society, responsible for creating alliances and fortifying infrastructures of power no less than for fracturing relationships and destroying community.

In the forging of bonds, gossip constructs and maintains personal and social narratives. Evaluating events is part of the ongoing development of self-identity through the storying of others. Each individual is, herself, positioned in the process, given shape, character, and distinctiveness by the boundaries she constructs. Gossipers situate themselves through their topic of analysis no less than their negotiation of motive, objective, personal meaning, social relevance, and determinations of success (did the dress look hot, or was it a hot mess?). Note that both comments made by Keisha assert her belief that Sara's actions are related to a narrative that involves inappropriate sexuality. In offering insight, Keisha may steer a discussion of Sara's purchase into a debate over Sara's motivations, beginning the process of socially storying personal behavior. This narrative simultaneously constructs Keisha's identity, not only situating Sara as *unlike* her but perhaps also disclosing that she is a prude or has an interest in Devon. Gossip circumscribes self, even as it defines other. Who is invested in what or whom (Sara is on their radar for some reason) is as significant, in its own way, as whether her behavior is endorsed, permitted, tolerated, or dismissed.

Exaggerations, embellishments, and oversimplifications emerge from this process and may begin to circulate in the social economy. Distorted speculations readily become toxic facts, as gossip smoothly segues into socially aggressive behavior. Sara may be denigrated further, as gossip networks expand, and by the time the prom comes around, there is little she can do that will not be interpreted in ways that affirm her spoiled identity. On the other hand, the whole conversation may be long forgotten by prom. Whoever identifies the events and individuals worth talking about or steers the direction of the ensuing dialogue controls the construction of a person's social identity, deliberately or unthinkingly. Individuals are defined into reality through characterizations that are shared (e.g., gossiped about). The attributes linked to them often (for better or worse) become real in their consequences.[5] Gossip creates significance. Yet the events and persons circulated in the cultural economy, once objectified, are burdened with ascribed meanings.[6]

It is the creation of significance that is key. Gossip may be merely a backdrop, securing social bonds by revealing, debating, and developing one's own positions, or it may be a central plot device in the scripting of self and the construction (or destruction?) of Other. These possibilities lie at opposing ends of a spectrum, and ascertaining the point at which gossip becomes relationally aggressive can be extremely difficult.[7] Positioning oneself in relation to the flow of actions, information, and others is *necessary* to both personal and social identity. When does the information circulating about Sara (or the act of repeating it) become cruel and destructive (and need this determination coincide with the point at which the gossip causes Sara emotional stress)? Further, *whose* perspective determines that behaviors have overstepped a vague social boundary and can be considered hostile if not malicious? Is she not allowed to grow, change, state opinions, alter alliances, or tell new friends the truth about former associates?

Distinguishing malicious gossip from informative, intimacy-creating sharing is difficult for numerous reasons, not the least of which is the assumption that they are mutually exclusive. Behaving in relationally aggressive ways toward a peer often creates intimacy within a group. It publicly affirms shared values, unifying and positioning the cohort against a particular individual. Gossipers assume the authority of a moral high ground—"I would never do *that*" or "Can you *believe . . .*" This ethical dimension not only licenses speculation but turns small talk into a force of social control, the foundation on which reputations rest. Note that Lexi and Jayde make comments that deflect moral indictment from Sara, as opposed to quips from the other girls that allude to suspect moral issues—the dress is a slutty choice; she is choosing it only to get with Devon; it might be a financially irresponsible choice, which makes her a wannabe; and finally, social protocol gives Jacqui, if she is an acquaintance of Sara's, dibs on the dress. As the discussion tacks between the dress itself and Sara's motivations in buying it, the implications move between impugning Sara's taste and her character. In this dance, Jayde might be seen as offering an unobtrusive bystander intervention. She does not overtly defend Sara and cause the group to turn suspicion on her but, instead, deflects attention from moral speculations. This small gesture holds out hope for Sara—and quite possibly sets up a coda for the whole conversation. It is a deft assumption of responsibility in a social process, one that establishes boundaries and polices group members without in any way destabilizing alliances.

Given the scope and depth of these varied functions, the question that arises is when is gossiping *not* okay?

The motivation underlying gossip is often considered the best indicator we have.[8] When the intent is to harm, malign, humiliate, and ostracize, gossip becomes a weapon of social destruction. But even then, is it necessarily wrong? What if those unsavory whispers are true? Is creating and saddling a person with a reputation she has earned really bullying, or is it simply not nice or perhaps even socially irresponsible? When does speculation and embellishment (perhaps coupled with other instances and incidents) cross a line?

Even if malicious motivations could be identified, attempts to establish norms circumscribing pernicious impulses would be futile, because even scapegoating has positive social functions. Gossip in the service of scapegoating ascribes attributes and inadequacies to victims that serve as a rallying cry for group coherence. It may help forge alliances or function on an intragroup level, maintaining boundaries and power structures. Scapegoating is routinely employed as a mode of conflict resolution within the peer cohort.[9] Casting out a group member sets an example, directly or indirectly addressing dissent or subtle threats to the balance of power. Creating a third-party victim is also a way to address strife and discord, as, for example, "when a dyadic relationship is in danger of splitting into two as a result of unexpressed conflict between the two parts. To stabilise the dyad, a third party is brought into the relationship and uncomfortable feelings are displaced onto this third party by one or both of the dyad" (Dixon 2007, 82).

Gossip circulated in the name of conflict resolution offers little or no possibility of redemption to victims, because the impetus behind Othering, or framing someone as Other, has less to do with individual character traits or behaviors than it does with the needs of the dyadic or group relationships. If the victim is a former group member, outsiders will rarely challenge her humiliation and marginalization, because they are unaware of the nuances and dynamics in play. Those in the group who are not directly involved rarely challenge her stigmatization and rejection either—even if they are uncomfortable with it. To do so may be construed as disloyal and threaten their own bonds of inclusion. Even if an outsider is the topic of conversation, dissenters tread carefully. Look again at Jayde's deflection of the moral overtones being linked to Sara's actions. Her topical assessment did not challenge claims but refocused attention, mitigating, even thwarting, the construction and circulation of devastating social speculation. This is precisely why insignificant observations have the potential to be pivotal. Her comment did not threaten her allegiance to the group or her bonds of friendship but might salvage Sara's reputation (if Sara were my friend or my daughter, I would be grateful for Jayde's seemingly insignificant gesture). It did not necessarily stop moral conjecturing, but Keisha's rejoinder to her, prefaced by "maybe," suggests that Jayde's comment challenged any certainty that was forming around Sara's motivations. It reined in runaway speculation that might have resulted in her stigmatization.

It is insignificant gestures like this that are going to change the culture of bullying. Bystanders *are* able to make them. Skeptical responses from peers are especially powerful, and onlookers need to own and exercise their potential. Emerging cultural norms, especially ones that encourage bystanders to move beyond the comfort zone of minding their own business, must be modeled. Merely a shrug of their shoulders in the face of cruel, speculative gossip signals a disinclination to either agree with or engage in suppositions, diminishing their social significance and often preventing gossip from successfully Othering its target. Carried out within sight or earshot of targets, this gesture alone *connects* with them, denying their social isolation even as it communicates an abashed helplessness to overtly challenge bad behavior. It signals, even for the briefest of time, inclusion.

Additional proactive strategies that interrupt the formation and dissemination of social knowledge include the redirection of focus and attention or subgroup speculation: "Why is Keisha so focused on Sara?" or "How pathetic that Keisha is saying that stuff about Sara just because she . . ." Subtle influencing is not always possible, not always allowed by the group, and at times not even desirable. But an increased awareness of the dynamics that might be in play, and a social skill set that includes deliberate hesitation before silently endorsing the judgments that others are passing, creates a toehold for bystander resistance to bullying. Pauses, hesitations, and small gestures can act as brakes on runaway emotional cruelty. Responsibility for applying these brakes lies with every member of the community.

Laughter

> Lexi was laughing at Keisha, not at me. Jayde could barely suppress giggles, as the whole Sara thing suddenly seemed absurd. Aaliyah picked up on her mirth, and suddenly we were all laughing together— all, except Keisha. She tried to smile but was unconvincing. It didn't matter. I was so relieved I could have hugged Jayde. I had been punished enough for chatting with Sara's friends in the cafeteria.

Laughter is universal. It is linked to neurological firings that produce complex interactions in the brain. Associated with happiness, joy, pleasure, and silliness, even, it usually occurs socially, a response triggered by external stimuli. Yet laughter is also an integral aspect of humiliation, scorn, and contempt, linking glee (gleeful degradation?) to the emotional violence bound up with bullying. The disparity between these two functions is not as great as it seems. As Konrad Lorenz notes, they are two sides of the same coin:

> Laughter produces, simultaneously, a strong fellow feeling among participants and joint aggressiveness against outsiders. Heartily laughing together at the same thing forms an immediate bond. . . . Finding the same thing funny is not only a prerequisite to a real friendship, but very often the first step towards its formation. Laughter forms a bond and simultaneously draws a line. If you cannot laugh with others, you feel an outsider, even if the laughter is in no way directed against yourself. (1963, 284)

As with gossip, sociologists configure laughter as a form of interaction intrinsic to the construction of social bonds. It articulates a particular relationship to an artifact (or an Other), demarcating boundaries between those who share that relationship and those who do not. Laughing *with* others produces social connection. Chuckles break down barriers, identifying and solidifying points of convergence, facilitating alliance (as in the fictional narrative at the beginning of the section: "suddenly we were all laughing together"). Public eruptions of laughter are contagious, beckoning social relating ("Aaliyah picked up on her mirth"). They even have the capacity to create rapport between strangers in situations that lead to no further relationship (e.g., the audience at a comedy club).[10] Like gossip, laughter positions those engaged in it, revealing sympathies and dispositions that at times require clarification ("Sorry I laughed; I couldn't help myself—just the *way* she said it was funny"). Finding something funny situates an individual interpersonally as well as socially: working-class humor often pantomimes the affectations of the rich, Republicans parody the political and social views of Democrats, and men caricature the logic of women.

Laughter not only reflects a relationship with the world we are socialized *into* but is how we are socialized *by* it. Consider early childhood, when the innocent faux pas of the young are a source of amusement for adults. Through malapropisms and category errors ("Doesn't the cat want nail polish too?") children induce laughter in those around them.[11] This response signals to a child (who courts affirmation in every interaction) that she has erred, has done or said something unexpected or wrong, and needs to reconsider her behavior. (Note that the self-awareness required for laughter to be experienced as humiliating may not yet have emerged.) Often intended as a gentle rebuke, laughter in this context is inclusive, reintegrative. Socializing laughter may even encourage a child to see her own behaviors as silly, taking herself as an object, allowing her continued connection with others *in terms of* the now-comical error.[12] In dispelling any tension arising from her failure to conform to social expectations, laughter reinforces social bonds through its reaffirmation of norms.

On the other hand, even in childhood, the laughter of others may be laced with sarcasm, hold mockery, and be experienced as humiliating. Far from inclusive, it is a reproach, a disruption of connection, and an assertion of superiority. Making fun of someone is laughing at not only the mistake but the person who made it. Children who are made into objects of ridicule learn to avoid missteps that expose them as inadequate. Reprimanded and belittled by laughter, a child also learns that adopting the other's perspective is the condition for reconnection, if not redemption. If she cedes her voice, she will be rewarded with approval and even reintegration. (And if she laughs at others, *she* will have power.)

In either scenario, laughter, which is ubiquitous in the socialization of children, instills a key behavioral norm: laughter is a—if not *the*—correct, deserved response to social inappropriateness. In learning what is funny, a child not only internalizes the norms circumscribing her habitus but masters the manner for articulating disapproval and sanctioning social trespasses. She not only learns to discriminate between same-as, or correct, behaviors and other, or wrong, behaviors; she learns that wrong behaviors are a source of amusement. Otherness is funny and can be mined for its entertainment value, even at the expense of the individual who has committed the faux pas.

In learning to be laughed at she learns to laugh, coming to recognize, interpret, and imitate all manner of nuances. Calibrations in volume, length, and tone communicate different social information, variously functioning to share delight, create social bonds, check behavior, identify blunders, scorn difference, or destroy relationship. Laughter is a social barometer with inflections that all children learn to read. It registers intent, the magnitude of missteps, and the extent of adjustments called for in the future.

A person's willingness to join in the laughter over her own gaffe or indiscretion can challenge and effectively subvert any negative implications that threaten to position her as an Other and become attached to her person. Laughing along keeps her connected, endorsing shared values from squarely *within* group boundaries. She may even, as a remedial strategy, initiate the laughter at her behavior, forestalling social reproof and preempting attempts to place her outside the group. In doing this, she manages laughter, keeping its focus *on* a particular action and not *at* her.

Attempting to manage the opinions of others by insisting that laughter be inclusive, even if one is well aware that exclusion is the intent, is a healthy psychological response. An ability to not take oneself so seriously gets beyond the vulnerability that inheres in an other-directedness, even if doubts and insecurities are quietly raised. Even a hollow laugh is a gesture of resistance, however fragile ("Ha ha, you're *sooo* funny"). Additional techniques for managing the meanings and values signified by laughter include outright denial of humor in the situation ("That's *not* funny") or turning laughter back on its originators. Laughing *at* the amusement of others is an act of defiance, a denial of the legitimacy of the ridicule, and a rejection of the personal reprimand intended by it ("You think that's *funny*? [*Snort*] God, you're pathetic!"). Aggressive parodies might even reemploy laughter to mock those who find humor in the situation. Nancy Reincke is not wrong in asserting that laughter in the face of derogatory narratives is an important part of the *process* of *creating* counterconstructions of knowledge—ones that emerge from the point of view of difference (1991, 31).

These nuanced cues are not, however, the full measure of laughter's complexity, as they give no indication of its ability to function in more than one capacity. Grins may stave off threats of social rupture even as they put an individual on notice. Ridicule may strengthen social bonds, as when mockery serves as a rite of passage, leveling group members only to more tightly bond them (gangs, the military, or sports teams). Mirth is a double-edged sword. Its intent may be indirect or serve multiple purposes. Bystanders are able to take advantage of this complexity in their own manipulations of laughter. Directed (or redirected) *anywhere but at the victim*, their mirth also has the potential to interrupt the dynamic in which bullies and their targets are locked. Intruding on the interaction, it disarms aggressors, diminishing their power and diffusing the situation. By breaking in on shaming in progress, laughter becomes a diversion, a site of social resistance. "Lexi was laughing at Keisha, not at me. Aaliyah picked up on her mirth, and suddenly we were all laughing together." Here, a bystander has used laughter to redirect the focus of attention. Bystanders can also pointedly refuse to be pulled in by laughter's appeal, resisting the invitation to join in the Othering. (We have all stood by and witnessed the awkwardness that ensues when laughter falls flat. Antibullying initiatives can deliberately encourage *active* nonresponse.) Social humiliation relies on the participation of bystanders and their affirmation of its intent. A refusal to be seduced by vicious jeering not only questions but perhaps undermines the intent (and the judgments) behind it. Clearly, when laughter goes unchallenged, when it effectively singles out, judges, and denigrates, when it denies connection and brandishes scorn and rejection as a social weapon, it realizes its destructive potential. Even less-obvious snickers of contempt and sneers of disdain turn differences into fault lines that separate and shame.[13] And if no attempts are made to challenge divisive laughter or its judgments, if the boundaries it draws are tacitly endorsed and ratified, victims have good reason to believe "*everyone* thinks that I . . ." and "*everybody* is against me."

Bystanders (i.e., everybody) often protest that they saw the victim laughing along and so assumed that the situation must, in some capacity, be inclusive. Their observations are not amiss, although their conclusions may be. Victims may laugh compulsively, a fragile resistance that manages tears or allows them to nervously stand their ground, as opposed to blushing, bowing their head, or becoming enraged. Even if distress is not apparent, or the public rebuke is deserved, any individual who becomes an object of ridicule will have added discomfort if others join in. During such spectacles, a small, seemingly inconsequential gesture by a bystander, such as refusing to lend her own laughter to the chorus, has the potential to minimize any snowballing effect. Nonparticipation refuses an endorsement of rejection. This act by a bystander poses nominal social risk even to insiders, as it is vague, indirect, and not necessarily a social challenge; she simply has something better to do.

Moreover, nonparticipation fits, hand in glove, with the prevailing ethos to mind one's own business, to not become involved. Ironically, such a stance deprives bullies of an audience. Public humiliation requires spectators, and refusing to be co-opted into this role is yet another option available to bystanders. Voyeuristic interest often prevents onlookers from routinely walking away, much as drivers often slow to take in the accident on the side of the road. Deliberately leaving the scene may be a refusal to lend support to bullies, even though it is, simultaneously, a refusal to support victims. If it cannot be determined whether the object of laughter is participating in the mirth, is a recipient of legitimate public humiliation, or is a victim of ridicule and social abuse, why lend voice to either side in the moment? Determinations can be made as social information is gathered and gossip is vetted, and appropriate responses can quietly be offered to one or the other participant after the public spectacle. A shrug of the shoulders—toward victims, aggressors, or other bystanders—does not communicate disinterest so much as an inability to judge, or even a deferring of judgment, a deliberate refusal to unthinkingly join in.

Rubber-stamp participation is often, unfortunately, more about *being seen*, more about cultivating the perception that one is in league with a dominant voice, than about humiliating a target. (If called out by an authority figure, these participants are the ones who truly answer that they do not know why they were laughing.) This is the sticking point with laughter—its ability to instantly create community. Heightened awareness of how such joining in is perceived by targets (e.g., media critiques of this response) may contribute, in a low-key way, to the sea change in progress (new behavioral norms may turn laughing along into bullying or cast tacit approval as uncool, wannabe behavior). One fewer person joining in, one person walking away, is *everybody minus one*, a good place to start. Eye contact, shrugging, or moving on may be noted by the victim and model alternative behavior to other onlookers.

In sum, the various functions of laughter, and the nuances communicated through it, make it clear that, like gossip, laughter is integral to normative social dynamics. It shares delight, creates bonds, polices boundaries, mirrors disapproval, offers resistance to authority, and destructively Others. As with gossip, cruel, derogatory laughter *at* difference can create intimacy between group members, even as it ostracizes and excludes. Also like gossip, it is caught up with intentionality, which places its meaning on a continuum that cannot be objectively defined or even subjectively agreed on. And again as with gossip, sites of resistance may involve bystanders intervening in unobtrusive ways, ways that play with and manipulate laughter's dual capacity. In response to the exclusionary laughter *at* a victim, a bystander may verbally affirm that she finds humor in the situation yet interrupt the laughter with words—"Yeah, yeah, we know, ha ha; now let's get out of here and . . ."—or she may laughingly groan at the whole situation, shifting focus from the victim and the spectacle with a "Not again—must you? Really?" deflective parry. These actions bend the emphasis of laughter toward bonds that are shared and away from differences that are Othered.

Stereotypes and Categories

Sara is a walking iconoclast.

Despite claims of full Cherokee ancestry, she has a round pale face, light eyes, and kinky, unmanageable hair (and can only shrug and laugh at the war whoops and rhythmic pow-wow drumming parodied in the hallways).

Other students are usually surprised when they discover that Sara is a cheerleader. She doesn't hang with the popular crowd or sport a 102-pound frame (in fact, her solid body type belies the athleticism that earned her a spot on the squad and routinely gives rise to snide lesbian-themed innuendos).

In addition, Sara and her family belong to the revivalist church outside town known around school as the Jesus-freak church. Although she spends hours at services on Sunday, Sara has somehow managed to resist being lumped in with the other members of the church (the so-called God squad), who are all but outcasts to the rest of Anytown High.

Stereotypes like the ones in this fictional narrative are "ready intelligibilities" (to borrow a phrase from Gergen and Gergen 1988). They code and further many of the differences that are played on by gossip and laughter, making them little more than prefabricated vehicles for Othering.[14] Built on the isolation and overemphasis of particular features, stereotypes caricature difference, often alleging inferiority on social or personal levels.[15] However, unlike other dynamics involved in the sorting of the social world, stereotyping, as a process, claims roots in cognitive functioning. It is hardwired into our brains. We break down and classify the world in which we live, reducing, sorting, and labeling reality on the basis of divisions we construct. This sorting and classifying is integral to the daily processing of an overwhelming amount of often complex information and warrants closer scrutiny.

Links between stereotyping and cognitive functioning (mental processes responsible for the breakdown of information) are well documented and seemingly legitimate the simplistic social classifications and relentless labeling at the heart of Othering. We process the whirlwind of people passing through our lives by using scant amounts of information to make inferences about them and even act on the basis of the conclusions we draw. Solomon Asch began studying this process in the 1940s and came to conclude that we interpret (stereotype) the personalities of others not well known to us according to what he called "central organizing traits" (Asch 1946). These traits condense overall impressions of others into distinct judgments about their personalities. For example, people who seem happy and outgoing are considered warm, while those perceived as aloof and indifferent are judged cold. These intuitive assessments not only influence the meanings attached to their behaviors but become the basis of additional characteristics we attribute to them. Outgoing people are often expected to be generous and sincere, while aloof individuals are readily typed as arrogant and calculating.

Further research established that we organize and classify the information about out-group members on the basis of static attribute categories that reflect physical characteristics (e.g., pretty, old, or fat), ascribed social roles (e.g., emo, God squad, or jock), and/or social evaluations (e.g., slut, bitch, loser, or fag) (see Linville and Jones 1980; Sedikides, Olsen, and Reis 1993). These embodied qualities, isolated and distorted, pack judgments into simplistic orderings that *become* social identities (Cherokee, cheerleader, solid body type, Jesus freak).[16] In contrast, in-group information is contextualized and interpreted in terms of unique personal qualities. Unlike the identities of outsiders, those of group members are rich and multifaceted, as intentions and motivations are factored into an understanding of their actions. Victims of bullying—whether they be former group members or those never allowed to belong—are caricatured and characterized by cliché, formulaic out-group typifications.[17]

If we process the actions of others in terms of in-group and out-group relationships, and if such cognitive classifying is inevitable, automatic even, then perhaps bias and discrimination are beyond our control. If stereotyping can be traced to neurocognitive functioning—if we cannot help but simplify, categorize, and stereotype—can we help but Other?

To more fully explore this question, Patricia Devine (1989) focuses attention on the relationship between classifications and their activation. Her studies not only confirm that stereotypes (caricatures of out-groups) are triggered spontaneously but demonstrate that they are activated *subliminally*. Sorting the world into preexisting social categories cannot be helped. The implications of this are stunning. Devine pretested for prejudice levels in her subjects and found no correlation between their levels and the activation of stereotypes. That is, she found spontaneous, subliminal sorting equally in individuals who scored high *and those who scored low* on prejudice rankings, suggesting that low prejudice is itself a response that attempts to inhibit automatically activated stereotypes.[18] Other studies corroborate these findings, documenting that stereotypes inform perception, influencing the information processing of individuals who have preexposure to them. This research has profoundly disturbing implications in our media-saturated world, in which even the most diligent of caregivers cannot prevent children from being primed with labels and social categories. Stereotypes are social shorthand and help navigate the social world no less than gossip and laughter—and, it appears, we are programmed to sort our world through prejudices and biases over which we have little control.

Or are we? Despite these findings and the fascinating body of work that continues to emerge in the relatively new field of social neuroscience, the conclusions indicated by this cognitive model (that we are hardwired to stereotype) need to be suspended. Viewed in a broader *social* context, several additional pieces of information disrupt what amounts to a scientific endorsement of social bias and prejudice. Consider, first, that within this research *stereotypes* themselves are undifferentiated from the process of stereo*typing*. A stereotype (noun) is the product that springs from the process of stereotyping (verb). The former are constructed socially, while the latter refers to a process with both cognitive and social aspects. Much cognitive research subsumes the social aspect (stereotypes) within the process (stereotyping), conflating questions about stereotypes with questions about the process of stereotyping itself. This conflation in turn legitimates prejudice and bigotry, reducing them to spontaneous behavioral tendencies.

Further, the process of stereotyping is often conflated with the process of categorization (by defining stereotypes as nothing more than social categories). This effectively blurs the line between cognitive processing and social construction.[19] While stereotyping involves categorization, and the tendency to sort is a *cognitive* process, categories—the basis of sorting—need not incorporate judgments. That is, both processes involve sorting, but cognitive functioning need not occur along the *social* lines established by stereotypes. In fact, stereotyping more accurately reflects a *social* process, as stereotypes, unlike categories, are constructed in relation to *subjectively defined, nonspecific norms* (e.g., pretty, old, or fat). Unlike the genus or species of biological taxonomies, they exist in relation to, and imply, a *relative, fluctuating standard* against which others are measured (and often found wanting). Othering may be linked to cognitive processes, but stereotyping differs from categorization insofar as its sorting is not based on fixed, identifiable characteristics (e.g., eight legs or exoskeletons). Categories have objectively verifiable attributes, not subjectively determined differences rife with connotations. Marginalization on the basis of categorization is nonsensical (when have Papilioninae looked down on Pyrrhopyginae?). Stereotyping, on the other hand, actively tends social boundaries, *creating* distance and denying connection or belonging to those who are culturally and socially constructed as different.

Stereotypes also cue emotional response. They overlay and integrate objective characteristics, called a master narrative, or master status (Sara's sex, race, and age), and other, clearly subjective social attributes (Sara's weight, cheerleading, and religious affiliation) with *beliefs, expectations,* and *feeling-based judgments.* Master narratives are *ascribed*—they are linked to primary (usually fixed) identifying characteristics that dominate the architecture of personal and social identity and are beyond the individual's control. Other categories are *achieved*—their boundaries are permeable and allow for movement. Importantly, it is not always possible to determine whether status is ascribed or achieved. For example, the statuses of weight and gender are hotly contested. Precisely because these attributes are believed by many to be within the individual's control, there is social animus against those who ignore—or flout—norms surrounding them. They are perceived to *choose* to violate social expectations and are rejected, shamed, and placed outside community on that basis. One is born a woman or Cherokee, but, it is argued, one is not born a fat lesbian. How responsible and reliable is someone who ignores or defies social norms, *choosing* to be either of these? A significant percentage of the population believes itself well within its rights to judge and condemn individuals who embody such traits. Ostracizing them is merely policing cultural boundaries and identifying threats to the organization of society.

Whether ascribed or achieved, these categories are narrative and rife with shifting social connotation. Consider what it meant to be a woman or Native American in the early twentieth century or what it means to be old today. Connotations, linked to *ever-changing* boundaries of difference, overlay social categorization with predispositions and prejudices. More than sort, stereotypes organize behavior. They type out-group members and inform interactions with them, prescribing and proscribing interrelating. And by ordering the world as if the content of stereotypes reflects rational, objective differences, we actively construct a society in which prejudices and subjective biases have very real and often unfair consequences.[20]

Abandoning social hierarchies that *we* construct (for example, along the lines of sex and race) does not threaten the functioning of society, although it does modify the dominant power structures within it. The recent deconstruction of racial and feminine/masculine stereotypes, the dismantling of emotional overlays that limited and typed these master narratives, has enriched individuals, society, and culture. Similar deconstruction of biases, beliefs, and attitudes linked to other stereotypes—notably those that oppress and reject "fags" and "fatties"—is long overdue. Cultural critiques must become invested in facilitating the creation of "'neutral' categories, within which each human being is evaluated in terms of specific information about him, and not in terms of a powerful evaluative frame of reference applying to the category of which he happens to be a member" (Tajfel 1963, 14).

Experience tells us that neutralizing stereotypes—especially those surrounding master narratives perceived to involve choice (weight and gender)—will be far more difficult than this formula suggests. Choice engages norms, and *choosing* to contravene them does not always call principles of self-determination (or respect for them) into play. Uniqueness must fall within an acceptable range of social behaviors. Recall that the desire to be oneself is not a desire to be fundamentally different from everyone else but rather an aspiration to situate individual differences within communal allegiance—that is, within the norms and values that unify a given community. As long as gender and weight are construed as *behaviors* within the individual's control, there is no reason for society to realign its values. Rather, it is the responsibility of the individual to act within a socially acceptable, *normative* range in order to be entitled to the protections and benefits society offers.

Constructed this way, choosing (to cross gender lines, overeat, overachieve, etc.) is directly related to the social brain hypothesis, discussed previously, in the section on gossip. It suggests that humans have valid evolutionary reasons for homing in on differences in any social sorting. To the extent that the world is appropriated in terms of social relationships, it is in our best interests to identify individual points of divergence that may signal threats to social bonds or the integrity of the group as a whole. Same-sex desiring or lack of personal control (overeating) threatens relationship boundaries and willfully subverts the norms of the collective—heterosexuality and a healthy, trim figure. Negative stereotypes surrounding either point to moral flaws, willingly embraced, and deserving of derogatory typing, social Othering, and even bullying.

That we appropriate the world in terms of relationship is no small part of the difficulty involved in neutralizing stereotypes. How can neutral social categorization be *meaningful*? We could group people with green eyes or people who stand between five feet six and five feet eight but toward what end? These are not socially significant categories. It is the *meaning* of differences that makes them significant to society. Can stereotypes be reconstructed in ways that retain meaning without locking individuals into hopeless, loathsome typifications? (What are the norms that surround sexuality and gender roles, as well as weight, and why does contravening them threaten the group? What is it about the differences that requires their marginalization?) As long as prejudice against particular attributes is normative, we need not understand those characterized by them in any complex way, include them in the distribution of social resources, or have reason to defend them against public ridicule (engaged in with the intent of policing social boundaries).

This raises a second critical question: What might motivate an individual to question the social judgments associated with one or another stereotype (especially those rife with negative connotations)? Foucauldians argue that social categories structure and maintain the hierarchies and power relations found in all groups. Stereotypes and stereotyping function to uphold the status quo, and those with social resources are invested in maintaining structures of subordination. As Michael Pickering put it, "The Other is always constructed as an object for the benefit of the subject who stands in need of an objectified Other in order to achieve a masterly self-definition" (2001, 71). If going along with negative stereotypes helps secure personal and social identity (even tacitly and indirectly), what might motivate individuals to reevaluate simplistic, pejorative social judgments and the people consigned to powerless, even reviled, social categories?

Heterogeneous, multicultural society will certainly be an asset in moving beyond simplistic Othering. If most members of society have at least one acquaintance who possesses a vilified characteristic, shifts are already being made. The derogatory characterizations that have kept overweight, homosexual, transgendered, Islamic, or other typed individuals in the out-group are disintegrating in the face of (even distant) relationship bonds. The fluidity and relativity of stereotypes, which differentiates them from categories, allows for revisions. Connotations change, and typing that does not lead to disenfranchisement is increasingly possible. These relationships themselves—the self-determination that allows us to choose whether to allow stereotypes to proscribe and prescribe interrelating—must be privileged.

The social media have no small role in this. Consider the recent rehabilitation of nerds or the acceptance of same-sex unions. Both stereotypes have been revised, and individuals placed in either category have overcome much of the stigma and rejection that social forces arrayed against them. This change attests to the malleability of entrenched cultural typifications (and the connotations linked to them). Nerdiness and homosexuality continue as social classifications, and individuals in these categories continue to cluster around traits (for example, social awkwardness). But these traits no longer exile them, no longer categorically confine them to out-groups. (In fact, select aspects of style that typified nerds in prior decades have become quite popular—repackaged and recirculating within the cultural economy.) Admittedly, advances in technology have helped open paths of redemption for both groups (in vastly different ways), while the media have endorsed and embraced characteristics previously scorned. Inadequate social pariahs now contribute to the richness of our social fabric, their one-time Otherness a relatively neutral attribute. Can antibullying campaigns learn from this shift? Can the revenge of the nerds help engineer the deconstruction of other devastating stereotypes? What positive characterizations might counter the purely negative valence of our most despised social categories, maintaining difference while imbuing it with potential?[21]

Competition

Stereotypes and stereotyping are supported by, even while they support, yet another social dynamic: competition. Competition, simply put, is about the struggle for control over resources—be it land, food, sexual partners, money, or social status. Situated on a continuum between conflict and cooperation, competitive behavior slides between antagonism and partnership in an attempt to negotiate obstacles to success. Requiring regulation lest it deteriorate into conflict, the contest to prevail, whether on Wall Street or in a sporting event, unfolds in terms of rules of engagement. Successes and failures are determined within established boundaries. Interestingly, and perhaps tellingly, the sole arena of competition that is relatively unregulated is the social. Only vague, informal, and largely unenforceable norms moderate social strivings. Few if any clear-cut penalties curtail engagement, which happens anytime and anywhere, often over nebulous stakes.

> Seating in the cafeteria was going to be a problem. Part of the outside wall had cracked when a drunk driver smashed into the building on Tuesday, and a whole section of tables was roped off. School officials claimed that the accident had interrupted cell phone and Internet service (though no one understood how it could be responsible for that level of damage), and everything was a bit chaotic. Tensions were high enough two days before prom without the stress of having to find each other and fight for seats. We *needed* a place to talk. Keisha had let slip some comments about Sara's dress, and we had to figure out how to do damage control. It wouldn't have been a big deal if Devon hadn't found out what Keisha had said and posted a response.
>
> I still didn't get what was so inspiring about Devon.
>
> Whatever.
>
> Frankly, the whole thing with Sara was beginning to realllllllly bore me. My brother and her brother hung out, and I don't have a problem with her, but Keisha was getting relentless. Why can't she just admit she's jealous? If anybody else saw the way she acts they would instantly say she's trying to compete with Sara.

In the preceding fictional narrative, several resources have sparked struggles: seating in the cafeteria, Devon, and the authority to define the group's relationship to Sara. Despite the urgency lent it by prom, the scramble for seats is hardly a core issue. The dominant, yet oblique, power struggles are over Devon and the social positioning of Sara. These struggles (occurring within and external to the group) organize and control actions, even though their underlying dynamic is ill defined and only beginning to be acknowledged. As competitiveness around both issues comes to a head, there are no clear boundaries that will contain it. The terms under which the struggles will be played out are even less certain, although it appears that gossip, laughter, and stereotyping all contribute to the drama that is unfolding. What, then, can be said about social competition; what norms are invoked in this tenuous social dance, what social and psychological dynamics drive engagement, and (how?) might they be influenced?

Competition is the infrastructure of capitalist society, imbuing economic, social, and personal relationships with tension. It undergirds the pursuit of grades, promotions, sexual partners, and sporting-event trophies no less than friendship and love. Little more than civilized conflict, it is the master meta-narrative of Western societies, prizing individual initiative and agency. As is well known, expanding cities, populated by relative strangers, were ripe for the deregulation of competitive social impulses. Values such as honesty, fairness, tolerance, and respect fell prey to the need to stand out and make a name for oneself in this secular world.

In American society, competitive behaviors came to be articulated by distinctly masculine and feminine norms and expectations. Sex and gender stereotypes, backed in some instances by formal law, ensured that women and men did not compete in the same way. Differences existed, and continue to exist, in content as well as *form*. While women and men both gossip (often with different vocabularies and at different length), laugh (often at different things), and create stereotypes (that may be disparate), they gossip, laugh, and stereotype *in the same way*. Distinctions occur primarily in duration and subject matter. The same cannot be said for competition. Its manifestations and the social and cultural norms circumscribing them (including means of competition, its objects, its arenas, and its rates) differ vastly for boys and for girls. Boys have traditionally been associated with physical contests, overtly vying for success—even against their best friends. Girls, on the other hand, have been denied arenas safe for the expression of rivalry (excepting county bake-offs, the cheerleading squad, 4-H, and of course, wardrobes and appearance) and have consequently become much more covert in their bids for success and jockeying for social position. Even today, when Title IX has literally evened the number of competitive playing fields, and increased liability has curtailed physical violence, blurring differences between male and female modes of engagement, qualitative, sex-based delineations can still be pointed to.

These differences have been variously situated by the nature versus nurture debate, through alternating emphasis on competition (theories linked to classical Marxist positions), competitiveness (theories linked to Freud), and survival of the fittest (theories linked to Darwin). Understood as an evolutionary force, competition was and is the impetus behind both adaptation and unimaginable destruction. Human survival has been a balance between the two. As a social force, competition is a double-edged sword. Not unlike gossip, laughter, and stereotyping, it can unite and facilitate belonging (foregrounding survival of the species, the success of the corporation or team, or the popularity of an individual) even while it oversimplifies, divides, Others, and destroys—especially if it is unregulated, as is the case with much social striving.

Attempts to regulate competitive social impulses will prove challenging in a heterogeneous society that continues to debate the *nature* of competition itself.[22] Proponents of the nurture side of this controversy (social psychologists and to some extent developmentalists) link competitive impulses to the differentiation and separation bound up with the emergence of a masculine identity (C. Gilligan 1982; Eichenbaum and Orback 1989). In this view, connection and intimacy are liabilities. They stunt the development of an assertive, self-determining (masculine) "I." Separation and differentiation—a goal as well as a process—foster competitiveness, a trait that boys are taught to display. They become versed in modes of engagement, openly measure their successes, and proudly take ownership of their accomplishments. An ethos of gamesmanship is caught up with masculinity, linking pride with getting back in the ring. Boys are taught to pick themselves up and keep going, to play through the pain in the struggle to be the best, to be number one. They match skill sets, resources, and intellect in the pursuit of success, with minimal risk to social bonds (e.g., they are allowed to openly compete with other boys for the same girl).[23]

Despite increasing options for identity outside competitive arenas, masculine stereotypes continue to circulate in the cultural economy. Expectations are still hung around the neck of too many male children in subtle and not so subtle ways (action-adventure movies, avatars in video games, toys). Denied displays of pain, compassion, caring, and love, boys have been left to negotiate their interdependence and connectedness to others in a relative cultural void—out of the public gaze, where they cannot be humiliated and held accountable for such feelings and dependencies (read, vulnerabilities). Competition (and, Carol Gilligan argues, a subsequent logic of rational, rule-oriented behavior) is not only encouraged but expected of boys and men, crossing barriers of race, class, and age. Those who refuse to engage, try harder, or be stoic in the face of failure or pain or who simply do not succeed (usually at athletic endeavors) are burdened with social and psychological shame. What are they to make of themselves? Where do they fit in the social order?

Femininity, on the other hand, was and still largely is contingent on *connection* and is vested in the continuation and furtherance of relationship and intimacy. Women continue to create and define self *and success* in terms of networks of inclusiveness and belonging.[24] They are socialized to maintain and repair webs of relationship.[25] In furtherance of empathy and nurturance, girls are still taught to avoid confrontation, often by suppressing overtly competitive urges. This has "led to the attribution of envy, jealousy, and competition to 'stepmothers' and 'stepsisters' [Snow White, Cinderella], forbidding those normal emotions between women" (Navaro 2007, 79). Cutthroat overambitiousness cast self-doubt, uncertainty, and even shame on girls' identity, for it fails to protect connection.[26] As a result, girls have become expert at competing in ways that are nonconfrontational, do not directly challenge relationship, and do not cast aspersions on their claims to femininity.[27] These include gossip, rumors, body language, and other relationally aggressive tactics ("Keisha had let slip some comments about Sara's dress").[28] Denied displays of desire or even feelings of covetousness and jealousy, they have had little choice but to negotiate adversarial impulses in the shadows, acting indirectly, discreetly, and in ways often quietly destructive of relationship. Today, girls appear less discreet, especially on social networking sites, and this visibility often devolves into unregulated conflict, public humiliation, and social destructiveness.

Fundamental differences between male-female competitiveness, which continue to be articulated and sustained through a variety of subtle cultural norms, can alternatively be explained by biochemistry. Rather than imprinting its expectations and roles, culture may do little more than reflect neurophysiology. Scientists in a range of disciplines who are proponents of the nature argument foreground biological distinctions to explain gendered behaviors. Neurobiologists, for example, cite varied hereditary testosterone levels (including prenatal testosterone exposure), augmented by hormones such as cortisone, as causal. Increases in both these steroids have been correlated with a greater degree of aggression, which in turn influences competitiveness.[29] While geneticists often acknowledge that environment and social factors influence the individual, they find physiological factors much more decisive in explaining competitive characteristics and traits. This amounts to suggesting that metanarratives of culture simply echo biological reality. Women are not hardwired to compete, and norms of femininity—ones that perhaps overstep and overstate physiological boundaries—have grown up around this biochemical fact.

Whether testosterone or culture is ultimately privileged does not alter the fact that competition has been promoted and encouraged in the lives of boys and men, although similar feelings and impulses have secretly informed significant aspects of women's interrelating. Bullying, if nothing else, identifies competitiveness as integral to social interaction, regardless of sex or gender. Dissimilar levels of steroids such testosterone may influence the intensity of competitive impulses, or lower levels might simply have allowed girls and women to more readily sublimate and deny these impulses.

While studies of covert competition are just getting under way, overt social competition, as well as the dynamics caught up with and influenced by it, has been studied for years.[30] The Robbers Cave experiment, undertaken in 1954, remains one of psychology's seminal studies, and its unexpected findings posed questions than are still being explored today. The study, which used only male subjects and did not consider sex-related differences, separated young boys into teams and orchestrated bonding, first through intragroup activities and then through the introduction of intergroup competitive tasks.[31] Researchers were surprised to observe how quickly competition strengthened the ties between team members while intergroup aggressiveness heightened, verging on open conflict. The experiment demonstrated how integral an out-group was to an (almost immediate) intensification of group identity. In addition, it documented how readily competition devolved into conflict. Researchers were stunned to realize that the competitive challenges they introduced between the two groups to facilitate in-group bonding needed to be curtailed. Cooperative challenges (requiring the two teams to work together toward a mutually beneficial goal) needed to be introduced ahead of schedule to defuse rising hostilities. Tasks *requiring* collaboration helped diminish and negotiate the overall animosity and heightened level of aggression that the challenges had fostered.

Although ethical considerations prevented the Robbers Cave experiment from being replicated, a variety of alternative protocols that manipulated its competitive elements corroborated these results. Introducing competition pushes individuals to try harder, invest more fully in outcomes, and in general, perform better.[32] In fact, research suggests that heightened results (in terms of both quantity and quality) *require* a competitive aspect. As a condition, it significantly increases motivation, which in turn enhances performances (when compared with individuals and groups in noncompetitive environments).[33] Cooperative conditions, on the other hand, facilitated positive relationships within groups, to the point that across some measures, productivity stands in an almost inverse relationship to feelings of happiness and belonging. That is, individuals do not compete, or do not compete well, in friendly, cooperative environments, because they privilege community over individual success.

These findings become even more interesting (and particularly relevant to our purposes) when sex is introduced as a control. Research that manipulated the male-female composition of groups produced results that suggest *social influences* are still key. Men, relative to women, were found to be more aggressive in mixed-gender *intergroup* exchanges (Van Vugt, De Cremer, and Janssen 2007). However, women were found to be "*as competitive as men when competing against women, but not when competing against men*" (Niederle and Vesterlund 2008, 449; emphasis added). In other words, women *are* competitive, especially against other women, but they seem reluctant to compete (i.e., overtly aggress or appear unfeminine) in front of men.[34] They struggle to best others in ways that are no less ingrained, instinctive, and integral to their being in the social world, ways that still appear to be regulated by cultural norms.

Studies documenting female competitiveness have tantalizing implications for bullying behaviors. Limited engagement is suggestive of social conditioning, but the roots of guarded aggression may just as readily lie in evolutionary survival tactics now hardwired in the brain.[35] Either way, competitiveness prompts a key question: *If* competition is normative and perhaps even hardwired (although its expression remains gendered), *if* competition motivates individuals and facilitates more impressive outcomes (e.g., greater quality and quantity) than cooperation, *if* an intensification of competitive behavior emerges when individuals are similarly matched (rivalry), and *if* gossip and laughter and stereotyping all help construct, maintain, and support power structures (perhaps fanning competition into conflict), can we realistically expect that any modification of norms will be capable of circumscribing the psychological forces and social dynamics that culminate in bullying? Simply put, *why* would anyone cease to act in ways that give him or her a social edge? Without some transpersonal force able to check competitive impulses, it seems unlikely that antibullying initiatives could possibly regulate aggressive social behavior.

Perhaps not unexpectedly, such a transpersonal force—one that has long since stepped into the void left by an omnipotent, omniscient god—can be pointed to. *Public opinion*, as ubiquitous as any divine fountainhead (and no less internalized) has the potential to exercise the power needed to limit social aggression, and many have begun, in earnest, to invoke it. Not surprisingly, members of a narcissistic society—one overly invested in the favorable opinion of others—are vulnerable to the active disapproval that is being called for in response to emotional and psychological cruelty. Even the mere cultivation of awareness has primed several levels of response. That we have begun to think about competitive social brutalities, have begun to decry public humiliation and advocate for intolerance of social violence, is helping create ready intelligibilities around bullying. The ability to hold, and share, negative estimations of aggressive behavior (and have others endorse them) will come to influence self-monitoring. In this way, the process of modifying social norms, even if to seemingly little direct, immediate effect, is crucial. It will slowly change expectations, thereby influencing social practices. Further, predicating this modification on principles that already function as "god terms" in society—the right to individuality, self-determination, and the pursuit of happiness—grounds changes in transcendent cultural values.

Referencing these existent principles will help promote *active* tolerance. *Tolerance* has too readily been translated as minding one's own business, which in turn has resulted in turning a blind eye to all sorts of behaviors, especially bullying. Instead of "indifference to alternative opinions and values," *tolerance* needs to actively foster fairness in social dealings. Respect for the differences of others and active intolerance of ignorance and discrimination need to be modeled, practiced, and reinforced. Paradoxically, this requires that individualism and self-determination be regulated. They can thrive only within limits—ones that privilege others' equal right to such freedoms and ensure the behaviors of any individual or group do not infringe on the self-same entitlements of others. Put differently, we are not enjoined to be tolerant of prejudice, ridicule, or social cruelties.

Regulation is not unprecedented. It became clearly necessary, and was successfully conceived, in the economic arena. Buy-in and adherence to market regulations did not benefit the individual, but they did safeguard her investment against dishonest, discriminatory practices. The regulations, put in place to guard the play of tensions that define and maintain the market—the dialogue of finance—profit a greater good. Aimed at supporting a healthy market no less than remedying its failure, regulations stand in opposition to schemas that promote the success of one or another vested interest. For example, insider trading prohibitions and antitrust laws prevent abuses of power that would restrain trade. Monopolies and unfair collusions quash competition, tipping the balance that sustains a robust market (the community). They are predatory (bullies), unfair, and prohibited. Regulatory practices artificially maintain a balance between conflict and cooperation, which would otherwise not exist. *Competition*, or the indirect conflict that achieves and is achieved by this balance, is sustained by formal and informal prohibitions.

Unfair social practices require similar injunctions. Individuals need to be protected from the predatory public humiliation and social insider trading (gossip, stereotyping, etc.) that is oriented toward illegitimate ends—including not only self-aggrandizement but also the alleviation of boredom (i.e., in the name of entertainment). These illicit goals trade on discriminatory practices and abuses of power that pervert sociation. Social profiteers trade on degradation, ridicule, and rejection (the social destruction of peers) to accrue social status and notoriety. More than anything, it is the addition of entertainment to the list of motivations that has blurred the lines and vaulted social competition to a whole new level. In targeting *audiences*, rather than victims, competitive social sport is unrelated to personal cost, which is capable of regulating its violences. Humiliation for entertainment *cannot* call forth the self-monitoring integral to social interactions between two parties, as it is oriented toward, and cued by, the amusement of bystanders. When "We were just having fun" is the rationale given, humiliation (or response to it, for which a victim can be mocked) *is* the goal. Bystanders, with social scripts that identify them as members of a voyeuristic audience, are content to be diverted, amused, and even titillated by perverse cruelties aimed at provoking a response from victims. Spectacles alleviate boredom, eliciting laughter at the expense of disposable targets and enhancing the popularity of aggressors.

Worse yet, the ability of socially disparaged nonentities to "take it" has made such ill-gotten social power appear victimless. A bystander's rationalization of "How was I supposed to know it upset her?" or simply "I didn't know" furthers passive uninvolvement, helping endorse the consumption of sadistic dominations and submissions. What social principles might question and challenge the social laissez-faire at the heart of this dynamic—the noninterference even denied to free enterprise?

Before principles can be referenced, those involved must *see*, understand, and legitimate the victim's pain. Only then will curbing social aggressions (and the mob mentality that supports them) become the responsibility of all citizens. *We* are the gatekeepers of sociation and must be enjoined to monitor and judge: if you see something, say something. Bystanders must be reminded of their power, unburdened of their indifference or fear, and begin to deny the humor in crippling psychological assaults (as orchestrated on reality TV no less than in the cafeteria). The potential residing in the dual nature of gossip, laughter, and stereotypes needs to be modeled so that it can more readily be marshaled to monitor and safeguard against rapacious competitive practices and abuses of social power. The ultimate reward is not being number one but gaining respect and success *within* community—belonging.

A reevaluation of failure must complement this shift. The sheer pervasiveness of competition in society requires a capacity to negotiate losing—coming in second, third, or even last place. Failure is normative. Someone has to lose. But today's cultural ethos is about winning. Winning is what garners attention and admiration and is something that narcissists, in particular, crave. Trying, but not succeeding, opens opportunities for shame and ridicule. Not to win *is* to lose. What happens then? Culture no longer speaks to or stories giving it your best shot any more than it narrates failure. Trying but not succeeding is failure, and failure is shameful. End of story. Young men learn to pick themselves up and return to the competition not because failing is a matter of course but because it is humiliating. The absence of second-place narratives (let alone last-place narrations) suggests that anything less than being number one is, in effect, unspeakable—unseen and unstoried.[36]

Healthy recognition of the commonality of failure and respect for trying will not only mitigate the pressure to succeed but help negotiate the emotional distress of falling short—in any arena (including the social).[37] This, in turn, may lessen the impulse to demonstrate superiority by mocking and humiliating those who try but fail, especially those who flounder in the face of popularity contests (pathetic wannabes). It is crucial that we, as a culture, figure out how anything less than being the best is to be negotiated (will it be the same for men as for women?).

Modified language games must reflect revisions to the rules of social engagement and to the terms of winning and mediation of failure (including possibilities for redemption). Role scripts for all those involved—competitors, bystanders, winners, and those who come in second, third, fourth, and last place—need editing. Even if changes and modifications to cultural narratives are not immediately taken up and put into play, they exist as a referent. Silence in the face of unfair social competition *produces losers and then denies their stories*. Without stories, there is no way out, no indication that it is even possible to redeem oneself or to coherently negotiate the social losses linked to unchecked social violence, no acceptable way to *be*. This opens the door for other, more literal annihilations of one's peers or one's self. Even if recent tragedies are not reactions to bullying, a correlation between the two has already become integral to social stories that are emerging. To the extent that violence is now seen as a viable counter to humiliation and social abuse, bullying affects each and every one of us and *becomes* our responsibility to address. Expanded roles for bystanders have the potential to head off the stigma, isolation, and shame that follows from social abuse. Refusing to participate in gossip about or laughter at a target's denigration (thereby furthering her degradation), deflecting negative attention being showered on her, or making slight gestures that acknowledge her pain opens the door for (re)connection, for *hope* of surviving her failure and shame, for terms of redemption.

Undeniably, all manner of cruel behaviors mushroom and flourish in places where society has trained itself not to look (for example, in the eyes of a victim). Adolescents live in these cultural blind spots, where relationally aggressive behaviors—displays of social power or popularity via strategies intended to hurt—have gone unchecked and now seem out of control. To address this situation, society's tasks are twofold: First, it will need to devise ways of regulating social competition, beginning with the inclusive capacities in gossip, laughter, and stereotyping. These social forces can be readily marshalled in the service of new norms, ones that question and restrain public humiliation. The dual nature of these dynamics signals regulatory potential and (re)integrative possibilities. Second, it will need to (re)narrate loss and failure, breaking the shameful silence that links inadequacy to victimization, especially the self-blame that helps maintain unfair social practices.

SHAME AND IDENTITY

Girls blush sometimes because they are alive,
Half wishing they were dead to save the shame.
The sudden blush devours them, neck and brow;
They have drawn too near the fire of life, like gnats,
And flare up bodily, wings and all. What then?
Who's sorry for a gnat . . . or girl?—
  —ELIZABETH BARRETT BROWNING, *Aurora Leigh*

Whom do you call bad?—Those who always want to put to shame.
What do you consider most humane?—To spare someone shame.
What is the seat of liberation?—No longer being ashamed in front of oneself.
  —FRIEDRICH NIETZSCHE, *The Gay Science*

There can be no outrage, methinks . . . more flagrant than to
forbid the culprit to hide his face for shame.
  —NATHANIEL HAWTHORNE, *The Scarlet Letter*

Shame. The *real* threat underlying gossip, laughter, stereotyping, and competition. The red flag identified by the popular media and insta-experts alike as the common, underlying (causal?) aspect of school rampages and teen suicides. If shame is (or is believed to be) the common denominator linking so many recent tragedies, why is it so little discussed and ill understood?

In all fairness, the media, as well as local and school authorities, moved quickly in their attempts to prevent further violence after the 1990s rampages, bypassing such questions as: What is shame? How does it arise? How does it function? How is it negotiated? Instead, they attempted to identify shaming *behaviors* and psychoanalyze bullies (or victims-turned-killers) while calling for bystanders to support peers who were marginalized and humiliated.[1] However, as soon became obvious, bullying defies attempts to operationalize its nuanced dynamics—especially those linked to shame. Despite ongoing efforts, authority figures remained (and remain) either unaware of or unable to address situations such as the one described by Laurie during our interview in the fall of 2013:

Here come Jean and—and—how surprising that I can't remember her name. I can see her, though—the two were Mutt 'n' Jeff. What was her name? Anyway, they have—they have already been unkind, but for now it was just unkind. Maybe it was just new-kid hazing they had put me through, and now they want to be friends with me?

Did I really believe that? Believe that after I had walked into a new class and had to find a seat and Jean sprang up and said, "Oh, I'll show you a seat," and literally took my hand and led me over to a seat in the back and sat me down next to a boy that even I knew was a pariah—the one—you know, pen protector, horrible glasses, extremely overweight, and—and she sat me down and said, "Here." And I got it.

Now, that just happened, and here I am at recess, writing to my friend Anne back in Marblehead, and the two of them come over, smiling, and say, "Whatchya doing?" And what I want to establish is—how I'm thinking is "I have a best friend," so I say, "I'm writing to my best friend in Marblehead." "Oh, really?" they say. "Tell us all about it." Basking in all this solicitude, I said, "Well, we love Man from U.N.C.L.E., and she's Napoleon and I'm Illya." "Oh, how wonderful," they say. "Tell us more." So I read them what I'm writing and [pauses] of course, off they go, the two of them, Napoleon-ing and Illya-ing with each other, literally calling kids over and doing it for them and pointing at me, alone, looking dazed and going, "What?" and then, "How stupid am I?" and [trails off].

I was laughed at in the hall, and they would walk behind me and imitate my walk—apparently I walked on my heels, and I'm very tall and skinny and [pauses] everything I do is subject to ridicule, and I didn't have a friend, and every class I was in I was—no one spoke to me that entire year, and then I would walk home alone and go down in the basement and play by myself, and that was my seventh-grade year.

The isolation was unspeakable and made me be—it's hard to describe 'cause I was both steely about it and—it just went straight in and stayed there. It just was, you know, being in the stocks, every day. That's what it was, you know; it was public shaming. That's what the stocks are for, and walking around in the stocks, everyone knows—every grade knows—that's how much of a pariah I was. You walk down the hall and people leave you space. [Pauses] Do not get close to her.

If scenarios like this one remain invisible to school officials or are ignored (because authority figures feel equally helpless), then the fallout from rejection and shame can (continue to) be devastating (personally and socially).

Raising awareness of shame's nature, its cost, and the avenues required for its redemption is crucial. Imagine if some of the kids these two girls called over, the audience they were mockingly posturing for, had conspiratorially rolled their eyes in Laurie's direction; or glanced at her, sighed or winked, and walked away; or said something to her in the hallway.

Shame: The Social Mechanics of a Social Emotion

There was a party. It was at a club, and I didn't really know anyone there, and I was out on a pier eating a hot dog and threw some bits of hot dog down. I had had some Hawaiian Punch in a cup, and I also set it down because I was feeding the seagulls and said something like "Let the birds have some of my Hawaiian Punch." And these two girls appeared—I knew them vaguely—and just turned to each other and got that thing going of repeating to each other what I said and doing their baroque imitation of me, and—and I couldn't—I couldn't see why. And on and on and on they went with it, and that was the—the crux moment, the isolate moment where you know you are "naked in a field of thorns," as my birth mother once put it, and that was—that one sticks in my mind, really. —LAURIE

Shame is a universal feeling state, an emotion or affect,* with cross-cultural physical manifestations.[2] These include blushing or blanching, downcast eyes, sweating, nervous tapping or twitching, bowed head, vocal tremors, and pitch irregularities.[3] Shame shows. It is embodied, emerging from within and occupying the space between the biological and the social, or put differently, is articulated at the interface between the individual and the group. Its distinct, corporeal displays betray an awareness that one's behavior is not in keeping with—perhaps even stands in violation of—norms and expectations.[4]

Clearly, the failure to behave in keeping with norms does not always—or even often—call out a shamed response. Unconventional behavior may, for example, be cited in support of uniqueness and individualism and even become tomorrow's norms—or at least the stuff of urban legends. It is only when unorthodox, idiosyncratic behavior, exposed and/or evaluated by others, *provokes negative self-judgments* that shame emerges. "The bearer of the social triggers of shame is the eye of the Other, the eye of the community" (Heller 2003, 1019). When the gaze of others prompts feelings of failure, inadequacy, and moral inferiority, causing one to be mortified, the experience becomes a site of humiliation. "The guilty party feels annihilated: she blushes, bends her head so she cannot see the judgment of the Eye, runs away or at least feels the urge to disappear or sink into the earth in order not to be seen" (1019).[5]

---

* *Affect* (noun) is a psychological term referring to an expressed or observed *emotional* response; *affect* (verb) means "to influence."

Others function as a mirror, reflecting her inadequacy in their response. They are the bearers of a standard (normative, ill defined, or even illegitimate) against which the individual is conscious of being appraised (and through which she appraises herself) and is found lacking.[6]

It is important to emphasize that others can trigger shame *only* if an individual is invested in their opinion. That is, only the impressions and judgments of others we care about and desire connection with can lead to shame.[7] Inversely, "shame alerts us to things, people, and ideas that we didn't even realize we wanted. It highlights unknown or unappreciated investments" (Probyn 2005, 14). An individual may feel uncomfortable but not shamed to discover she has violated a norm when travelling internationally, or a teen may remain unfazed by the accusations of inadequacy made by an authority figure. Neither is significantly invested in the other, thus neither experiences degradation, let alone a sickness of the soul, in response.

> The thing that moves us to pride or shame is not the mere mechanical reflection of ourselves, but an *imputed sentiment*, the imagined effect of this reflection upon another's mind. This is evident from the fact that the character and weight of that other, in whose mind we see ourselves, *makes all the difference with our feelings*. We are *ashamed* to seem evasive in the presence of a straightforward man, cowardly in the presence of a brave one, gross in the eyes of a refined one and so on. We always imagine, and in imagining share, the judgments of the other mind. (Cooley [1902] 1922, 184–185; emphasis in first two sentences added)[8]

Charles Horton Cooley's insight constructs shame (and pride) as a feedback loop, one continually connecting the embodied self to others and society, linking physical and psychological effects (and affects) to the environment. These feelings become embedded in further interactions, implicitly maintaining—or explicitly exposing—values and investments linked to identity:

> As is the case with other feelings, we do not think much of [social self-feeling] so long as it is moderately and regularly gratified. Many people of balanced mind and congenial activity scarcely know that they care what others think of them, and will deny, perhaps with indignation[,] that such care is an important factor in what they are and do. But this is illusion. If failure or disgrace arrives, if one suddenly finds that the faces of men show coldness or contempt instead of the kindliness and deference that he is used to, he will perceive from the shock, the fear, the sense of being outcast and helpless, that he was living in the minds

of others without knowing it, just as we daily walk the solid ground without thinking how it bears us up. (Cooley [1902] 1922, 208)

In focusing on the *social* relationship within which self-feelings occur, Cooley calls attention to interdependency. Despite (psychoanalytic) culture's attempts to situate an independent self, self arises, and is maintained, intersubjectively. However, society's ongoing homage to independence "prevents us from seeing how much people are really driven by their concern with others' opinions. Our belief in individuals, with its focus on the person as the sole author of his or her actions, blinds us to our interdependence with others" (Cohen 2003, 1100). Other researchers have echoed this observation, noting that a capacity for shame and pride speaks to interconnectedness, despite that being "a great deviation from the very foundations of Western thought. Western culture has at its center the embedded idea of the isolated, self-contained individual. Since . . . shame . . . implies that our self-feelings are dependent on other people, it violates the principle of the self-contained individual" (Scheff 2005, 156). Not only is dependence on others ongoing, but self and other are interrelated in a way that quietly positions affect as central in human functioning. That is, individual behavior and relationships continue to be managed by threats of humiliation and shame—in short, by emotions.

These emotions connect us to others and motivate behaviors integral to sociation. What does this mean? Vulnerability to the opinion of others facilitates self-regulation in social interaction and a sensitivity to the impact one has. Silvan Tomkins (1962–1992) characterizes this connection as "interest," while Thomas Scheff and Suzanne Retzinger (1991) refer to it as "attunement." Attunement produces a heightened awareness of others' expectations and of our own ability—or willingness—to meet them. The social dance that emerges from this interrelating, and the self-control that pride and the threat of shame fosters, is integral to the functioning of society. Erving Goffman (1959, 1963) painstakingly chronicled this other-orientation, contextualizing and giving form to abstract insights. He exposed the *social scripts* underlying social order and the norms orchestrating social discourse. Daily life involves highly synchronized patterns that require familiarity with numerous social roles and attunement to the moves and responses of individuals co-enacting them. Self is situated in the articulation of these roles—correct, expected, or otherwise. The elaborate moves and countermoves through which individuals negotiate and maintain their public images, including impromptu riffs that establish or salvage their identity in social discourse, were likened by Goffman to the theater. In his parlance, social actors always have one eye on the (social) mirror, gauging themselves as objects, appraising their performances on the public stage. Performances are offered in the quest for validation and self-affirmation and geared toward an avoidance of negative, embarrassing feedback.

Like Cooley before him, Goffman was especially intrigued by the *social forces* that referee these exchanges, particularly embarrassment. His work focused on the ways that social actions are tailored to the avoidance of awkward social situations (especially through the management and promotion of identity). In addition, he studied the rituals through which individuals attempt to refute or overcome social stigma, once conferred. Taking Cooley one step further, Goffman contended that all social interaction is bound up with the threat of (or attempts to manage) embarrassment. It "lies at the heart of the social organization of day-to-day conduct . . . [and] plays an important part in sustaining the individual's commitment to social organization, values and convention. It permeates everyday life and our dealings with others. It informs ordinary conduct in areas of social life that formal and institutionalized constraints do not reach" (Heath 1988, 137). While the examples that populate Goffman's books are dated, they still powerfully convey the extent to which self-monitoring determines action (i.e., the importance of presenting oneself correctly) and the complex social dances inspired by (often tacit) efforts to avoid exposure of ineptness or subterfuge. Goffman was at pains to illustrate the lengths to which individuals will go to manage their effect on others and the types of manipulations that carry performances. Appearances matter. As Laurie explained, "What I want to establish is . . . 'I have a best friend,' so I say, 'I'm writing to my best friend in Marblehead.'" Laurie wants to signal to peers at her new school that she is not a social outcast and is worthy of friendship. The response to her attempt to establish social credentials gives credence to Goffman's contention that "there is no interaction in which participants do not take an appreciable chance of being slightly embarrassed or a slight chance of being deeply humiliated" (1959, 243).

Because of this, attempts to preempt exposure, ridicule, and possibly rejection routinely introduce a component of calculation. Premeditations on how to act or deliberate exaggeration in order to appear authentic, competent, trustworthy, or likeable (to target audiences) help ensure the desired response. However, should this contriving and impression management be exposed, authenticity and sincerity become suspect, throwing the desired outcome into question. Credibility is damaged, threatening other social identities and often one's moral integrity as well.[9]

Goffman had little interest in exploring the ramifications of such exposure and rejection for the individual or in deconstructing the nature of embarrassment itself, despite it functioning as the linchpin of his social theory. He did not ask what a negative social status implied for individuals whose performances were rejected or how rejection influenced the construction of personal or social identities. Hand in hand with his refusal to discuss the implications of a spoiled identity was Goffman's unwillingness to discuss the self that exists behind social performances. Yet a backstage self, not unlike a puppeteer, is referred to throughout his work and crucial to his vision. This private, presumably authentic self stands behind the identity a person projects, orchestrating and managing impressions—even inadvertently ruining performances by letting slip, or "giving off" (1959), information that discredits her. Goffman did not speculate on the ontological status of the self that exists behind the performance or whether its construction, or very nature, was ultimately intersubjective or even other-oriented. Grounding his work in the judgmental gaze of the other, Goffman focused on the implicit infrastructure of social interaction and, in particular, the forces that regulated sociation while helping negotiate public identity. His work is rife with narratives of discrediting, all of which illustrate the role of the audience, or bystanders, in each performance. These individuals assess presentations of self, endorsing or discrediting the performance and often the performer. Goffman was interested in how enactments of identity, once disrupted (either for or by this audience), are managed, as well as how face, once lost, is restored. He seized on the fleeting, often visceral embodiments of embarrassment that offered cues and clues, analyzing responses to them, as opposed to the self responsible for them.

It was left to one of his students, Thomas Scheff, to take up questions that emerged from the universality of visceral indicators (blushing, stammering, downward gaze, etc.) and unpack the implications underlying the disruption of social dances. Scheff shifted Goffman's dramaturgical focus from the verity of social performances and the ways that audience members seek to acquire information regarding their authenticity to the significance of the social bonds being constructed. If Goffman was correct in his assertion of the paramount importance of identity management and the function of embarrassment in social interactions, what can be said of the nature of social bonds that performers went to great lengths to maintain?

In raising this question, Scheff focused on the importance of social connectedness and the magnitude of any threats to the social bond. He looked beyond the social discomfort that foregrounds Goffman's presentation of self, penetrating the surface of scripted social exchanges and coming face to face with the enormity of the social consequences threatening the individual. If the potential to lose face has the importance Goffman attributed to it, embarrassment, linked as it is to social stigma, must reference more than particular situations or isolated behaviors. And as soon becomes clear, performances are *inter*actions that levy moral demands on their audiences. They orchestrate a social identity (and reality) in which others are asked to invest and even participate.[10] Should the performance be discredited, shown to be contrived or insubstantial, the individual is held accountable for a moral violation. Labeled inadequate, a liar, or a pathetic wannabe, her failure is measured by the degree of diminution of others' trust and the extent of their lessening investment in relationship. Trust informs social bonds, and if called into question, the convictions and expectations that animate relationship are attenuated; credit is withdrawn. Failed impression management, *itself an inadequacy*, casts doubt, often weakening social bonds. Doubt challenges others' belief in her, eroding her right to make claims on them. Each and every presentation of self is open to scrutiny, requiring ongoing vigilance and an anticipation of and ability to manage misunderstandings (the *way* they are handled also references and reveals aspects of her backstage authentic self). Insofar as each performance can be linked to moral character, no less than social and personal identity, each discrepancy risks more than blushing awkwardness and temporary self-consciousness. Discredited social performances threaten the destruction of self—through shaming.

Shame severs connectedness.

It exiles.

It inscribes the social flesh and brands the psyche.

Shame bears witness to the perversion of the self that *I*, and *others*, believe me to possess.

Helen Lynd argues that an experience of shame is devastating because it is not linked to "an isolated act that can be detached from the self. . . . Its focus is not a separate act, but revelation of the whole self. The thing that has been exposed is what I am" (1958, 50–51).

Shame entails a moral indictment that disrupts—if not *ruptures*—social bonds.

The threat of lost connection strikes deep into the heart of (wo)man, ripping well-being and contentment from her, denying interrelationship.[11] Shamed (shameful) behavior evidences a human stain and has "the effect of cutting [a person] off from society and from himself so that he stands a discredited person facing an unaccepting world" (Goffman 1963, 19).[12] "By definition, of course, we believe the person with a stigma is not quite human. On this assumption we exercise varieties of discrimination, through which we effectively, if often unthinkingly, reduce his life chances" (Goffman 1963, 5).

A shamed individual (particularly one with visible differences, whom Goffman had in mind) is often complicit in this discrimination, diminished by her own self-judgment. Identifying with the (shameful) self-object others perceive her to be, she accepts and participates in the denigration of self (and the disassembling of any other identity; see the discussion of master narratives and stereotypes in Chapter 2).

Joining in the gaze of others, turning a critical eye on self, she becomes subject to a level of psychic distress that may affect her ability to function:

The self system is caught in a bind in which the ability to act or to continue acting becomes extremely difficult. Shame disrupts ongoing activity as the self focuses completely on itself, and the result is confusion: inability to think clearly, inability to talk, and inability to act. (M. Lewis 2003, 1187)

Internal chaos, occasioned by public humiliation and damage to social bonds, often gives rise to confused, desperate attempts to salvage relationships. Anxious absorption with self-presentation and frantic attempts to please signal and highlight the ongoing import of *acceptance* and *belonging*.

Acceptance and belonging are key to the functioning of both society and the individual. (Recall Laurie's anguish, years later, over her social isolation in school: "I didn't have a friend, and every class I was in I was—no one spoke to me that entire year, and then I would walk home alone and go down in the basement and play by myself, and that was my seventh-grade year. The isolation was unspeakable and made me be—it's hard to describe 'cause I was both steely about it and—it just went straight in and stayed there.") Psychologists, echoing Émile Durkheim's 1897 *Suicide*, assert that acceptance, belonging, and an individual's relation to her community have a direct bearing on psychic health.[13] The body, shaped by thoughts, memories, and emotions peculiar to it, must yet feel itself fitted to the social organism, must believe it is part of something that transcends self. Helen Block Lewis (1971), a pioneer in shame research, understood this need to be biopsychosocial. In her view, shame is a *social instinct* that signals threats to the social bond. Belonging, placed on a par with biological needs for food and water, relies on fine (instinctive?) attunement to nuances of interaction to gauge and negotiate the gaze of the other. Any lessening of connection or failure of inclusion may be a precursor to further degrees of emotional and psychic distance and responsible for a variety of ill effects.

Roy Baumeister and Mark Leary advance Lewis's view, asserting that

> many of the emotional problems for which people seek professional help (anxiety, depression, grief, loneliness, relationship problems, and the like) result from people's failure to meet their belongingness needs. Furthermore, a great deal of *neurotic, maladaptive*, and *destructive behavior* seems to reflect either desperate attempts to establish or maintain relationships with other people or sheer frustration and purposelessness when one's need to belong goes unmet. (1995, 497; emphasis added)

Belongingness is considered a requirement of psychic coherence[14]—a *need* that "takes precedence over esteem and self-actualization" to the extent that "aversive reactions to a loss of belongingness should go beyond negative affect to include some types of pathology" (500). If this construction of belonging is correct, then, as Goffman (1959, 1963) asserted, much of human motivation springs from a need to avoid being left out, cast out, shamed, or Othered.

Recent findings in neuroscience support these claims, offering proof that neediness is a justifiable and even appropriate disposition. C. Nathan DeWall's research, for example, establishes that "social exclusion represents such a basic and severe threat to human well-being that the body encodes the experience of social exclusion in a manner that is similar to physical pain" (2009, 201; see also MacDonald and Leary 2005). This neural overlap between physical pain and the psychological distress resulting from rejection or exclusion is probably the result of evolutionary adaptation. A break in connection resulting from maternal rejection or social exclusion would, like physical injury, threaten survival (suggesting that wearing the right pair of jeans may well be more important than we have supposed). This level of embodiment is discussed at length below and in Chapter 4. More immediately, the relationship between belongingness needs and shame requires further consideration.

Shame and Anger

Given the import of belonging, individuals go to lengths much greater than Goffman documented to maintain control over the identity they project (and others' investment in it). If that identity is challenged, they may attempt to wrest back control by appearing more compliant or by aggressing against the threat. Heated displays enable individuals to vehemently, even violently, challenge the assertions of others, and aggressive responses are well documented in psychoanalytic and criminology literature. If shame is a significant component in the ordering of experience and the reordering of relationship, anger reflects attempts to manage and resist such reconfiguring—though often the connection between the two remains obscure.

The pattern between anger and shame was first documented by Helen Lewis in 1971 in transcriptions of analytic sessions. Lewis noted that when an experience of shame arose in therapy, a significant number of patients all but instantaneously masked it with anger; many even cycled back, then becoming ashamed of being angry.[15] In other words, patients frequently appeared to "have emotional reactions to their emotions, and . . . this loop may be extended indefinitely. [Lewis] called these reactions 'feeling traps'" (Scheff 2000, 95).[16] Seemingly incapable of acknowledging their shame, let alone grasping its nature, patients lashed out, attempting to regain control, to "make it [their feelings] stop." In this way, they became locked in a pattern of reactivity, spiraling further and further away from a genuine ability to act in the world.

Since Lewis's research was published, a small but growing number of psychologists, sociologists, and criminologists have grounded their work in her findings, testing, refining, elaborating, and applying her theories. Notable among them are Thomas Scheff and Suzanne Retzinger, June Tangney and Rhonda Dearing, Michael Lewis, Mark Leary, Roy Baumeister, C. Nathan De-Wall, John Braithwaite, James Gilligan, and Jack Katz. What follows here is a brief introduction to much of their work, intended to familiarize readers with the body of literature while bringing it more fully into sociological conversations around bullying.

———

To begin, it is important to establish that Helen Lewis's recursive shame-rage cycle, each emotion calling out and feeding on the other, finds support outside the therapeutic encounter. In 1988, Jack Katz released a study that analyzed hundreds of criminal acts (spanning the spectrum, from property damage to extreme violence against others). In a majority of cases, he discovered that the perpetrators felt humiliated, and the commission of the crime was inextricably intertwined with this feeling. Their actions were *reactions* concerned with redressing, and thereby assuaging, the inadequacies and shame called out by a prior insult or degradation. Katz's interviewees lived—and continue to live—in the minds of others. And righteous indignation at the assault on their dignity often became a stepping-stone to violence. Manifestations of anger redressed the damage to connection via a *demand* for respect.

James Gilligan also spent decades working in prisons, and his work reinforces Katz's claim. Over and again he was struck by "the frequency with which [he] received the same answer when [he] asked prisoners, or mental patients, why they assaulted or even killed someone. Time after time, they would reply 'because he disrespected me' or 'he disrespected my visitor (or wife, mother, sister, girlfriend, daughter, etc.)' In fact, they used that phrase so often that they abbreviated it into the slang phrase, 'He dis'ed me'" (2003, 1149). Again, the *desire* for affirmation and respect emerged as integral to their violence. Being dissed was shameful, signaling a change in the balance of power within relationship, including a lessening of interest in it. This change may, in turn, lead to psychological states that are intolerable and require relief. Distraught states indicate a significant investment in relationship. Even if the investment is not reciprocal or the relationship not intimate, it has functioned to buttress personal identity. Over and over again "in the prisons and on the streets of the United States, such behavior [killing] appears to be committed by people who are so tormented by feelings of being shamed and disrespected by their enemies that they are willing to sacrifice their bodies and their physical existence to replace those intolerable feelings with the opposite feelings of pride and self-respect, and of being honored and admired by their allies and at least respected by them" (1151).

Shame, it appears, is lent power and force by its somatic nature. It is embodied. Individuals may be so distressed, agitated, troubled, or even crazed by humiliation and a sense of inadequacy (or worse yet, others' belief in their inadequacy) that the ability to register their own physical pain is overwhelmed, especially if incurred in the throes of a violent response. *Reactive* violence is the *body's* resistance to psychic annihilation.[17] It confirms the "common neural overlap between social and physical pain mechanisms" and attempts to alleviate the suffering by addressing its root (DeWall 2009, 201). Desperate attacks, on self or other, promise to mitigate the agony of humiliation and disrespect by (re)asserting both agency and authority, reclaiming dignity. It is bodily begotten social redemption—and socially begotten bodily redemption. The interconnection prompts Elspeth Probyn to ask, "Is shame cultural or physiological, or does it—and this is my bet—demand a way of rethinking such oppositions? Does shame disconcert us because we feel it simultaneously in our bodies, at the core of our selves, and in our social relations?" (2005, 4). Violence against others seeks to restore balance by redressing slights, proving one is respectworthy and deserving of investment in relationship.[18] It resists severance and refuses alienation, restoring legitimacy to presentations of self, allaying self-judgments and the need to reconfigure identity. It is an extreme attempt at impression management, aiming to restore positive self-feelings by setting the record straight.

Gilligan is at pains to note that while humiliation, whether acknowledged or unacknowledged, appears to be a necessary condition for violence against others, it is obviously not a sufficient cause of it. His experience led him to posit three additional provisionals necessary for violence to result. The first involves the perpetrator's capacity for emotions that inhibit violence—namely, guilt and remorse. Gilligan suggests their absence is the result of a developmental lack, but June Tangney and Rhonda Dearing contend that shame itself "may actually interfere with empathic responsiveness. Shame is an acutely painful experience, involving a marked self-focus that is incompatible with other-oriented empathy reactions" (2002, 83). In either model, the pain animating shame is uninterrupted or unassuaged and comes to dominate the individual's actions in the world. It is difficult to know whether and to what extent it may be possible to interrupt this cycle of violence, as its continuation is vouchsafed by the sociocultural silence surrounding shaming experiences. We do not know what should be done with shame or how to negotiate self-judgments, severed connections, and self-narratives of inadequacy. Anger, which is active, interrupts this helplessness. It counters challenges of inadequacy through its very agency, bending situations and self-conceptions to its authority.

The second condition Gilligan cites has already been noted—namely, that the pain caused by shame and humiliation is so intense as to threaten the viability and cohesion of the self. Interestingly, while the cohesion of the self may be threatened, it may be more than the *feeling* of acute pain that causes this cognitive disorganization. Neurological findings, discussed in the next section, suggest that intrapsychic configurations are more complex. Third, Gilligan argues that the individual does not sense that she has sufficient nonviolent means by which to save or restore self-esteem. This paucity may, in part, be linked to the narcissistic personality traits discussed in Chapter 1. A substantial body of research links rejection to anger and aggression, and clearly, the sting of rejection is particularly incisive—even defining—to individuals with grandiose self-conceptions in need of constant affirmation.[19] Studies confirm this, finding that "narcissists who were rejected reacted with greater anger and aggression than participants who scored low in narcissism" (Leary, Twenge, and Quinlivan 2006, 119).[20]

Finally, and crucial to the argument Gilligan makes, boys have been socialized into roles of masculinity that have taught them to quash and deny emotions such as shame and embarrassment in order to do gender properly. If keeping these feelings in check involves violence, then these are the times it is appropriate to become violent.[21] Violent acts prevent one from being emasculated—from being thought a fag.[22]

In addition to these conditions, Gilligan elaborates on the role of what he calls "secret shame" (1997, 75). Helen Lewis (1971), John Braithwaite (1989), and Scheff all emphasize the unnamed, unidentifiable nature of shame in contemporary culture, noting the destructive potential of shame that remains unacknowledged. Scheff, in particular, elaborates on embodiment, arguing that unrecognized shame has no possible way of becoming resolved. It is either violently discharged or burrows deeper and deeper into the self, manifesting as extreme, alienated emotional withdrawal or depression. One anonymous interviewee was well aware of this:

> I think I turned the anger against myself. I wasn't angry—I could say I was furious with them, but the truth is because I took it [social cruelty and bullying] so personally, I turned it against myself.

Disturbing possibilities are linked to shame that is denied cognitive appropriation. Attempts to respond to bullying that do not explore the full implications of shame, its surreptitious miring in the body, where it anonymously organizes relationships and identity, will fall short. This can hardly be helped, as antibullying interventions and support for victims reflect cultural denial and are handicapped by culture's inarticulateness. Shame's affect, a social consequence, remains destructively incarnate.[23]

Scheff and Suzanne Retzinger (e.g., 1991) have long decried the denial of shame that has been institutionalized in modern societies and have attempted to pull it into the mainstream. They suggest that rejection is equally unacknowledged, occurs routinely, and if unresolved, stockpiles in the psyche, contributing to a backlog of hidden shame. How could it not? Culture's only terse narrative for rejection involves self-blame. To avoid feelings of inadequacy linked to rejection, individuals—especially boys—are coached to pick themselves up and keep going, to be unworthy of, and able to preclude, humiliating social repudiation. "When there is considerable backlog, then any new incident is felt in itself, but also seems to reactivate the backlog, making the new incident, even if seemingly trivial, extremely painful" (Scheff 2011, 456).[24] Unacknowledged, denied, or unsuccessfully negotiated, these slights increase social alienation, loosen social bonds, and add to the burden of worthlessness the individual carries—a burden that may eventually lead her to desperate acts.[25] Consider the potential role shame and rejection played in the backstories of school shooters that Katherine Newman and colleagues analyze in *Rampage* (2004). Research revealed that Michael Carneal, the fourteen-year-old student who opened fire in the lobby of Heath High School in West Paducah, Kentucky, in 1997,

> was the victim of one very public incident of teasing that haunted him for months to come: A gossip column, "Rumor Has It," in a school newspaper . . . implied that he had a homosexual relationship with another boy. . . . Michael was humiliated by the allegations, particularly when other students began to tease him and call him "gay" and "faggot." This very public teasing—which somehow escaped the attention of the staff that was supposed to supervise school publications—felt like character assassination to Michael and did indeed have lasting consequences. It precipitated an avalanche of bullying, teasing, and humiliation that followed Michael for the rest of middle school. Michael was unable to escape and unwilling to fight back or enlist the help of adults. Instead, he buried his rage, expressing himself only on paper in an essay he wrote for an eighth grade teacher. Michael's writing . . . lapses into incoherence at various points, a symptom of his increasingly disorganized thought process. (Newman et al. 2004, 27)

In profiling thirteen-year-old Mitchell Johnson, half the adolescent team responsible for a rampage in Jonesboro, Arkansas, in 1998, Newman and colleagues again note that the gunman felt publicly humiliated. In their description of the incident involving Mitchell, who by all adult accounts was a polite, yes ma'am, no ma'am student, the humiliation is obvious, as should be its link to rage:

> Mitchell wore a baseball cap to school even though he knew that was against school rules. The ISS teacher, Beverly Ashford, ordered Mitchell to take the hat off. He refused. She insisted, called another teacher for help, and the two of them wrestled the hat from Mitchell. . . .

> Mitchell was humiliated, furious, and unrepentant. . . . He fumed over
> his humiliation. (2004, 36)

Newman and her colleagues' own words—their linkage of "humiliated, furious, and unrepentant"—bring together shame and anger and add to them a defiant characteristic, not backing down: I will restore my image and manage my shame by *demanding* respect. Mitchell had no way to process the brew of volatile, even conflicting, emotions he felt, save through fantasies of retribution. In an essay he was ordered to write during detention, he obliquely threatened a reckoning. A backlog of unacknowledged shame—perhaps coupled with narcissistic character traits—might certainly have added to, and provoked, the magnitude of response Mitchell Johnson, as well as Michael Carneal and others, eventually made. Mitchell's writings suggest he did what countless others in the same predicament do—he fantasized and schemed of ways to right the wrong done him, the wrong that *humiliated* him. The question here becomes to what extent, if any, does his writing reveal an awareness of rejection and shame? Forcibly stripped of his baseball cap—reduced to a child, with no autonomy, self-determination, or ability to garner the respect of his peers—he was left with few options: Was he going to take it (swallow the abuse so as to not further disrupt social bonds, perhaps becoming chronically depressed and alienated as a result), was he going to tattle (run crying to an authority, be a mama's boy), or was he going to be a man (take control) and redeem his reputation? No other template for processing his anguished humiliation, for redressing any damage done to social bonds, or for redeeming himself to peers was available.[26] Beyond hope of social reintegration and belonging, his personal self challenged and discredited, he set out to prove himself and force others to see him differently.

Dylan Klebold and Eric Harris, the Columbine shooters (whom I have otherwise omitted from this discussion, as Harris, the clear leader, is believed to have had acute psychopathologies), were also subject to shaming.[27] Public humiliation might have added to the other disturbing factors linked to their spree. Ralph Larkin cites a report claiming that

> people surrounded [Harris and Klebold] in the commons and squirted
> ketchup packets all over them, laughing at them, calling them faggots.
> That happened while teachers watched. They couldn't fight back. They
> wore the ketchup all day and went home covered with it. (2007, 87)

While shame, especially secreted, unacknowledged shame, may well have contributed in significant ways to the tragedies that followed, there is no simple connection between it and school rampages. Millions feel—if not *are*—shamed daily and do not resort to violence. Teachers, bosses, and parents routinely show up their charges, addressing lacks in knowledge, skill, or competency in offhand, even callously critical, ways.[28] Do these less-than-gentle criticisms damage bonds and threaten connection? Are their emotional consequences stockpiled in the body, silently informing the very flesh of sociation? Are they defused and diminished by counterincidents that induce pride? Does biology endow some of us with long fuses and others with short ones? Clearly, these questions are important and point toward an overarching consideration: are there tipping points, and are they biologically, neurologically, psychologically, or socially weighted? Further, can balances be recalibrated, socially? Shame alone does not explain dire responses to victimization, even if it appears to factor into them. It is experienced in combination with personal traits, neurobiological limitations, and social circumstances, all of which are linked to shame's embodiment. Neurobiological research has recently shed light on this incarnation, uncovering startling connections between physical and social pain. These relationships and correlations are summarized and considered in the sections that follow.

The Psychodynamics of Anger and the Neurodynamics of Pain

While bullying is disrespectful, intimidating, and shame inducing, not all social humiliation, not even all *ongoing* humiliation and public disgrace, leads to violence. Individuals may quietly marinate in ignominy for years, stockpiling shame, allowing it to build and influence their lives in a variety of ways. They may overcompensate, become bitter and alienated, or quietly sink into depression, as it erodes their ability to engage self, other, or even life. Or they might negate its effects through shrugs of genuine indifference, rational or even calculated discourse, or their own counterachievements. None of these responses preclude anger. Anger might trigger explosive reactions to shame, productively manage and negotiate shame, or inform a variety of responses between these poles. This is because *not all anger is expressed aggressively or leads to violence.* That is, anger and aggression are not synonymous.

This is a crucial distinction to make. Anger, per se, is a negative *affective state*—a feeling, a somatic reverberation, even—that *cannot be equated with one or another particular behavioral response.* While anger involves attribution or blame, it is *aggression*, "a *behavioral response* aimed at causing harm or distress to another" that entails violence—whether verbal or physical (Tangney and Dearing 2002, 98; emphasis in original). This difference is important to have in mind when unpacking bullying, violence, and victimization and developing responses to social aggression (although it is also important to note that even if bullying ensnares victims in a shame-rage feeling trap, it is unclear whether rage is an affective state or a reactive state that situates individuals in an intense, relatively immediate—and unmediated—response). It would appear that, in functioning to manage shame, rage response follows relatively quickly upon the emergence of the feeling it looks to quash—that rage, unlike anger, is a deep somatic response demanding release.[29] Yet before rushing to affirm the equation of rage with angry, even out-of-control, aggression, it is important to pause and consider that the careful planning of most school rampages suggests much more deliberateness and control than this cycle implies. Is it possible that rage, like anger, does not always lead to aggression (in fact, may not always be visible) or that the dynamics involved in this feeling trap cannot be reduced and oversimplified, let alone operationalized, and articulated as guidelines around which interventions are constructed?

It seems plausible to assume that addressing the potential for violence requires society to acknowledge and constructively address shame. This might begin with an affirmation: the affective aspect of responses to humiliation—whether anger or rage—is legitimate (and, it would appear, need not lead to aggression). Instead of rushing to erect metal detectors that will, ostensibly, forestall violence, we need to spur the development of social Geiger counters able to register and gauge humiliation, in addition to modeling the productive negotiation of intense emotions that may follow it. This latter task—expanding and popularizing options for the negotiation of anger (or rage)—may be the more important project.

In distinguishing between anger and aggression, a difference grounded in the research of James Averill (1982), society opens a space between the two, into which alternative responses (on the part of bullies and victims alike) can be scripted and promoted. Scripts are, in fact, already in use, as Averill's research illustrates. Although destructive, maladaptive responses (including indirect aggression, displaced aggression, repressed aggression, or self-directed abuse) appear and are functionally significant, his research also documents constructive, nonaggressive, adaptive behaviors in incendiary situations. These include discussions with one's antagonist, actions that move to fix a key aspect of the situation (as opposed to affixing blame), behaviors that defuse the situation (a sarcastic comment that changes the topic or an offer to have coffee, shoot hoops, or engage in some other activity that sidelines the antagonism), escapist behaviors, and cognitive reappraisals (reinterpreting the situation and reevaluating responses to it).

None of these alternatives is currently a viable option in bullying scenarios, which may help explain the strong correlation between maladaptive expressions of anger (or rage) and shame.[30] Humiliation and the felt experience of inadequacy seem to preclude negotiating anger in a proactive way. Perhaps the emotional distress called òut by humiliation overruns the space between anger and aggression, making productive response all but impossible. If this is the case, it would not seem overly effective to call for new narratives against displacing shame or violently acting on the anger that follows from it. Even if public opinion were marshaled in support of new, normative expectations, these may be less than compelling in the face of deeply resonating somatic responses. The upshot would be a series of namby-pamby social stories that gloss over intrapsychic, even neurological, impediments to resolution.[31] Since these physiological aspects may be key, as *they* threaten to diminish or eradicate the space between felt experiences of anger and response, it is important to better understand their nature and *its* susceptibility to manipulation. To what extent, and how, can the separation between anger (or rage) and aggression be maintained and capitalized on when humiliation is the trigger? (The calculation involved in rampages suggests space between affective state and response.) Put differently, is anger in the employment of shame *able* to preserve this space, or does it rush to trample it though any number of unproductive behaviors? Perhaps this is the space of stockpiling, where pressure might be released, options explored, and aggression defused. Or perhaps a much more complex neuro-psychological dynamic is in play.

———

Social pain, long dismissed as whining oversensitivity, has recently been located in the pain centers of the brain, where physical trauma is registered and regulated. That is, the same mechanisms that are activated in instances of tissue damage come into play when one is cut off from acceptance and belonging—for example, when one is shamed. This overlap is arguably a consequence of evolution: "Social pain hurts because social inclusion was and is key for human survival" (MacDonald and Leary 2005, 205; see also Baumeister and DeWall 2005; DeWall 2009).[32]

If this is correct, it would appear that the shame-rage cycle is mediated by pain. Rage, in this model, is the response of an organism that is overwhelmed by injury and reacts violently, if not aggressively. Put differently, shame taps into a pain circuitry and sparks automatic neural mechanisms primed for quick reaction, including threat-defense responses, as social pain signals that future relationship with the group may be jeopardized. These reactions include *fight* (aggression) as well as *flight* (or *freeze*).[33] If social exclusion is linked to a biochemical chain reaction, interrupting responses (many of which are, today, socially maladaptive) could prove extremely difficult. Reflexes hardwired in the brain have been tripped.[34]

Even so, common sense and the ubiquity of shame, but not of violence (impotent or otherwise), suggests that any hardwired biochemical response to pain or to the threat of pain is a bit more complex, thus sustaining hope of interrupting a shame-pain-aggression sequence. In fact, laboratory experiments that manipulated conditions of belonging and exclusion (or future exclusion) in an attempt to better understand social pain found that neither rage *nor any other elevated emotional response* was provoked.[35] This startled researchers and did not immediately make sense. Links between shame (social rupture) and maladaptive anger (aggression) are well documented (see Leary, Twenge, and Quinlivan 2006 for a review of this literature), leading researchers to fully expect that exclusion (social pain) or threats of exclusion would heighten arousal and emotional distress. Recall that "human beings evolved to rely on group interaction as their main biological strategy. With no fangs, no claws, no fur . . . human beings are not well suited to living alone" (Baumeister and DeWall 2005, 54). Social exclusion is a precarious condition, one that other research indicates is painful, as it threatens the well-being of the organism. Yet time and again, studies show that the loss of connection *does not trigger heightened affective response*, despite the fact that a lack of belonging is linked to personal devastation. Violent, even aggressive, reactivity—rage—was not found.

Perhaps this might be explained by the controls: Did they fail to adequately simulate exclusion? (Subjects may not have been invested enough in the relative strangers who rejected them to feel anger or shame or overly concerned with a far-off future-alone scenario.) How else does one explain the absence of emotional arousal or the distress one would expect to be associated with a negative social experience? What can be made of findings that were opposite of those that were anticipated? Data indicate that in the face of rejection and social exclusion—distinct threats to, if not severance of, social bonds—individuals became detached and indifferent. Instead of distress induced by pain or even agitation associated with anger, researchers found flatness.

This flatness, the absence of any increase in anxiety or emotional distress, prompted researchers to turn their attention to social pain itself—its cognitive effects as well as the neuromechanisms regulating it (see Baumeister and DeWall 2005; DeWall, Baumeister, and Masicampo 2009). Although failing to measure any increases in emotional arousal in rejected, excluded individuals, data indicated (1) a significant increase in aggressive (although not reactively rageful) tendencies, (2) significant impairment to the executive functioning of the brain (self-regulatory and cognitive systems), and (3) a marked decrease in ability to demonstrate empathy, implying a decreased capacity for emotional responses that are linked to prosocial behavior. In the following I touch on each of these in turn, after first considering the larger issue: why responses to exclusion—and perhaps shame—are not primed by extreme agitation or even anxiety. Although exclusion is clearly a threat to the social bond and is, perhaps, shameful (one is not good enough or has done something egregious), no heightened emotional response—let alone reactivity—was discernable.

While seemingly paradoxical, this lack of distress is not unrelated to pain. In keeping with the theory that social exclusion activates many of the same neural mechanisms associated with physical trauma, it can be argued that social pain is linked to neuromechanisms that are hardwired to detach from, and thereby regulate, pain. In this hypothetical model, agonizing social experiences, no less than acute physical pain, are linked to the potential production of endorphins, which have an analgesic effect. Endorphins block pain, and emotional numbness ensues. This makes sense. Analgesic detachment protects the individual from being overwhelmed by emotional wounds.[36]

The implications of this are startling: if social exclusion and isolation do not necessarily imply a short-circuiting to inflamed, irrational knee-jerk response (as documented in shame-rage sequences), then it is disruptions to executive functioning (namely, the cognitive abilities linked to self-regulatory capacities) that are more directly linked to maladaptive behavioral responses. Put differently, there is no evidence of a *violent, reactive* exclusion–social pain–aggression sequence, suggesting that there is not necessarily one for the shame–social pain–aggression sequence either. Shame might be managed by rage or by numbness. What is certain is that rejected individuals do not think clearly (links between this disruption to cognitive functioning and depression are explored in Chapter 4).

In light of this deadening, it is reasonable to expect that shame leads to a decreased capacity for empathy. A heightened threshold for pain (including painful feelings about self) should also inure subjects to the pain of others, negating any sympathetic responses called out by their distress.[37] Data support this inference. Deadening and withdrawal correlate with a decrease in prosocial behavior, as "social exclusion saps the capacity for the emotion system to function properly, leading excluded people to behave selfishly" (DeWall 2009, 214). Shut out and rejected, they are less concerned about, unable to empathize with, or unable even to have tolerance for the distress of others. This finding appears capable of extension to responses that follow shame, for which the emotion system seems equally impaired. Shamed individuals are absorbed, on many levels, with self and seem incapable of concern with, or feeling for, the misfortunes of others. Indictment—especially public exposure—induces a tremendous preoccupation with one's inadequacies, drawing focus away from other-orientation. As Tangney and Dearing (2003) contend, a focus on (shameful) deficits precludes an ability to think about much else, contributing to an inability to feel connected or be concerned with others.

Despite this preoccupation with self, individuals trapped in shame-rage cycles appear to remain overly sensitized to what others think of them (hence the rage). Analgesic-related social indifference does not seem to correspond to this state (though a decreased capacity for empathy can certainly be pointed to). This leads to questions concerning impairment to the emotion system and whether vastly dissimilar responses link to it in similar ways. Research on such questions is barely under way, and preliminary findings are fragmented.

Scientists are not sure "why rejection sometimes causes people to become very emotional, whereas at other times they become affectively numb" (Leary, Twenge, and Quinlivan 2006, 114). However, it does appear that emotional distress *and numbness* signal an increased propensity for aggression. The organism is on high alert, and resources linked to self-control become diminished, *even if distress is not apparent.* (In protocols that replicated a lack of emotional distress in the face of exclusion and rejection, researchers began to specifically look for, and found, an increase in aggressive behaviors.) Individuals cut off from or denied connection have shorter fuses and a greater capacity—and propensity—for hostility (even if the *reactive* affect we are accustomed to identifying with such behavior is missing). Exclusion and rejection, it turns out, are strong *predictors* of aggression—whether it be immediate, deferred, unleashed on a different object, or manifested as antiempathetic responses.[38]

Additionally—and significantly for our purposes—Jean Twenge and W. Keith Campbell (2003) found that test subjects who scored high on narcissism pretest measures reacted to rejection with significantly greater anger and aggression than participants who scored low on these measures. Their inflated self-images, which attempt to compensate for the inadequacy and emptiness they feel, are precariously balanced and threatened by even the slightest detraction. Further, when confronted with evidence that contradicts their grandiose self-images, narcissists tend to externalize blame. Rejection interrupts their lofty views of self, challenging inauthentic strategies and exploitative behaviors that manipulate the esteem of others (on which they are overly dependent). They respond to the disruption of identity directly, suggesting a proclivity for shame-rage response. Research even documents that narcissists are "likely to aggress against an innocent third party after experiencing a social rejection" (268). This suggests that, to the extent that culture fosters narcissism, it facilitates increased aggressive responses, which it fans with the violent images it normalizes and circulates.

In the face of these chilling findings, researchers point to data that suggest that imbalances can be addressed and a degree of equanimity restored to cognitive functioning. While analgesic effects vastly diminish a capacity to feel the pain of others,

> social rejection does not decrease the *absolute ability* of victims to self-regulate but rather decreases their *willingness to exert the effort necessary to do so.* . . . When given sufficient incentive, rejected participants were able to match the self-regulatory performance of participants in other conditions [of the study]. Inducing self-awareness also allowed rejected individuals to self-regulate as effectively as other participants. (Crescioni and Baumeister 2009, 267; emphasis added)[39]

Self-regulation may not equate with empathy, but it suggests that cognitive dysfunctions linked to maladaptive responses may be overridden or reversed. Individuals *know* how to behave proactively, even if their emotional responses are not in sync with their behavior. And given sufficient incentive, they will.

While further research is clearly called for, these preliminary findings need to be introduced into the conceptual framework currently under construction. They go far toward explaining the apparent inconsistencies and unexpected findings on bullying, victimization, and social pain (as it manifests in the playgrounds, hallways, and cafeterias of our children). In addition, they imply that the space separating anger and aggression, no less than that separating pain and reactivity, is the arena for intervention. Emerging social narratives would be well advised to insinuate *acknowledgment of victims* (a form of connection) in the wake of social rejection, interrupting social pain and numbing through simple signals and body language that become the responsibility of bystanders. Even passing recognition gives rejected individuals reason to strain intrapsychic resources linked to self-regulation by providing them encouragement, even *hope*, and a reason to negotiate their feelings in more prosocial ways. A compassionate glance at the victim and a helpless shrug of the shoulders or rolling of the eyes in the presence of outrageous behavior blunts the force of bullying and may go far in negating its insidious fallout (as opposed to silently endorsing its cruelties). Conspiratorial eye contact or body language stanches social pain, perhaps forestalling numbness or reactivity and aggression. Bystanders might even impede analgesic effects with their empathetic responses. An unwillingness to publicly champion the victim need not preclude myriad invisible gestures and emotion work, all of which have the potential to interrupt the effects of shame, rejection, and ostracism. As one anonymous interviewee affirmed in no uncertain terms:

> *Yeah, I think there is something they could have done. I think they [by-standers] could have put words to it. I'm thinking of "bullying." . . . Instead of—even if they didn't have the courage to stop it at the time or didn't know, afterwards they could have pulled me aside—they could have signaled to me—just a wink or a nod—or they could have tried to let me know.*

Dan, another interviewee, believed that

> *if people [had been] indifferent—if they'd have even just walked away— that would have been great, that would have been less a mess, and any one person saying something would have been huge. So anytime, like, someone would do something nice or whatever, that was huge; it would make all the difference—'cause otherwise you're just like, "Aaaaaugh!"*

While such overtures to victims seem reasonable, even possible, their likelihood is significantly reduced when the targets of bullying are culpable (yet not deserving of the extreme social repudiation their behavior has called forth).[40] Offense aside, it is important for society and, ironically, for bullies that victims continue to *care* what others think, continue to be *capable* of pride and shame, of *feeling*—that is, continue to be connected to self and other, retaining hope of atonement and forgiveness. Nurturing this possibility is difficult when (1) the climate created by administrators (and faculty) gives free rein to predators in public spaces, inadvertently fostering inequality, discrimination, and shame by modeling noninterference. This so-called tolerance is disastrous to any sense of fairness and justice young adults often harbor and is especially problematic when (2) shame, rejection, and exclusion are legitimately employed—she *has* made a mistake. Shame and rejection, not unlike gossip and laughter, are dynamics of social control. They enable groups to police normative boundaries and maintain order. Calling attention to breaches of these boundaries—to social inadequacies—*is the point*. In this, shaming is *not* the problem. It is the follow-up, or absence thereof, that needs to be addressed. Ruptures must not be irreparable. Merely the *potential* for remediation challenges the effects of rejection and shame, ameliorating social pain, although narcissists may be a bottomless pit of need. Because our brains continually adapt "in both positive and negative directions . . . establish[ing] a nurturing relationship may well be capable of triggering genetic expression in ways that can decrease stress, improve learning, and establish a bridge to new and healthier relationships" (Cozolino 2010, 223). The first step in such a relationship is the hope of righting a wrong, overcoming an inadequacy, and moving beyond a lapse in judgment, all contingent on a belief in connection. Shame and rejection require monitoring and regulation, the maintenance of belief in the future possibility of trust and reciprocal relating, however faint.

Perversely, ongoing public humiliation might help maintain that belief. It is a *confrontation*, a connection, and as such differs from routinized exclusion, social marginalization, and invisibility. Spectacles marshaling the derogatory gaze of the community *acknowledge* inadequacy and in so doing acknowledge the individual. She is important enough to merit attention. Being confronted by one's peers radically differs from being confronted, daily, by silence and isolation (no press is bad press).

Moreover, negative connection—unwanted and perhaps unwarranted attention—is visible and can be addressed. While social norms allow for spectacles, for making examples of perpetrators in an attempt to forestall further transgressions, the very publicness of this practice, at times played out under the nose of authority figures, opens the process, extent, and duration of her disgrace and humiliation to the gaze of bystanders, to examination and monitoring. The same cannot be said for exclusion and ostracism, which deny connection in quiet, even insidious ways. With no fanfare, the shame attached to social invisibility is incapable of being seen or identified and addressed. Whether left to their own devices or pointedly ignored, these outsiders are disposable: unseen and incapable of mobilizing intercession. Bystanders are hard put to empathize with silence and social invisibility. Public shaming, by contrast, is all too visible (see Williams and Nida 2009). And spectators to public rebuke (or harassment) are acutely aware of acceptable means and measures of disapprobation. Even though she might be deserving of public censure, even though everyone might be going along with it, there is a line, a point at which public derogation, cyber manipulations, and malicious gossip turn undeniably cruel and overwhelm. Peer cohorts often have a distinct sense of when that line has been crossed.

Can bystanders monitor the justifiable policing of social norms, gauging such elusive variables as severity, intent, and sincerity of repentance? Can they offer acknowledgment—even if the briefest of connection—to those who try and do change and extend tolerance to those who cannot, even while continuing to join with others to rebuke those deserving of disapproval and reprobation? Determinations of culpability and evaluations of social censure are made, on a regular basis, despite norms admonishing us to mind our own business. The question is can norms support bystander involvement in this process, encourage them to look more closely at the claims and behaviors of both parties, and even champion their interventions? As even the smallest of gestures has the potential to reverberate, I suspect the answer is yes. Difficult, perhaps. An unwanted responsibility, even, but yes. By Laurie's description, Sarah's patronage of her, although hardly covert, illustrates the ability to walk this tightrope and the magnitude of such gestures, even decades later:

> Sarah . . . managed to pass [with the popular crowd]. She was perfectly aware that girls that she would speak to and befriend and go over [to] their house and do sleepovers with were girls no one else would talk to or indeed would talk about in the halls, and she nonetheless did these things. . . . So she didn't take on her peers but had the courage of walking side by side with such a person as myself—it was extraordinary. She understood what it was to reach across no-man's land.

Notwithstanding the extreme strategies that social pain may force individuals to adopt for survival, negative outcome is not inevitable; nor is damage suffered irreversible. Daily dynamics of support and disapprobation point to constructive responses already in play: reparations being made, bonds mended, and even bullying interrupted. Relationships are woven and rewoven daily, and the regulatory logistics involved in this process need to be highlighted, encouraged, and rewarded. Everyone has experienced shame—

without it having cost them an ability to feel or triggering extreme, maladaptive responses. Why is that?

Guilt

Just as not all anger results in maladaptive, aggressive behavior, not all humiliation results in the rupture of social connection, withdrawal, or pariah status. This leads to an important question: What makes for the difference? Is there a tipping point, a level of psychic intolerance, a danger zone that signals damaging levels of social abuse, or is there a hidden, qualitative element?

Without a doubt, additional factors, including social opportunities, family background, personality, and an ability to negotiate pain socially, psychologically, and biologically are in play and contribute to variations in response. To this list must be added a capacity to hive self, to separate behavior from identity. The productive versus unproductive management of shame may be related to an individual's ability to orient toward an action for which she assumes responsibility but not identity. In other words, it may be linked to her ability to resist the routine indictment of self through a capacity to experience *guilt* or to transform shame into it.

Guilt is a self-reflective emotion that shares striking similarities with shame yet differs from it. Both emotions reference the self, might be called out by the same situation, and are often used interchangeably by researchers as well as the public. They are members of the same affect family, differentiated only in terms of their purview, or scope, which Helen Lynd summarizes in terms of a sole implication: "Guilt can be expiated. Shame, short of a transformation of the self, is retained" (1958, 50–51).[41] Helen Lewis elaborates:

> The experience of shame is directly about the *self*, which is the focus of evaluation. In guilt, the self is not the central object of negative evaluation, but rather the *thing* done or undone is the focus. In guilt, the self is negatively evaluated in connection with something but is not itself the focus of the experience. (1971, 30)

Guilt, like shame, occasions anxiety and self-reproach. While its intensity is often not distinguished—or distinguishable—from shame, its link to specific behavior fosters the belief that effects of the behavior might be righted and any incurred debt repaid.

> While both guilt and shame are excited by what others think of us, shame goes further. Shame is deeply related not only to how others think about us but also to how we think about ourselves. Guilt is triggered in response to specific acts and can be smoothed away by an act

of reparation. Shame, however, demands "a global [re]evaluation of the self." (Probyn 2005, 45)

Guilty individuals often attempt to fix the situation, to assume responsibility for what they have done and compensate for the fallout from their behavior (possibly believing that they can fix a situation but not their entire self). Thus, guilt, like shame, is a moral emotion, one that provokes negative self-judgments. Unlike shame, however, it holds out the possibility of atonement, restitution, and forgiveness. Whereas shamed individuals feel exposed and are more apt to cover up, attempt to hide, accept broken connection, withdraw, and even covet isolation, guilty individuals often feel compelled to reaffirm relationship. In separating object from identity, they believe themselves able to exert control over future experiences. Put differently, insofar as it does not involve a global self-measure, guilt allows for adaptive social response and the possibility of redemption and may be called out simultaneously with shame.[42]

A cogent example of this difference can be seen in the varied response a woman might have to rape: "A woman can blame herself for having walked down a street alone at night or for having let a particular man into her apartment . . . or she can blame herself for being 'too trusting and unable to say no' or a 'careless person who is unable to stay out of trouble'" (Janoff-Bulman 1979, 1799). The former response is linked to guilt and allows her to change her behavior and in so doing exert control over outcomes, while the latter, linked to deficits of self, does not afford ready adjustment.[43] Adaptive, even proactive responses reflect the *hope* that exists within the possibility of righting the wrong and of negating the ramifications of inappropriate behavior. The opportunity for redemption is retained, damaged bonds are salvageable, and the discharge and resolution of emotional states is possible.[44] Self-blame and shame stand in opposition to this, striking deep into the body, even, as Katherine Young puts it, becoming "the flesh of memory" (2002, 47).

Ronnie Janoff-Bulman's research with victims of trauma suggests that variation between a guilt response and a shame response produce "very different relationships to many aspects of psychological adjustment and social behavior, including psychological symptoms, narcissism, sociopathy, interpersonal empathy, anger, aggression, constructive anger management strategies, and aspects of interpersonal perception" (2002, 30). These variations may be linked in important ways to the relationship between trauma, shame responses, and the narcissistic tendencies fostered—even cultivated—by contemporary culture. The character type of late twentieth- and early twenty-first-century Western culture (whose existence may be more descriptive than clinical; see Richard Kilminster 2008) involves a comprehensive, global sense of self, much like shame. Narcissistic individuals are identified by self-absorption, chronic boredom, and ongoing moral and psychological crises that they are unable to address and instead minimize through hyperconsumerism, risk taking, self-gratification, and instant intimacy. Preoccupation with self and its voracious need for admiration and approval compromises their ability to invest emotional energy in the concerns of others or to see in them anything other than a reflection of self (with dire consequences if the reflection has negative valence). Increasingly unable to grasp Others as genuine objects in their own right, narcissists have difficulty relating to others in a truly empathetic fashion, causing interpersonal relationships to atrophy.

Narcissistic tendencies may also signal a difficulty in feeling guilt. Guilt presupposes distinct others, as well as a synergistic relationship between them and the individual. Its orientation is outward, toward others, and its responses defy rupture to connection. Roy Baumeister, Arlene Stillwell, and Todd Heatherton contend that not only does guilt preclude severed connection; it "serves to protect and strengthen interpersonal relationships" (1995, 256).[45] In contrast to guilt response, narcissistic rage reactions belie shame and its comprehensive threat to the shriveled, inadequate self. Such responses, situated in terms of the individual's sense of entitlement, are prompted by perceived threats to social status, which are in turn linked to perceived attributions of deficiency. Narcissists are intent on cloaking insecurities and reasserting superiority, as opposed to fixing an inadequacy. In addition, because narcissistic individuals perceive the mirrorings of others to reflect a global sense of self, any capacity for hiving may be limited.

While guilt and shame often overlap, making clear distinctions little more than heuristic devices, the potentials identified with guilt might serve to orient both cultural and individual attempts to negotiate shame. Although the degree to which the two are correlated may influence how much proactive solutions will be sought, reparation must begin to be encouraged and *be allowed*; hiving must be sponsored.

Re-visioning Shame: The Strengths and Weaknesses of a New Paradigm

This protracted analysis of shame and its brief, pointed differentiation from guilt identifies it as integral to the extreme acts that give bullying national headlines. Perhaps more importantly, it identifies shame, the root of social pain, as loss of connection (responded to reactively or with disquieting detachment). That guilt does not signal this loss, may even, in its attempts to set things right, articulate empathy, is extremely significant. Guilt's ability to retain connection, to compensate on the basis of ongoing responsiveness to the other, the group, or society, may be the concrete stepping-stone that is needed to translate narratives of victimization into stories of redemption. It is the model used in Alcoholics Anonymous, an organization that helps shamed, inadequate, broken individuals reconfigure and *redeem* self. It is also the springboard from which Scheff and Retzinger, leading scholars in shame research, call for the reconceptualization of shaming.

Scheff and Retzinger situate their theories in an analysis of the roots of violence. Casting a broad net (illustrating the repression of shame by noting that "in the Old Testament there are references to pride and shame but very few to guilt. In the New Testament this ratio is exactly reversed: there are many more references to guilt than to shame" [1991, 5]), the authors conceptualize shame following Helen Block Lewis (1971): it is underground, disenfranchised, and potentially destructive. Secreted from self and other and thus incapable of transformation into healthy guilt response, modern-day shame has little or no possibility of resolution.[46] This is the crux of the matter. The myth of individualism (little more than a defense against the pain of threatened bonds), helped institutionalize this repression. In not acknowledging belonging as a human need or the interdependence and intersubjectivity that form the basis of social order, the self-sufficient individual stopped being accountable to others, believing she could stave off social and psychological wounding.

Scheff and Retzinger's response to the predicament in which the individual and society find themselves is formulated in terms of a much larger theory of social action, one informed by the work of John Braithwaite. Braithwaite is best known for his theories of restorative justice[47] and his proposals for shame management, criminal justice practices, and reintegration.[48] His work engages crippling social stigmatization (a secondary punishment meted out to convicted offenders) through counternarratives that temper censure with the possibility of forgiveness. In this re-visioning, the all-important social bond is not fully, irreparably severed by the shaming attached to and arising from a guilty verdict. Instead, the possibility of reintegration remains available and is carefully tended. Ongoing but fragile connection is, in large part, predicated on the nature of the shaming itself—is it *reintegrative* or *stigmatizing*? Does it allow repentance and the assumption of responsibility to exonerate the offender, or is she stigmatized and branded with a reprobate master status? In large part, Braithwaite calls for shame to be associated with the offense, not the offender, allowing reparation, redemption, and reintegration into the community. His focus is on society and the moral and emotional aspects of social order.

Scheff and Retzinger's focus shifts to the individual and to society's role in her ability to process shame. They believe that a reintegrative shaming *style* (a benignly paternalistic penal system?) in addition to a focus on offense will allow shame to be acknowledged and accommodated. A reintegrative style fosters normal shame, which, in being "acknowledged rather than denied, is of brief duration—usually lasting less than a minute—and serves as a signal, allowing for the repair of damaged bonds. ('When I do something stupid, if

I say "That was stupid," everyone laughs and we get on with it.')" (1991, 29).[49] Social gestures that sponsor reintegration, in conjunction with the individual's affirmation of culpability and of humiliation, set the stage for shame to be hived or discharged. Not unlike Old Testament shaming or the dynamics of guilt, connection is retained and redemption remains a possibility.

Scheff and Retzinger dub the model they construct the (Helen) Lewis-Braithwaite hypothesis, which states, in part, that normal shame and reintegrative shaming practices produce social solidarity, whereas pathological shame and stigmatizing shaming practices produce alienation. Elaborating on this foundation, the authors attempt to draw out and shore up the potential for change by identifying conditional *ifs* under which productive shaming in a larger population might occur. Key to their model is an ability to

> distinguish productive from counterproductive shame sequences. Shame provokes violence when it is (a) unacknowledged, and (b) communicated disrespectfully. Shame prevents violence when it is acknowledged and when it is communicated respectfully. The crucial feature of respectful shaming is that it shames a deed which is perceived as wrong while refraining from rejecting the wrongdoer as a person. (Scheff and Retzinger 1991, xii)[50]

In this re-visioning, any attendant distinctions between normal shame and guilt are blurred and glossed over, as the authors focus on constructing and elaborating a bridge between acknowledged and unacknowledged shame. Whether a comprehensive indictment of self can be forestalled is not an immediate concern and may or may not be implied in the severance of bonds and separation from community that becomes of central import. The authors argue that one way to forestall alienation and social isolation is through a focus on *behaviors* that prompt humiliation and rupture, another is to be aware that the *communication* of censure may itself be shaming or conciliatory. A focus on communication potentially limits the social effects of shame without denying its emotional devastation, prompting acknowledgment through the promise of ongoing connection and suggesting that the trespass might be remediated. In other words, it does not drive shame underground. This seems straightforward enough and tailored to a narcissistic culture, as it aims to save face. *Respectful communication* quietly modifies social dynamics to enable shame-inducing situations to become productive experiences, or at least not stockpiled, deadening ones.

This oversimplified representation of the Lewis-Braithwaite hypothesis is modeled on parenting practices already in use—practices outlined in Chapter 1. Recall, for example, Chapter 2's distinctions between the processing of in-group and out-group information. Children are often the innermost in-group, individuals whom adults not only cherish, support, and teach but forgive, often not expecting their young charges to know better. One cannot co-opt this model without co-opting the relationships that make it function—relationships that are absent in society at large and markedly missing in instances of bullying-related social shaming.

A second, not unrelated concern might be posed like this: If reintegrative shaming is being modeled in homes, in the communications of caregivers, why is it not translating into interactions in other arenas? Why is bullying and social humiliation on the rise? Perhaps child-centered parenting is helping produce a generation of more entrenched narcissists? Might overattention to self-esteem be nurturing grandiosity, entitlement, emotional neediness, and an inability to negotiate criticism, rejection, exclusion, and even shaming?[51]

A final, more fundamentally troubling issue (should overcoming outgroup mental processing and links to narcissism not prove sufficiently challenging) is that the Lewis-Braithwaite hypothesis rejects the *social element* of shame and shaming—namely, the rupturing of social bonds. In privileging communication styles, Scheff and Retzinger attempt to preclude the severance of bonds, phrasing the possibility of reparation and redemption in terms of ongoing connection. In turning the usage of shame on its head and introducing a moral function into the *practice* of humiliation, the authors negate the inherent nature of shame, denying it the capacity to rupture, to sever, to disconnect, even momentarily. In other words, shame should *not* shame. Moreover, they situate primary responsibility for social change and the transformation of shaming experiences with the shamer. For a more complete representation of their argument, see Appendix C.

This is problematic. Respectful communication would much better serve the process if it did not seek to subvert the nature of shame, to delegitimate its social functioning, but rather to offer *hope* of future reintegration (postshaming). Rejection, stigmatization, humiliation, and exclusion are all aspects of a *social* dynamic that is bound up with the maintenance of boundaries, order, and control in society. There will always be gestures that deliberately destroy connection, whether they are called shame, justice, or bullying. In their wake, future possibilities are situated along a continuum, by the shamers no less than by the community that interprets and enforces their acts. Respectful communication as Scheff and Retzinger conceive it may be adapted by a justice system whose purposes are better served by appearing benevolent, but such a solution does not allow us to think about humiliations that are ongoing, indictments of self that are reiterated, and shaming that appears unremediable.

What, then, can this model contribute to the negotiation of deliberate shaming linked to social abuse? The narrative needs of bullying stories require the foregrounding of an intent to shame, reject, degrade, and cause social pain. Bullies set out to stigmatize, to deliberately create a pariah status for the victim. They are invested in the cruelty of their communications, employing shame as a social weapon. But bystanders need not be invested in that same cruel severance. In fact, it seems possible to transfer the responsibility Scheff and Retzinger claim for the shamer to bystanders—to the "public" in public humiliation. The community needs to assume responsibility either for its silent endorsement of bullies or for mitigating the experiences of humiliation that lead to ongoing exclusion and alienation. Bystanders are able to facilitate "normal" experiences of shame by fostering the capacity to recover from its losses—by communicating hope, which extends a liminal space of possibility to victims. It is imperative that those who watch come to understand that they are not a latent power, a mere presence throughout spectacles of shaming. Rather, they are a silent social force, one integral to the *creation* of spectacles. Social humiliation requires the eyes of others to witness and affirm disgrace. Only then does individual degradation ripple and reverberate socially. Everybody not only knows; they endorse and even bond with shamers, laughing, gossiping, and *creating* social consequences.

Or they bond with the victim and begin actively creating the possibility of future redemption.

Although habitually viewed as a backdrop to shaming, bystanders are integral to it, enforcing or rejecting the break in connection, shunning or offering vague hope to the victim. They hold the key to re-visioning the processing of shame, to manipulating its ability to redeem even as it destroys. Should they choose to reject silent bonding with bullies, they will temper the power of shame. ("Sarah . . . didn't take on her peers but had the courage of walking side by side with such a person as myself.")

New social dances and new roles, exchanges, and dynamics cannot, however, simply be mandated. They require grounding, a social basis from which to position themselves, legitimate themselves, and act, a social norm through which to sustain their orientation. Such grounding is implicit in the answer to a single question: Why shame an individual? A bully is clear about this: to humiliate, reject, and cause pain. But it is bystanders who must engage this question. Does it involve a confrontation over group norms? In-group bonding? Entertainment? Punishment? Bystanders must whisper, "Why are they treating Laurie that way?" and on the basis of coconstructed answers, police shame's usage and outcome.

There is scant language for such assessment (excepting articulation of self-serving motivations—"better her than me") or precedent for acting on it. If bystanders are unclear about the function of the shaming (or even the difference between legitimate and illegitimate uses of shaming) and vague about its desired outcome (is there a desired outcome other than social destruction?), they are unlikely to take issue with public spectacles or foster conditions that limit its effect. They have no way to orient themselves toward displays of degradation, and no norms prompt a response other than silence (mind your own business). How can they adopt new roles, or even be clear about the cost of shaming, if culture itself is evasive as to its appropriate use? What situations *should* call out a shaming in response? How should the possibility for reintegration be calibrated? (We know well the nuances of laughter—tone, length, duration, and the like—and are equally capable of learning to nuance shaming.) Responses to the question *why shame* are not scripted into the language games of culture, as the question itself is never asked. A consideration of *why*, directed at the actions of victims, the behaviors of shamers, and the norms of a culture itself, would orient response, implicitly suggesting a how-to for negotiating and discharging shame (providing that atonement is a cultural and social possibility). Without an expansion of language games, there are insufficient conditions and options for response on the part of those who witness public humiliations or are privy to vicious gossip.

Legitimating discussions around shame—its affect, effect, and implications—sets the stage for remediation and redemption. "Why has she been humiliated?" "Is disgrace a condition of her atonement?" and if so, "What more do we want from her as a condition of her reintegration?" need to become commonplace considerations, able to guide the variety of social and personal responses now emerging. In not knowing why we shame (or are shamed) or, as bystanders, why we collude in the creation of spectacles of social disgrace and uphold the social consequences of shaming, shunning the wrongdoer or promulgating an unsavory reputation even after she has suffered and attempted to make amends, it becomes clear that shaming has lost a social language. It is no longer able to calibrate its own functioning. (This capacity is needed, within community, independent of culture itself having fractured, or lost, its moral compass. For despite this, an ability to humiliate attests to an ongoing morality in play—one that has become, quite literally, unspeakable.) Bystanders are discouraged from assessing, evaluating, and forming judgments (ironic in a democratic society). Their silence is in keeping with the mantra of individualism: mind your own business. But when they are co-opted into participation, as spectators, the spectacle becomes their business.

Language games that obscure key aspects of shaming are only reinforced by the cruelty for kicks showcased for our amusement on numerous channels every night. Reality TV illustrates the challenges posed by shaming's lack of value orientation. We take prurient interest in, even voice a titillated OMG! at, the orchestrated escalation of cocontestant degradation or the mean quips of judges and then are puzzled and upset over the uncalled-for nastiness of kids on the playground. We do not connect the two. Moreover, *Access Hollywood* and *e-TV* do not follow up with losers, unless, tragically, they are reporting on the suicide of a former contestant. Those judged inadequate on national television are sequestered in therapist's offices, made invisible, the cost of their humiliation far from the public eye. Cruelty is funny, and contestants, no less than kids on the playground, are obligated to take it.[52] "Get over yourself" or "I was only kidding" are responses that degrade the experience of shame itself, denying ramifications and ensuring secrecy. While school tragedies, contestant suicides, and even discussions of taunting in the National Football League have reinserted shame into public discourse, we have done little more than nod at its significance before glossing over its implications. Instead, we need to begin a dialogue, perhaps by asking, "If we disgrace individuals for fun, how can we simultaneously attempt to reclaim the *moral* authority contained within this social force?"

Disturbing events have broken the vast silence surrounding shame. It is now incumbent on culture to acknowledge its importance and begin developing a language that, in itself, will reconnect us to this experience. It can be anticipated that growing dialogue and a call for bystander participation will, inevitably, raise the issue of *intent*, which leads to a slippery slope. A discussion that opens such a conversation might ask, "When is it *not* okay to shame—not okay to call for global indictments of self (especially considering there is little or no possibility of redemption)?" It is likely that Johnson, Mitchell, Corneal, and others felt they had no options, no (safe) way to acknowledge, discuss, and begin negotiating inadequacies (or the pain associated with them) and no way (storied by culture) to reconfigure themselves on a sociopersonal level. Recall that social and personal identities closely reference each other in a fishbowl, school environment, making the loss of face—even the imagined loss of social standing—potentially devastating. We continue to need to belong, even to potentially belong. Without the benefits of belonging, why curb and control impulses?

Summary

The ongoing importance of belonging is often overlooked because the ideals of individualism, hand in hand with multiculturalism and diversity, eroded communities built on unifying cultural norms. In so doing, they dismantled the transcendent (if not transsubjective) moral authority that had grounded shame in atonement-redemption paradigms. Seduced by the freedom and promises of power held out by a psychologistic cultural paradigm privileging the self, individuals actively worked to *undo mechanisms of guilt formation*, while culture repudiated guilt-inducing mores on a larger scale. Such mechanisms had, however, been a stepping-stone to processing shame, allowing and guiding reparation and reintegration, facilitating continued connection, hiving, and even facilitating bystander support. Reclaiming this possibility by positioning bystanders as arbiters of second chances, which legitimates the possibility of reconnection, allows victims—culpable or innocent—to begin negotiating their felt experiences or, perhaps more importantly, to continue feeling.

One final note: Connection, hiving, bystander involvement in reintegration, and the interruption of maladaptive anger responses are not the only options. Emerging cultural stories barely allude to the intrapsychic potential that exists in the acknowledgement of shame—in the potential for overcoming, for rising up from the ashes—even if the malicious intent of bullies and the passivity of bystanders continue to compromise social possibilities. Acknowledgment reestablishes connection and, at the very least, situates individuals in a limbo space, where connection to self and to pain (and possibly to community) has the potential to be reconfigured. It retains transformative potential. To deny shame such potential is to forfeit the possibilities that *inhere* in its *very nature*. The disruption of social bonds transforms an individual's world and, reciprocally, her self, opening opportunities to constructively re-vision her embodiment in it. Probyn notes that "shame, as the body's reflection on itself, may reorder to composition of the habitus, which may in turn allow for quite different choices" (2005, 56). And it is in the intrapsychic space where self as subject and object interface that transformation is possible (this potential is explored in depth in Chapter 5).

GRIEVING AND GRIEF WORK

Negotiating Social Pain and Personal Loss

At the time, there would be only incoherence. As though
meaning had slunk out of things and left them fragmented.
. . . As though the intelligence that decodes life's hidden
pattern—that connects reflections to images, glints to light,
weaves to fabrics, needles to thread, walls to rooms, love to
fear to anger to remorse—was suddenly lost.
  —ARUNDHATI ROY, *The God of Small Things*

If shame signals a break in connection, a change to social and personal identity, then bullying must be addressed in terms of this consequence. If the cruel convictions of peers sever bonds, loosening identity from inter-subjective moorings, then means to resecure this lifeline must be identified. Placing the responsibility for making it stop squarely on the bullied person's shoulders, requiring that she either stand up to her abusers or trivialize her emotional distress, has been the response of a culture that does not fully grasp the conditions of shame (investment in bullies or the culture they represent, embodiment of humiliation, and desire—even need—to belong) or the social dynamics that compound the cost of public rejection. This culture accepted no responsibility for oversight of shame (tacitly legitimating the unrestricted use of social force) and positioned her as a culpable victim (otherwise, it would not be left *up to her* to overcome her social disenfranchisement). Regrettably, it has taken horrific acts of violence to challenge this response. Suicides and school shootings (even if not directly linked to bullying) demand an assessment of the social dynamics linked to public humiliation and psychological cruelty and a reassessment of strategies that support victims.

Social scripts promoting bystander intervention are being drafted, and bullying workshops are big business. But a full understanding of shame's social nature and responses that foster the negotiation of pain in terms of severed connection are alarmingly absent. If shame ruptures bonds, then emerging social narratives would be well advised to appropriate the cultural stories and infrastructures of support that surround loss of connection in other contexts. They must, quite simply, orient themselves around facilitating the negotiation of grief.

It is important to be clear about this.

Victims have *lost* important relationships and connections to society, and even if shaming is legitimate, the community needs to begin monitoring the sentence imposed, including its severity and duration. Understanding shame and responding to it in terms of loss provides a toehold into the constellation of emotions that often overwhelm victims—notably, the stressors that emerge from changes to relationship. It also suggests that coherent ways to begin supporting victims are already in place and that culture *and* society will benefit from fostering psychological processes associated with grief work. Broadly speaking, this means the community will begin to affirm, assess, and make accommodation for a victim's pain. What was her relationship to the object of her loss (e.g., best friend?), why was it lost, and how does culture frame and support this level of loss in other arenas? Is it comparable to the loss of an athletic competition? The loss of a position in the starting lineup? The loss of a job? The breakup of a romantic relationship? The loss of a parent through divorce? The loss of a pet? The death of a mother, father, sister, brother, or friend?

Only death and divorce—dramatic instances of shattered connection—are recognized as losses whose potentially disorienting pain and numbing require social support. Experience of either is stressful, confusing, and often associated with feelings of depression. Marital breakup often involves a belief that one party had some control over outcome, increasing the potential for feeling demoralized, rejected, and a failure. Society recognizes the magnitude of these upheavals and allows those grappling with either to stand outside normative behavioral requirements. They are given tolerance, personal space, grief narratives, and mourning rituals to support their processing of social and psychological dislocation. Norms and the emotional support of others (through social sympathy rules) safeguard the space of people who are dealing with loss as they reconfigure changes to social status, roles, and identity.[1]

Loss in a competition, on the other hand, is qualitatively different. "It was only a game," "There will be other games," and "Better luck next time" are sentiments that, while consoling, recognize that the loss itself can be recouped tomorrow, next week, or next season. The upheaval is transitory and negotiable—even if social status and identity are in play. In a very real sense it is these sentiments that most closely parallel those offered to victims of bullying and relational aggression. "Why all the drama?" and "She wasn't a good friend to you anyway" dismiss the severity of the loss and insinuate that moving beyond it is only a matter of putting the whole in the right perspective—something that should not be too difficult to manage. Social relationships are put on a par with other forms of competition (in itself quite telling), and loss in this context does not—or better yet *should* not—involve profound turmoil or devastation.

While there may be no repairing it, it is of negligible consequence, and there is always another game to be played or relationship to be formed.[2]

And often enough, this is the case. Sociation is an ongoing dance, one in which partners change, tempos intensify and resolve themselves, and individuals need to keep up with new steps or sit the dance out. Bullying is simply a part of this dance, its cruelties absorbed into the music, or so we have been led to believe. In reality, however, psychological and emotional violence often *interrupt* this dance. Crescendos break through and explode connection, partners whirl away, orientation becomes lost. And yet the music plays on, stopping for no one. Disoriented dancers stumble to the sidelines or are helped there, attended to, and encouraged to sit and regain their balance. Supportive gestures, even on the part of relative strangers, are not unknown or even unfamiliar. These social courtesies now require broader and more frequent applications. Bullying disrupts the rhythm and flow of life, and those who struggle to keep up, in the face of humiliation and rejection, need reintegrative possibilities. Small gestures *are* reconnection to the social group, thereby cultivating *hope for* or even *belief in* the possibility of overcoming rejection.

Offering even minimal social courtesies is often forestalled by the belief that the stumbling and out-of-sync dance steps of a victim or outcast are indicative of larger inadequacies, for which she has *only herself to blame*. And on the basis of this belief she is further jostled, while any pain or grief she experiences is *disenfranchised*.

This apt term was used by Kenneth Doka (1989, 2002) to describe pain and mourning over losses that society does not recognize and that therefore do not warrant sympathy (e.g., there is no recognition of grief—or even the right to grieve—over the death of felons or junkies, just as there is no right to mourn the abuse one suffers as a homosexual, an overweight individual, or a burqa-clad Islamist). The invalidation of pain—itself a rejection—reinforces social distance and Othering. Not surprisingly,

> shame is the psychological force that prevents the experience of grief from occurring and that may outright foreclose the experience of grief. . . . [I]f a loss is not recognized as loss, it is not realized as grief—just as directly and magically powerful as that. Shame is the psychological regulator allowing and disallowing recognition of grief. (Kauffman 2002, 63)

And if shame is not recognized, how can grief be?

In incidents of bullying, the original shame is compounded by a secondary shame over the pain and vulnerability a victim feels, doubly interrupting an ability to process the experience, fostering a denial of both. She has not only

been humiliated and cut off from the benefits of belonging; the grief she feels
over this is itself shameful ("Grow up," "Don't be such a crybaby," "Get over it,"
"Deal"). We are, as Dov Cohen (2003) contends, a culture ashamed of shame
itself.

> Being disenfranchised is itself a loss, a loss that is a narcissistic injury
> to one's self-regard and to how one experiences, values, secures and
> defines oneself. Disenfranchisement is an injury that blocks the pos-
> sibility of mourning; self is turned inward, wishing repair, but instead
> it repeatedly attacks itself with its worthlessness. (Kauffman 2002, 63)

Denial now frames and positions self. Discredited at every turn—victimized, then disallowed not only complaint but the pain itself (only crybabies admit pain)—the intrapsychic coherence of the self is violated. Pain and shame
are repudiated and driven underground, triggering all manner of maladaptive
responses. Alienated from body and mind, she becomes increasingly desperate to resist the disintegration of *being*. Her tenuous relationship to society
becomes an increasing risk factor in this, as reality belies *her* experiences, and
her identity loses its mooring.

As Laurie explained:

> *I hated myself for decades and was suicidal into my thirties. Very nearly
> killed myself each night over a stretch of months. By that I mean I really
> had a plan—a plan that could be enacted within the next twelve hours.
> And it could have gone either way, or it felt like it could have gone either
> way, and I never—it's not that I never analyzed what the self-hate thing
> was about. It was—it would be like analyzing why I'm left-handed or
> something. I think it began with my speech impediment. [Pauses] Um,
> you know, you know, "inferiority" is a word—but you're still on the scale
> with inferiority. It's being off the scale, it's being different, it's the expo-
> sure of being wrong, being made wrong, that self-hatred, and I think
> that's the way I would describe myself. I was made wrong—certainly gay
> kids feel they are made wrong—absolutely and innately. How can they
> excise or expunge the thing that they're made of? It's not less than, it's
> other than. You're not inferior; you're alien. Being a pariah was a way of
> being, like being depressed.*

An anonymous interviewee described the maladaptive responses in terms of
embodiment:

> *[I've] been abused [pauses], tormented, bullied at a level that had
> me make decisions about myself in the world that were not true—I*

told myself lies, but I took them to be true. Thing is, they're not fully psychological; they're lodged in my body, so what happens is that even when I change my thoughts, I'm surprised. Often I'm having a response, my body is having a response, that triggers thoughts and feelings, so thoughts and feelings can trigger the body, but the body also triggers thoughts and feelings. And unless I'm aware of what's going on, I could retreat in situations that are very safe because I feel unsafe, even though they're not unsafe.

Ongoing experiences of bullying, with all their disruptive violences and disconnects, are (and need to be acknowledged as) on a par with death and divorce. Both are normative yet nonetheless resonate deep within the body, often interrupting the flow of life. Ruptures and severances may involve a prolonged, dramatic dance, as hope of repairing the bond delays acknowledgment of the break. Or separation (rejection, exclusion) may be swift, incomprehensible, and irreversible. Either way, loss and grief, grounded in investment in other, disrupt psychic balance. As does the loss of peer relationship. Social bonds coconstruct and validate identity and are thus equally integral to sustaining self. Their interruption, which is of no small consequence, trails disorientation (especially during adolescence, when identity is under construction). This holds even if there are valid reasons for public humiliation, sanction, and exclusion—as there are legitimate reasons for death and divorce.

Bullying, contextualized in terms of loss, requires cultural and social responses aligned with existing grief narratives, protocols, and etiquettes. Piggybacking onto norms regulating grief, grieving, and displays of sympathy redefines emotional violence in terms of social and personal cost, helping bridge consequences to coping strategies. Constructing this connection requires familiarity with conceptualizations of mourning as well as an awareness of the key pitfalls associated with grief: rumination and depression. Appreciation of these risks will help define and shore up effective support of victims.[3]

One of the functions of any society is to validate the legitimacy of a loss, and individual experiences of loss are judged by the social norms of that society.
—DARCY HARRIS, "Oppression of the Bereaved"

In conferring legitimacy (enfranchising grief), culture establishes when, where, why, how, and the extent to which emotional responses are appropriate. It determines not only who are considered victims and in what circumstances but also how victims and those surrounding them are to behave. Unfortunately, even though death and divorce are recognized as legitimate losses, "death and grief signify vulnerability, which is a sign of weakness. In a social system that is based upon competition and acquisition, weakness is not tolerable, and so grief goes underground" (246). Bereavement-leave policies (one to three days, sometimes a week) are correlated to the logistical needs surrounding death (travel, final arrangements, memorial services) and only granted to immediate family members (those responsible for arranging and playing central roles in death rites). Policies are not in place to support the process of grieving but, rather, the practice of grief. Pain, loss, and their negotiation are private matters, given play in brief, formal rituals and then closeted and accommodated informally.[4] (It is, in fact, shameful if a grieving person does not get a grip and quickly return to a semblance of public functioning, despite her ability to meet workaday demands being compromised.)

Expressions of grief are equally regulated on an informal level, and interpersonal support is guided by norms and sympathy etiquette. For example, culture holds that death-related grief should run its course in three to twelve months and that its expression be gendered (women are expected to be distraught, responsible for outward emotional displays, while men ought to comport themselves with strong, stoic affect). In addition—as Candace Clark so insightfully documented nearly three decades ago—a unique set of norms and reciprocities guide the practice of sympathy. (Sympathy is a form of currency in the emotional economy, within which feeling rules inform such things as the intensity [strong vs. weak], duration [fleeting vs. lasting], and direction [positive vs. negative] of an emotion, as well as its display and response to displays.)[5] Deference is largely contingent on whether a victim is perceived as sympathy worthy or to blame for her misfortune. This distinction determines the sympathy margin, or amount of leeway an individual is entitled to and given.

> One's moral worth and network ties affect how many emotional commodities, including "units" of sympathy and compassion, can be claimed from others and that others feel they owe. . . . [This sympathy margin] . . . must be *ascribed by others*. Since we all interact with a variety of others, we may speak of people as having many margins of variable widths—one with each specific other in one's network. . . .
>
> Each group member has . . . what amounts to an "account" of "sympathy credits." . . . A certain number of sympathy credits are automatically on deposit in each of the sympathy accounts of the ordinary group member, available for cashing in when they are needed. They are a right of group membership. (Clark 1987, 300–301; emphasis in original)

All members of society are entitled to at least minimal support. Claims are made and responded to on the basis of belonging (although not all claims for sympathy are honored). This poses a significant dilemma around support for those who are publicly shamed, as they are visibly, even violently and intentionally, cut off from community and the benefits of membership. They are Othered in response to behaviors (or omissions) for which they are deemed responsible and thereby denied any claim to sympathy. They are deserving of their pain. And it may be this deservedness of social consequence that has, in large part, negated bystander response. Humiliated and cast out, shamed individuals are not legitimate objects of deference, support, or compassion (and should have no expectation of it). They have no account.

Clearly, social abuse needs to be legitimated as cause for cashing in sympathy credit—in fact, additional credits need to be created in the name of emotional violence. Even minimal, formulaic responsiveness—perfunctory expressions with no genuine sentiment behind them—will address the root of the shamed person's pain. These gestures themselves are overtures of (re)*connection*, validating her suffering and confusion, communicating that in some capacity she belongs. Thus, the overweight, acne-prone, poorly dressed girl is owed units if she is shamed and abused, as are culpable but overly stigmatized and ridiculed social outcasts. They are *due* the potential for redemption and the hope of more intimate inclusion. By incorporating sympathy credit into emerging narratives, culture normalizes this potential. Rote social overtures of sympathy connect bystanders to victims in an active way. And importantly, as a socially scripted response, they do not signal a personal invitation to greater intimacy. In fact, Clark (1987) argues that to solicit more from a sympathizer is to lose one's credibility as well as one's entitlement to sympathy in the future. Rather, such gestures are a simple acknowledgement of cost and signal that a victim's need of space has registered with peers. This is not to suggest sympathy is *owed* every victim by every individual. Acts may be unforgiveable to those who suffer their consequence and perhaps to many bystanders as well.

Once a person's membership in community, however marginal, is reestablished, her grief process itself becomes the focus. Culture understands grieving as a series of stages that chart and benchmark her coping. External expressions of sympathy confirm that she has been given space and time to negotiate and resolve her loss. Stage theories provide maps of grief work that guide her while also supplying a progress plan to those in the community, enabling them to measure her headway. They are the blueprint of cultural beliefs informing loss and the social dynamics surrounding it, including emotion norms and feeling rules, as well as a vocabulary of oral and bodily articulations.[6] Expectations of mourners, no less than bystanders, are so integrated into our stock of cultural knowledge that they would require little discussion were they not currently contested and in the throes of drastic reformulation. This re-visioning emerges from critiques that allow a more ready adaptation of the process of mourning to the needs of the bullied and begins with the deconstruction of stage theories.

Traditional Conceptualizations of Grief

Coping with loss has traditionally been seen as a process, one structured around foundational assumptions contained in Freud's seminal essay "Mourning and Melancholia" ([1917] 1974). Freud's reflections led to the mapping of grief into stages that articulate it in terms of personal psychic economies. These exist in relation to the objective of all grieving: *relinquishing attachment to, or investment in, the lost object*[7]—that is, to letting go. Importantly, each stage was believed to be identifiable by its affective correlates (emotional states), which were, and for many still are, a gauge of the nature and degree of investment remaining in the lost object. Plainly put, how close is the bereaved to letting go? This goal marks the point at which she has returned to the psychical equilibrium that existed prior to the loss and can move on and form new attachments. Stages monitor progress, measuring advances and setbacks to the individual as well as to the community that supports her.[8] The immediate concern is to get beyond the temporary period of confusion that surrounds broken connection and surmount any neediness or dependency occasioned by the loss. Communities extend themselves to meet interim needs, tolerant of lax productivity, disorganization, emotional outbursts, and preoccupation. Their allowances informally sustain her, as she gradually gets back on track and resumes a life in keeping with cultural ideals of independence. The returns on this support are the victim's own efforts, which can be charted (see, for example, Talcott Parsons's "sick-role" [1975]).

Although Freud's model has been updated and revised (e.g., Bowlby's [1969] flexibly occurring phases of shock, yearning and protest, despair, and recovery or Kübler-Ross's [1969] stages of denial and isolation, anger, bargaining, depression, and acceptance), stages still dominate the way we think about the (rational) process of grief resolution. No matter their content, a linear progression continues to orient sufferers toward the end goal of relinquishing investment in the lost relationship.

In shepherding mourners through the grieving process, stages, with their objective, identifiable characteristics, serve additional functions. First, they lend the experience of loss a coherence by containing and controlling the raw experience of pain. Their identification and labeling of expected response at various stages bundles reactions, ordering them, making disorientation intelligible. Second, stages provide a language that enables discussion of complex, changing feelings. Identifying, articulating, and sorting responses creates a common ground, promoting understanding, support, bonding with other grievers, and a measure of stability. Third, they allow the individual to establish her location along a trajectory, providing her with a sense of control. Where she is and *where she is going* become anchored in the process itself, thereby keeping a void of meaninglessness at bay (and, as long as she is progressing, allowing her to continue to claim support from the community). Finally, a measurable march toward a clear end is in keeping with cultural norms of rationalism. Stages prompt and foster resolution, furthering culture's streamlined, use-value orientation by holding that it is the individual's responsibility to sever relationships that are no longer active in her life, that no longer support her life, and that in any way prevent her from getting on with her life, whether these relationships are to the living or the deceased.[9] Understood thus, it seems that stage theories might be modified and readily adapted to support victims of bullying. They could provide bystanders with an indication of how bad the rupture is and script prompts for support at one or another stage, again, offering the possibility of intervention without extending the offer of intimate friendship. Stages could also provide victims with a language for their (legitimate) pain, a goal for resolution, and a sense that they belong to a larger community in which their pain is understood, validated, and accommodated.

However, while monitoring the internal state of individuals suffering rejection, loss, and intrapsychic instabilities is important, lest they helplessly spiral into maladaptive responses, including depression, stage theories contain shortcomings that are not insignificant. In this model grief is standardized along economies of psychic energy. It is linked to a closed internal system that does not take account of the external circumstances—either those surrounding the loss (was it betrayal by a best friend, exclusion by the group, mockery by the popular kids, or foreseeable, even warranted, rejection, or is it *ongoing* violence, perhaps humiliations that alternate with acceptance?)—or the impact of others' responses on her (bystanders may inflict additional cruelties, ignore her, or intervene and support her in some capacity). Stage theories level the original no less than ongoing relationship to the loss (as well as to the lost object) and assess a victim's response in relation to an assumed and undifferentiated psychic toll. While it might be countered that these variables are addressed informally (by the extent of sympathy that is extended) and reflected in the three-to-twelve-month range allotted for mourning, informal accommodations do not reflect differences in relationship that should *ground and define* her response as well as her process (see Janoff-Bulman and Frantz 1997; Seale 1998; Neimeyer 2000a; Moss and Moss 2002; Ribbens McCarthy 2006). By imposing cookie-cutter templates on all varieties of severance, stage theories artificially isolate loss, assuming it is a relatively identical experience for all. Their framework of absence establishes an end goal that positions the individual and orients her negotiation (negation?) of loss, stage by stage. In operationalizing response, they ignore circumstances following the break, as well as the *ongoing* significance of social factors. (These aspects of renegotiating relationship to both self and community are extremely salient in recovering from experiences of bullying.)[10] Ongoing bonds, changing connections, and the relentless *social* repositioning and (de)construction of self are all precluded.

A second assumption in the stage-theory model—that the intent of the grief work is to restore the psychic balance that existed prior to the loss and that to do this the person must let go—is also suspect. The formula for resolution—gradual divesting of investment in the lost object—is expected to return her to an assumed preloss equilibrium. This goal is not only presumed desirable but *possible.* Professional and cultural endorsement of this objective notwithstanding, individuals have managed to relinquish severed relationships about as effectively as victims of relational aggression have been able to believe that sticks and stones will break their bones but names will never hurt them—which is to say, not very well at all.[11] In spite of lip service to this end (and psychotherapists' pursuit of it), individuals often maintain investments in lost relationships, even intentionally allowing them to continue informing their daily lives: "I know she is looking down on me and can see that I . . . ," or "I always feel that she is looking over my shoulder and criticizing," or "I want to make her proud of me." Influence does not cease once the tangible bond has been lost. (Consider the girl who is rejected and picked on and moves to a school in another state. Although no longer ridiculed, she continues to incorporate a sense of self in relation to the bullying she suffered, reflecting an ongoing investiture in the internalized gaze of this other, which may, in a variety of ways, inform her fresh start.) Relationships are not and cannot simply be reduced to (severed) psychic investments, dangling emotional threads that need to be withdrawn (decathected) to be reinvested. The particulars and significances that make for emotional investment are interwoven with identity and suggest a much greater complexity.

In fact, this weave suggests an *inability* to relinquish ties. Failure to disconnect from lost objects points to a coconstruction of self, an *intersubjectivity* that stage theories fail to recognize:

> Fundamental assumptions about self and reality are not individual productions but joint constructions often achieved through conversation. [Ronnie] Janoff-Bulman (1989), for example, contends that significant others aid us in determining whether the world is a benevolent or malevolent place, whether life is fair or unfair, whether we have control over events or are powerless, and whether life is meaningful or random. The [loss] of an important other may contribute to the total collapse of this basic structure of assumptions about the character of social reality. (Forte, Barrett, and Campbell 1996, 34)

Individuals develop self and identity with and through others, *enacting* their lives in terms of others' gaze. Social, psychological, emotional, and corporeal knowledge has been and continues to be coconstructed in terms of these dialogues. Their absence, no less than the terms of their loss, is profound. The collaborative infrastructure animating the physiology of the social has collapsed, and to the degree that a person has internalized others' voices, it is their silences that now inform her.

Stage theories miscalculate her needs because of their inability to grasp self as an artifact of interrelationship or understand how severance fundamentally changes her. Bonds tether her to a shared social reality, and their rupture alters the very basis of her *being* in the universe. To be cut loose from social mooring *transforms* the conditions—and perhaps the framework—of her interaction with the world. Thus, loss itself is transformative. The process of negotiating the changes it entails—the social, biographical, and physiological realignments at the heart of grief work—constitutes metamorphosis. Stage theories deny metamorphosis, orienting her toward the past, calling for *return* to an equilibrium that might never have been optimal to her. How can she return to whomever she was prior to the (d)evolution of self that occurred in—and in the loss of—relationship? To how she inhabited and appropriated the world while the other was incorporated into her navigation of it—for better or worse? To constructions of self that prevailed before that other, who provided "the social context for understanding, organizing, validating and defining feeling, action, values and priorities, was removed" (Rosenblatt 1988, 68)? The answer is she cannot. Letting go of the lost object occurs at the cost of *letting go of narratives of self.* Seen in this light, severance calls for a precarious balancing act, one that cannot always be struck or struck without significant challenge to identity. Stage theorists little recognize this aspect of loss or, consequently, the end they are championing.

In response to this oversight, and in keeping with attempts to minimize and contain disruption to self, an ongoing relationship to the lost object (other) must be affirmed yet repositioned. Continuity is key to narrative coherence. However shaken, her (coconstructed) conceptualizations of self will be decisive to her ability to connect past to future, as well as to how she connects them. Facilitating this bridge work, transitioning past relationships into new narratives, is integral to the new blueprints of support being drawn for victims of bullying. Bystanders who recognize her needs in this provide the social space for her self project: transitioning to her future in ways that confer meaning on the pain of her past. Importantly, "when bereaved individuals are unable to negotiate this transition they may feel constrained by a life story that is radically incoherent, leaves important experiences 'unemplotted,' is devoid of thematic significance, or is no longer organized around a 'fictional goal' that leads toward a meaningful future" (Neimeyer 2001, 267–268).

Contending that relationships *cannot* be let go and instead require re-configuration voids many banal responses to bullying (e.g., "Just ignore her," "Why do you let what they say bother you?"). Recognizing the ongoing import and influence of damaged or lost bonds or frustrated investments allows affirmation of—even deference to—the victim's ongoing connection to her abuser(s), be it tacit, explicit, or reluctant. Connection, even to bullies, *maintains a coherent identity structure.*

Letting go, or radically repositioning self on an interpersonal level within social realities constructed by others, poses another level of difficulty. Past relationships tie a victim to a specific social identity—one that may be soiled, repudiated, and firmly entrenched in the (intersubjective) reality maintained by others. (Cruelly, personal bonds may be severed, but she will be denied the opportunity to socially reposition herself, to move on, to reestablish psychic equilibrium and salvage, if not redeem, self. She has become a social cipher and is not allowed to let go of her public identity, making letting go of or even modifying her personal indentity constructs seemingly impossible, especially in a small community.)

Relinquishing—even revising—the identity constructs linked to social bonds is particularly difficult if the individual has been complicit in her own victimization, if she has embraced the critical voices and judgmental gazes, anchoring identity in negatively valenced feedback.[12] Her at times desperate, heartbreaking attempts to recover damaged, broken connections are attempts to control for the ontological upheaval that loss of even a deficient self will entail. Grief narratives that promote the need for transitions, fostering cultural and bystander support of her process, forge an infrastructure for—while at the same time legitimating the possibility of—change. They provide social backing for her bridging project.[13] Grief work occurs in the liminal spaces that, if society cordons and supports them, become key to her healing process. Bystanders will influence *that* she reweaves relationships as well as how she reweaves them—to self, to other, and to society. New social norms that speak to the *creative, transformative potential within the process of grieving itself* will allow her to effectively reconfigure her relationship to attachments: "The life story disrupted by the loss must be reorganized, rewritten, to find a new strand of continuity that bridges the past with the future in an intelligible fashion" (Neimeyer 2000a, 263).

New Models of Grieving and Grief Work

Critiques of stage theories have sparked renewed discussions about the nature of grief, facilitating the emergence of new, dynamic theories that ask not only, "If letting go is not the goal of grieving, what is?" but also "How do we go about it?" Response to these questions clarifies *how* the needs of the grieving self are being redefined, setting the tone for new grief-work narratives and their support.

Margaret Stroebe and Henk Schut are leading voices in this change, proposing a dynamic new paradigm that abandons the truth and certainty of letting go. Their approach (first proposed in 1999) fits well with a diverse, multicultural society in which no fixed, universal prescriptions can be made or institutionalized. Its dynamic framework dissolves the staid, singular understanding of loss into individual experiencing (fitting well with the ethos of individualism and self-determination that characterizes Western culture). Ends are not given but emerge and cohere around a *relational* positioning of the subject to the loss.[14]

Understanding grief and grieving as subjective, relational experiencing responds to critiques of stage theories, but Stroebe and Schut's dual process model (DPM) is also tasked with proposing coping strategies, as leaving each individual to her own devices hardly constitutes a new paradigm. To mediate the subjective configurations of a single objective fact (there has been a loss), the DPM explores coping strategies in terms of dynamic cognitive processes. It identifies grief and grieving as multidimensional experiences revolving around two distinct stressors: *loss orientation* and *restoration orientation*. Loss orientation refers to making sense of severed connection. It is the personal (intrapsychic) grappling with change and, more importantly, with the terms of change. Significantly, this includes a confrontation with and attempts to work though and get a handle on overwhelming and potentially incoherent aspects of the experience. (Why would God take away my child? Why was I put in a concentration camp? Why would Brianna do that to me?)[15] It may, at first glance, seem almost scandalous to include nasty interpersonal ruptures (e.g., Brianna's actions) with larger, philosophical questions that engage the meaning of life itself. But because social abuse emotionally cripples individuals, sometimes for life (and can even elicit violent actions against self and others), these questions belong in the same category. Emotional violence and psychological abuse have the potential to upend ontological security, causing confusion and doubt about the order of things and how one is to *be* in the world. Extreme instances disrupt mental functioning, no less than other experiences of severed connection that occasion chaos, and cry out just as plaintively for incorporation into personal narratives and larger life schemas. Attempts to endow experiences of cruelty with meaning may be ongoing, almost compulsive, causing an individual to withdraw from other investments in life, becoming inattentive to the demands of her body, her environment, and the needs of others. Increasingly consumed with *why* questions, she pays little or no attention to social regimens in which she is embedded.

On the other hand, she may avoid thinking about the loss, distract herself with activities that take her mind off it, focus on pragmatic, day-to-day chores, and set new tasks for herself. Preoccupation with activities related to day-to-day living in the world swings her behavior toward the second locus of grief work, which Stroebe and Schut call "restoration orientation" or "restoration coping" (1999, 2001). *Restoration coping* refers to the concrete ways the individual restores coherence to her life. Through a focus on tasks at hand (What is needed for her to get through the morning, the day, the week? Through homework, exams, job responsibilities, or long stretches of silence?), she keeps the void of meaninglessness, and even the hurt, at bay. Often this focus involves the assumption of new social roles. Prior (lost) relationships had cast her in specific social roles (significant other, best friend, group member) associated with particular functions (study partner, designated driver, social coordinator, peacekeeper, or even clotheshorse). These roles opened particular opportunities to her (invitations to parties, getting algebra answers, skateboarding, borrowing clothes, going to the movies, and just hanging out) that are now closed. Bereft of self-defining roles and expectations, she may welcome new obligations that distract her from the gaps in daily life. Focus on these responsibilities is a segue of sorts, fending off isolation and even depression and despair. They *actively* preoccupy her, requiring movement in the world, forging a new social identity.

In separating functioning from meaning making and positioning the two in a dynamic relation to each other, Stroebe and Schut set up a fluid model that, however much in possession of a tangible infrastructure, cannot, in itself, indicate the direction through her pain: "Being oscillatory in contrast to linear stage theories, [makes] it . . . impossible for [grieving] to become normative: no expert or well-meaning family member can tell the mourner what is 'normal' after, say, six months" (Walter 2007, 132). Individuals negotiating loss are tasked with processing their feelings as well as working out practical concerns, and to the degree they are able to oscillate between a focus on one and the other, they resist becoming engulfed in denial or alienation. The space between the two opens the possibility for silver linings, repositioning an individual in relation to self and world.

Clearly, this model can be mapped onto the needs of victims of bullying, assisting the community in untangling and supporting them. Broken connection—especially ruptures that de- and then reconstruct the social world in ways that exclude a victim (divorce, as well as the death of a spouse, often ends relationships with the other's friends, coworkers, and in-laws, no less than social rejection ends participation in the activities of the inner circle)—requires social frameworks. Rejected, humiliated victims of social aggression are in need of cultural narratives that prescribe and model the scaffolding of options and next steps. These need to be scripted with the following questions in mind: What is the nature of the bond that has been broken by bullying, or what future social relationships have been jeopardized by relational aggression? How and to what extent has day-to-day life been orchestrated in terms of these investments and connections (implicitly or explicitly)? How can a victim address ongoing needs when shame and social censure are ongoing and/or are not undeserved? Finally, it must be kept in mind that in instances of bullying and relational aggression the victim is often challenged to reconfigure personal and social functioning in a fishbowl environment. Opportunities for restoration coping are limited, as may be the possibility to replace role relationships (and make other friends). What is the basis of hope, and how can she transform self?

Bullying: A Special Case of Loss and the Pitfall of Rumination

Attempts to reconfigure social response to bullying are frustrated by the impossibility of knowing what incidents radically challenge bodies, psyches, *being*. Not all pain involves loss, and not all loss is a traumatic rupture calling for coping strategies and reconstructions of meaning. Most episodes of nastiness—even extended periods of ostracization and Othering—do not appear to require extensive reorderings of the life world (although this cannot be certain, as the disenfranchisement of shame and grief have quashed all but the most dire of signals indicating distress). Infractions, innuendos, and insensitivities that regularly prick insecurities and threaten relationship, social sour notes, *are* often absorbed into the music of the dance. Is this because shame and grief are immediately ushered underground and danced over, or might it suggest that means to both address and redress social loss are already in play and perhaps need little more than elaboration and expansion?

> In the ebb and flow of everyday interactions, as has been conveyed so effectively in the work of [Erving] Goffman, there exist numerous opportunities for small psychic losses, exclusions and humiliations, alternating with moments of repair and optimism. [Thomas] Scheff (1990) has sought to understand this quality of everyday interaction as consisting of cycles of shame and pride as the social bond is alternately damaged and repaired. The experience of loss and repair is, then, a daily event. In this sense "bereavement" (and recovery from it) describes the continual daily acknowledgement of the problem of human embodiment. (Seale 1998, 193)

Social life initiates us into experiences of loss as well as habitus-determined rituals for reparation patterned on atonement paradigms (Is an apology warranted? A public post? An admission of culpability to others? An offering such as chocolate or wine? Or is distancing to be expected and accepted?). These ebbs and flows familiarize us with disruptions in connectivity to others and socialize us into means of restitution, whereby a continuation of relationship is possible.

Bullying moves beyond this (expected) rhythm, as the actions of others are often unwarranted, unrelenting, even unfathomable, and unremediable. Increased familiarity with the dynamics of shame and grief, while instructive, will not put meaning into how malice is experienced or diminish a person's ongoing pariah status. But with social acknowledgment of her pain's significance, increased understanding will help story her loss. Most importantly, social recognition and condemnation of bullying and sympathy for its cost allow individuals to continue to stand within the narratives of culture, to have status and position and even supportive scripts, although Danah Boyd and Alice Marwick (2011) make it clear that identifying oneself as a victim or labeling interactions as bullying may be beyond the ability of many young people. An example of inclusivity has, as Boyd and Marwick note, already emerged from youth culture. Rather than viewing themselves as helpless, hapless social (and personal) failures, victims see themselves as caught up in dramas. Dramas are inclusive and normative and continue to situate stigmatized—even guilty—victims within larger, unfolding stories. The languaging of experience as "drama" is rather remarkable, confirming that inclusivity is precisely what targets of social aggression often need. As a metanarrative, drama normalizes interpersonal conflict, acknowledging ongoing social and personal narratives that recognize *all* parties—protagonists and antagonists, victims and bullies—as participants.

Several factors thwart any attempt to identify at what point dramas cross a line and meanness moves beyond expected (and acceptable) social rhythms. Not the least of these is that, in bullying, loss is often not definitive. The severance is inconsistent, jagged; rejection is incomplete; and an ebb and flow still appears to be in play (though the play may be sadistic and the ebb much greater than the flow). A person may, in fact, be led to believe that the relationship is not lost and its salvaging is still somewhat in her control. Grieving and struggles to reposition the relationship and renegotiate meaning may all be unnecessary and (understandably) deferred. When things are worse one day and better the next, the relationship is potentially recoverable. Loss of connection is not inevitable: hope remains, severance may be forestalled, and grief work is uncalled for.

Inconsistencies in the response of peers redouble attempts at sense making, which usually occur in terms of personal responsibility. (This is to be expected—it is the social function of shame. Self-reflection and adjustments to behavior are the socially desired outcome of negative response to actions and/or presentations of self.) Questions such as "Why is this happening?" are an attempt to answer the question "What can *I do* to make it stop?" For girls in particular, reflections on agency may more readily move to global indictments on, and judgments of, their very *being* in the world, calling for more than adjustments to patterns of behavior.[16] Gender inequality weaves a greater degree of inferiority into girls' everyday lives, making inadequacy a familiar social experience, one that too well acquaints them with the position of supplicant. Moreover, a girl is less comfortable claiming self-determination in defense of differences. To the extent that inadequacy is familiar and self-blame does not interrupt her understanding of her position in the world, recourse to reparation and self-redemption involve little more than habitual self-deprecation. Assuming responsibility for broken connection reaffirms a known, predictable social reality, one that (ironically) she can influence. Reassertion of flaws and deficiencies and further self-denigration is preferable to grappling with an arbitrary, even absurd and unforgiving world. Desperate to restabilize her identity, she endures, even endorses, censure and rebuke. Self-blame does not require the overhauling of the whole assumptive world, only revisions to her pathetic, sketchy, inappropriate comportment within it. Acknowledging that she *is* inadequate and cannot fix herself is less alarming than taking on meaninglessness, which poses a much greater threat to self-coherence.

As she surrenders self-narrative to the constructions of others, her ability to know and trust herself in the world is undermined. As sites of resistance implode, a victim loses the ability to independently assess the situation and question the behavior of others; she no longer notices or questions why they do not say anything about x's clothes or hair or behavior, or she resentfully complains, "It's not fair that . . ." Once this internal dialogue stops, she ceases to see herself as someone deserving of equitable treatment, reasonable answers, or inclusion (and forgiveness?) and is well on the way to forfeiting self. Acceding to, embracing, and *becoming defined in terms of* her inadequacies, she is authored by others, lost.[17]

At this point, healthy self-reflection devolves into ruminations (which may or may not overlap with the meaning-making axis in grief narratives, in which she may become stuck). When no answers emerge from re-reviews of behavior, from searches for unintended infractions, hidden meanings, or should-have options and when attempts to remediate the situation or to change self are unacknowledged, dwelling on *why* questions—What did I, should I, could I do?—becomes counterproductive. As aspirations of forgiveness, redemption, and reintegration begin to disintegrate, the replaying of misunderstandings, of laughter, mockery, incomprehensible sneering, or just plain mean incidents (that are, perhaps, compounded daily) may threaten chaos: a void of meaninglessness. Inability to reverse damage to reputation or negotiate a pariah social status undermines hope and shores up helplessness. She is pathetic, even to herself. This downward spiral appears inevitable, because she has no option but to continue rewinding and replaying events, re-viewing them from an increasingly numb perspective.

Rumination and Depression:
Social-Psychological-Neurological Interface

Pain, whatever else philosophy or biomedical science can tell
us about it, is almost always the occasion for an encounter with
meaning. It not only invites interpretation: like an insult or an
outrageous act, it seems to require explanation. —DAVID MORRIS,
"The Meanings of Pain"

Downward ruminative spirals lead to a morass, a place seemingly beyond reclamation. "Rumination is defined as engaging in thoughts and behaviors that
maintain one's focus on one's negative emotions and on the possible causes
and consequences of those emotions" (Nolen-Hoeksama 2001, 546; see also
1991). At some unspecified point, ongoing rumination traps an individual in
a loop of unsuccessful attempts to make sense of, and incorporate, shame and
rejection (the beginnings of cognitive impairment, discussed in Chapter 3).
Failure to negotiate and resolve the meaning of socially isolating cruelty and
to incorporate it into coherent self-narratives (even habitual self-deprecating
threads of coherence) causes self-reflection to devolve into self-annihilation
and nonreflective account giving. Mired in a loss orientation, active engagement in *effective* problem solving (restoration coping) eludes her.

Susan Nolen-Hoeksema notes that the ongoing stuckness of ruminators
may cause any support they do have to fall away. We all know such people,
whom we come to avoid, as they "go over and over their loss and persistently
discuss their feelings and grief-related symptoms without making much progress toward 'resolving' their loss" (Nolen-Hoeksama 2001, 551). Their ongoing
self-absorbed negativity is a violation of social norms and exhausts any sympathy margin they may be entitled to. Increasingly isolated, these individuals' circling, repetitive thoughts become embodied, etching mental grooves
that slowly damage ongoing self-narratives, preventing future orientation and
change. Distant, hunched, and lackluster, they "feel they have stopped delud-
ing themselves, and are now seeing things for how bad they really are. Such
thoughts are extremely compelling and would be difficult to put aside for the
sake of lifting one's mood" (552). Social exclusion only reinforces this conclu-
sion, as a person comes to confirm, in her bowed shoulders and crumpled
spine, that she is the waste-of-space, loser, sluttish, fat, ugly, stupid, sorry,
pathetic, or lying wannabe that her tormentors have constructed.[18] Resigned
acceptance replaces most vestiges of active agency, fostering a passivity that
is, itself, fodder for increased depressive states and self-loathing. Depressed
individuals come to have an expectation of failure, often taking details out of
context (or negatively skewing neutral comments or experiences) in support
of their global evaluation of self.

Ongoing taunts, humiliations, and/or exclusion exacerbate this mental state, reinforcing negative self-images and encouraging an increasingly imbalanced processing of experience. This differentiates bullying from more conventional losses, separating the grief work needed by a victim from that occasioned by death or divorce. Bullies can promote open-ended self-blame, denying her the possibility of making claims on others, of redeeming self, or of renegotiating personal and social identity, *driving* her into and maintaining ruminative patterns (or numbness that deflects the torment). Because she cannot "just ignore them" (well-worn advice that, in ignoring her pain, seeks to promote a semblance of restoration coping and moving on), she becomes trapped in patterns of thought that themselves deny the possibility of future social relationships, complicit in grinding down hope and securing isolation. As one anonymous interviewee put it:

I mean, I don't think I ever was to the point of suicide that I would do it, but I thought about it because it hurt so much. But I also had love in my life, so I was able—like I remember as a child feeling love for people. I would think about my grandparents and focus on that—being loved—so it wasn't like I was completely isolated from that, but there was deep, deep, deep, deep, deep, deep, deep, deep sadness.

As ongoing marginalization (social ostracization and/or shamed collaboration in one's own exile) forecloses hope or severs it completely, her ability to feel (or even to shrivel at shame itself) deadens. The implications of this are extremely significant. If, as discussed in Chapter 3, relationships are our natural habitat and belongingness is on a par with food and water, then ongoing social deprivation can be expected to impair the functioning of the organism. It affects the emotion system, altering the manner in which the body responds by producing a higher pain threshold and decreased sensitivity. *Along with a heightened ability to tolerate her own privation and pain comes an expanded ability to witness the pain of others* (Crescioni and Baumeister 2009; DeWall 2009). Her capacity for other-orientation, for sensitivity and prosocial behavior (acting in ways that show concern for the welfare of others, taking their feelings into consideration, even benefiting them some way), becomes attenuated.[19] This lays the psychological preconditions for all manner of atrocities.[20]

Equally important is that the *executive functions of the brain*, notably the ability to process information and self-regulate, *are impaired as a result of rejection*. The disruption of cognitive processing often contributes to—and reflects—a depressive downward spiral. When torment is ongoing and questions of *why* or *why me* cannot be adequately answered, ruminative states may devolve further, seguing into *cognitive deconstruction*. Cognitive deconstruction, a psychological state associated with lethargy, absence of emotion, lack of self-awareness, perception of meaninglessness, fixation on the present, and perhaps even presuicidal conditions, is considered a defensive mental strategy. "People enter into a deconstructed state when they experience personal failure or when it becomes abundantly clear that they are inadequate on some personally or socially desirable trait. When in a state of cognitive deconstruction, people are prone to make irrational decisions and to show unwillingness to delay gratification so as to meet their long-term goals" (DeWall 2009, 204). (Note the overlaps between the description of this state and descriptions of response to shame.) In particular, they are unwilling to engage in the self-control that is integral to relationship and group coherence. Not gaining any of the psychological benefits that accrue to group members, these individuals are not only less able but less inclined to manage their impulses, becoming aggressive and unhelpful—which only furthers their rejection and spiral into isolation. "Many of the responses that follow from experiencing social exclusion *likely preclude the possibility of excluded people regaining a sense of social belonging*" (203; emphasis added). However, as noted in Chapter 3, there is still an ability—albeit a *lessened* ability—to self-regulate and exercise control if the victim has reason to do so.[21]

Unfortunately, that reason is often not offered. The social conditions promoting wound repair and healthy scarring while curbing impulses are absent; cognitive deconstruction and the analgesic reduction of sensitivity accompanying social pain are not allowed heal—to return to their original stable state. This is the real crux of the matter. The more antisocial and insensitive an individual becomes (in response to gossip, laughter, and humiliation), the less likely she is to be included, be invited to join, or feel connected to the community. And the less included she is, the less invested she is in others or even in her own desire to belong. This social cycling—Scheff (2011) dubs it a recursive social loop of rejection and isolation—is caused (or supported or accompanied) by neurophysiological responses that numb her pain and limit her capacity for empathy. Socially destroyed, consumed by the deficits and inadequacies of self, these individuals are not (are unable to be) concerned with or connected to others.

If responses to pain come to preclude other-orientation, then offering hope (connecting with her and giving her incentive to care) is an even more pressing responsibility of bystanders. Failure to understand victim nonresponsiveness as mistrust, as active resistance to annihilation, involves their own failure to empathize. Tacit assent looms as malicious solidarity, silently endorsing inadequacy, undesirability, Otherness, and even repugnance. It is a moral strategy in the communication and reinforcement of group values, an absence of connection that reverberates in and through her body. In addition to breaking this silence, it is important to determine how society (bystanders, professionals, caregivers) might slow the deterioration of cognitive functioning. How do we forestall a slide into chaotic mental states? Can coherence and productive cognitive functioning be prompted?

————

The ability to sponsor an enhanced cognitive capacity rests on the ability to isolate productive from unproductive rumination—from a mere focus on negativity to an embodied, cognitively destructive morass of self-deprecation—but on what possible basis? Critical self-reflection, which includes replaying events over and again, questioning behavior, and even finding it inadequate, is central to healthy psychological growth as well as successful social adaptation. It is the organic connection between self and society, crucial to sustaining intersubjective realities and reconfiguring self. Further,

> the ability to face distressing emotions (e.g. to grieve a loss fully, to acknowledge and "work through" major disappointments and setbacks) has long been viewed as a hallmark of mental health; and *experiencing and expressing negative affect has been considered an important ingredient of successful responses.* (Rude, Maestas, and Neff 2007, 844; emphasis added)

In apparent contradiction to this, there is "a large body of evidence indicat[ing] that individuals who ruminate—who focus attention on the self and symptoms of distress, and the meanings of those symptoms—are more likely to experience prolonged suffering" (843). How can the two be squared? Why and at what point does reflection begin to feed on itself, contributing to a belief in worthlessness and a loss of agency and control? If critical, even painfully unflattering self-reflection is not only normative but healthy, what triggers its deterioration into counterproductive ruminative states? Sustained exclusion, compounded by gossip and repeated, humiliating, public laughter can provoke disruptions to cognitive functioning, but this outcome is neither inevitable nor predictable. Short of typing and cataloging internal and external factors, rumination appears impossible to operationalize. A unique array of environmental factors and situational circumstances interface with neurological predispositions, muddling any such attempt (for a hint at its would-be complexity, see Appendix D). This impasse leads to the question: Might there be an x factor, an overlooked constant (aside from lost connection) that transitions one to the other, crippling, eventually negating, her ability to function in the world?

Nolen-Hoeksema's lifework exploring rumination (and its correlation to gender, depression, coping strategies and bereavement, thought suppression, etc.) often incorporates this question. Does ruminative thinking exist along a subjective continuum, and if so, is some identifiable factor likely to trigger its slide into negativity? Is it a slippery-sloped scale, or is this the wrong model?

Gradually, the data obtained from ongoing research yielded an alternative conceptualization, a dual-response model. In this revised conceptualization, *all* ruminative thoughts simultaneously exhibit an *active, self-reflective* and a *passive, repetitive* component (Nolen-Hoeksema, Parker, and Larson 1994; Nolen-Hoeksema, Larson, and Grayson 1999; Nolen-Hoeksema 2001; Treynor, Gonzalez, and Nolen-Hoeksema 2003). These aspects function in complementary ways, balancing the process itself (not unlike components of the DPM). When they cease to inform each other—especially when self-reflection is co-opted by other's voices—individuals become trapped in overwhelmingly passive, dysfunctional patterns. Productive self-reflection does not slowly morph into maladaptive low-level responding but, rather, *exists alongside* resignation and convictions of incompetency, inadequacy, and undesirability. Withdrawal and nonproductive rumination reflect an imbalance in these dual properties.

While it seems obvious that the response of others plays a key role in this imbalance, what is less than obvious is the trigger. Is it simply a quantitative ratio? Does the positive, self-reflective component become overshadowed by ongoing negative feedback? (This puts researchers back on the same slippery slope: How much is too much?) Or is there a qualitative element linked to imbalance and cognitive disruption? The *coexistence* of active and passive tendencies suggests that productive self-reflection is not linked to a zero-sum game and thus can be bolstered, even while lethargic, unproductive states continue to orient an individual's being in the world. But how?

Again referencing the dynamic of the DPM, it seems clear that what is needed (especially for preteens and teens) is a viable version of restoration coping: a way to counterbalance the quagmire of meaning making that smothers the self's capacity for productive reflection and repositioning of self. But how *can* one engage the higher-level thinking that might reevaluate connections; how *can* she get beyond the numbing perils of rumination and (re)engage (which should not be conflated with reestablishing self-esteem)?[22] While breaking the silence of bystanders interrupts *ongoing* victimization, it does not preoccupy her with or invest her in new roles; nor does it necessarily promote productive self-reflection. How might she get at, and maintain, higher-level thinking?

In place of strategies more readily available to those negotiating death and divorce is a deliberate, considered tactic: the exercise of cognitive abilities through *expressive writing*. The benefits of these exercises have been well documented since the mid-1980s, when James Pennebaker began studying and qualitatively assessing the positive impact that writing about traumatic experiences has and pioneering measurement of distinct physiological correlations (see Chapter 5). In writing, a person has the opportunity to organize her experience, giving voice to her deepest pain, fears, and confusion. She can further devise, revise, and actively re-vision outcomes and renarrate ruminations, allowing them to admit of intentions, context-rich explanations, apologies, and attempts at remediation. Such exercises promote the cognitive structuring and restructuring of the trauma, shaping and reshaping social parameters, personal response, and adverse effects on the individual (but they must be carefully distinguished from uncritical revenge fantasies). They recall active engagement with hows and whys of experience, the cognitive efforts to grasp and remediate social sanction.

The process itself seems redundant (the active replaying of events, of what-ifs, has not proven productive) and its focus paradoxical. Promoting further reflection would seem to risk ushering victims into deeper negative cycling, furthering apathetic acceptance. Countless school-age diaries, journals, and blogs offer daily laments, entries characterized by increasing self-blame and nonreflective account giving ("She said . . . then she did . . . then she said . . ."). They are unremarkable testimonials, artifacts documenting uncritical, low-level, repetitive mental functioning that seemingly attest to stuckness and dull, passive ruminating. What differentiates these school-age blogs and journals from expressive writing exercises, which, in study after study across the country, have produced productive, self-reflective writing samples (across such disparate variables as sex, gender, ethnicity, and depressive tendencies)? This question is at the heart of the next chapter. But before turning to it (through a fuller consideration of expressive writing's ability to promote cognitive functioning), it is important to conclude the discussion of rumination. Research on rumination informs an understanding of the dynamics at work in expressive writing and allows it to be more closely adapted to the needs of bullying narratives. It does this by identifying a trigger for unproductive reflection, an explanation for the diaries and blogs that are little more than tedious, negative ruminations on troubling life experiences. (Such accounts are not absent from the data accumulated in almost thirty years of varied expressive-writing research protocols. Every test population has participants who do not benefit.) Why do some individuals focus on negativity in ways that are beneficial to them, while for others, this very focus appears detrimental?

Situating this question at the center of their research, Eva-Maria Gortner and colleagues (2006) and Stephanie Rude and colleagues (2007) set about testing a unique hypothesis: that the degree of *judgment* that accompanies an individual's focus on unpleasant experiences is *the* factor separating what they call reflective emotional processing from passive, dysfunctional rumination. It is "likely not the focusing of attention on problems and their attendant distress that drives harmful effects of rumination, but rather the negative judgment of the experience" (Gortner, Rude, and Pennebaker 2006, 294). Critiques of the RRS (the Ruminative Response Scale, the standard scale used to measure rumination) were central to this hypothesis.[23] For more than a decade, researchers had noted a degree of self-criticism implied in some questions on the scale, a tacit judgmental perspective overlying the recounting of painful, traumatic, or unpleasant experiences. For example, some questions suggest that the respondent should examine her responses for clues as to why she did not respond as she "should." Implied judgment, which was not present in all questions on the scale, might well explain the divide between brooding, unproductive, and even destructive responses and beneficial reflective processing.[24] Perhaps interrupting debilitating global indictments of self, as well as the passive, unproductive cycling of thoughts that maintain them, hinges on the *nonjudgmental* contemplation of experiences (including the pain and loss associated with them).

Data support this hypothesis, confirming that self-judgments are key: if self-criticisms and the negative emotions caught up with them are separated from appraisals of traumatic experiences, the brooding, depressive aspects of rumination are lessened, and distinct, repeatedly verified benefits accrue to those engaged in sustained reflection. In other words, self-judgments—overarching evaluations of deficiency—preclude constructive appraisal of the experience, heading off avenues of escape from passive, repetitive, dead-end derogations, including those that might emerge through the process of grieving. (Interestingly, emotional distance aids in the practice of mindfulness, perhaps allowing numbing to be harnessed for its positive, productive potential.) These results are consistent with the rationale behind Thomas Scheff and Suzanne Retzinger's (1991) promotion of reintegrative *styles* of shaming. If the individual does not feel her whole self to be judged and branded with a master status, if she is not alienated by humiliation but instead able to acknowledge culpability while retaining connection to self (and potentially to other), she is able to experience, productively process, and discharge her shame.

The findings of Gortner and Rude and their colleagues have profound implications for victims, as well as for emerging cultural scripts and social interventions. Expressive writing prompts that encourage participants to identify and then perhaps screen out encompassing, self-judgmental aspects of their recountings can readily be devised. Such exercises can be incorporated in various curriculums at several levels, becoming an embedded classroom tool—one that supports the humiliated student who is unable to focus on or care about anything unrelated to charged social experiences (while giving students who are not troubled by shame and social rejection a skill set for future use). Objectifying and languaging (through expressive writing) recurring incidents, exclusion, and all the pain and grief these dramas entail opens possibilities that are unavailable as long as shame is unacknowledged, pain illegitimate, and rejections and humiliations unremarkable. Current norms of denial offer a person little choice but to internalize suffering and blame self on increasingly global levels. Self-blame offers her control over negative experiences, as well as the possibility to negotiate forgiveness and redemption in a world whose functioning remains coherent and intact. Were she, instead, prompted to focus attention on reinterpreting events; separating out criticisms, recriminations, or even protests against their outcome; probing for reasons above and beyond negative self-characterizations; and acknowledging the pain of rejection (and renegotiating relationship to self and other on the basis of it), she might be capable of a more balanced (even transformative) response.[25]

A focus on neutralizing (global) self-judgments dovetails with, though it is not identical to, the hiving that distinguishes guilt—a productive emotion— from isolating, recursive, self-negating shame. Exploring *situations* and perhaps even tendencies associated with self encourages an alternative packaging of experiences, dislodging ruminative stuckness, although it might seemingly do little more than return her to initial atonement responses, which are overshadowed by the memory of their inadequacy. The critical sting of social cruelties is lessened if behaviors are, and remain (or again become), compartmentalized or if the whole is viewed as an unfortunate series of events in which she has played a part.

A less-optimal hiving, *avoidance* (on par with denial and stockpiling), may well be standing in place of self-reflective compartmentalization by victims. One anonymous interviewee was quite aware of this:

> *My coping strategy was not remembering—to ignore it, actually. To try and put it away and to compartmentalize it. . . . I would think about the love of my grandparents, focus on that.*

A Final Note

It is important to at least mention (before turning to expressive writing) that self-deprecating rumination is forestalled, with apparently few ill effects, by transcendent understandings of traumatic events, such as "Karma's a bitch," "God works in mysterious ways," or simply "Shit happens." In other words, if unfair cruelties are explained by impersonal rationales, the victim can skirt the psychological pothole of repeated, unsuccessful attempts at self-centered meaning making that results in low-level cognitive processing (at the risk, of course, of skirting any responsibility). Consider, for example, the productive rationale of another anonymous interviewee:

> *You know, one of the things that gave me peace only a couple of years ago—I have a doctor friend who has young kids, two girls and a boy, and he said he noticed something about them when they were five years old. This gave me peace around the bullying, this many years later.*

What he said he noticed is that, up to five, they're loving, and then what happens—he noticed they start pushing away people who are different. And in the animal kingdom, you know, that behavior is part of survival—you know, like women choosing men who are [pauses] you know.

I wasn't sure that I was gay or whether I was just rejected by women because I was different.

That's why it supports me, the way my friend spoke about it, because otherwise there's a tendency to personalize it, try to figure out, well, what did I do, what did I say? When I go down that road, it is a very unhealthy place—to try and figure it out. I can't go there. Even today my mental thinking would take me there. I have to be very careful, or I try and understand what's not understandable, try and figure out, keep saying it over and over again: why would they do that, why would they do that, what did I say?

No data exist to tell us to what extent an avoidance of personalized meaning making is optioned, but because bullying often labels individuals and because culture bids us reflect on negative experiences (lest we repress responses, cultivate denial, and invite a host of ill effects), victims tend to search for meaning. Nonetheless, subscribing to an overarching perspective that limits substantive engagement with *why* questions is an alternative means of curtailing the impact of negative experiences and the self-judgments they may spawn.[26] Incorporating pain and loss into a larger narrative that simply accepts suffering as part of life grounds its meaning outside self, ultimately depersonalizing the experience. Lumped together with all manner of misfortune, bullying can be repositioned and negotiated on an equally impersonal level.

Secularized transcendent perspectives readily translate to a diverse, multicultural populace, believers and nonbelievers alike, and can even be specifically promoted in expressive writing exercises, even if the trauma is ongoing. The only foreseeable hindrance to this process (aside from the absence of a personal, overarching perspective) involves the difficulties that may arise from the languaging of shame itself. Rumination may remain inarticulate about experiences of humiliation, limiting a person's ability to engage in productive reflection and the cognitive reevaluation of social, affective, and behavioral responses. Unacknowledged, her shame is uncommunicable, ungrievable, and unrestructurable.[27] Reflections in an unstoried nether space might remain low-level descriptive accounts if active, productive, self-reflective reevaluations have no basis, no narratives, and no support. Vast linguistic wastelands may continue to promote resignation and embodied articulations; shame and pain still silently informing her "gestures, manners, and small ways of being and inhabiting social space" (Probyn 2005, 49). This is the only way that the body, denied the legitimacy of its experience, is able to speak.

The *cultural* inroad through silence, low-level thinking, and pain (or numbness), the insight that must inform storied responses to bullying, is the recognition that her experience, like all grief stories, is a *joint story. All* those connected to her are coauthors of a bullying and loss narrative. Horrific tragedies have served to validate her pain, but thus far strategies for lessening *her* responsibility for it, no less than *her* responsibility in negotiating it, have fallen short. Constructed jointly, as a socially recognized loss, her pain becomes embedded in larger, metanarrative scripts that tap the empathy—and stories—of others. The fear conjured by loss, the terror of a world without significance— or perhaps even without rhyme or reason, without connections tethering her to roles, expectations, and belonging—produces affects that strike deep into the heart and are called into play by shame and bullying no less than by death and divorce. We are *neurologically and corporeally* affected by the severance of bonds. Yet "fear and terror can be burned out by simple human contact" (Probyn 2005, 47).

NARRATIVE WRITING AND THE
RECONSTRUCTION OF SELF

Stories do not simply describe the self; they are the self's
medium of being. . . . The self-story is not told for the sake of
description, though description may be its ostensible content.
The self is being *formed* in what is told.
—ARTHUR FRANK, *The Wounded Storyteller*

L oss, on its deepest level, can be characterized as *being* the pain and
grieving, that process by which we come to *have* the pain; to hold it,
to mold it, to construct a future tense in which it shapes us, even as we
shape it. Grief work requires a holding space, a protected pause in which in-
terruptions to pain might be enacted and hope emerge. In the absence of grief
work, attempts to salvage coherence often come at the expense of the affective self by deadening desire, investment in others, and engagement with life.
Key to the reclamation of a self so deadened by trauma and loss is the storying of experience in ways that move beyond passive low-level account giving.
The process of articulating and (re)narrating self reconfigures frameworks of
connection, reconstructs memories, and even re-visions ways of being in the
world. Cultural, social, psychological, and neurological correlates support this
process. Might it be adapted to bullying, fostering a victim's ability to negotiate rejection and emotional violence? To recover voice, re-vision the future,
and even transform self?

Overview

Storying experiences, meaningfully structuring daily exchanges and encoun-
ters, creates coherence between the events in our lives and allows us to share
them with others. Sharing stories is "a critical means by which we make ourselves intelligible in the world. We tell extended stories about our childhoods,
our relations with family members. . . . about last night's party [and] . . . may
even create a story to relate how we cut ourselves shaving. . . . We use the story
form to identify ourselves to others and to ourselves" (Gergen and Gergen

1988, 17). Inviting others into our stories solicits their active participation in our narratives: as cointerpreters of events, purveyors of moral support, or facilitators of critical reflection. We have coffee, meet for drinks, or Skype, sharing backstage intimacies and daily annoyances, authoring self through the mirroring gaze of others. Telling friends what happened, we seek sympathy, encouragement, and advice as we try on interpretations and craft responses. (Importantly, many modes of cyber-networking—texting, instant messaging, tweeting, vining, snap-chatting, and so on—do not facilitate reflection and storying as much as they foster low-level account giving. Facebook threads may be an exception to this.)

Who we are emerges and comes to be through the stories we tell and the varied audiences who receive them. Self-narratives are not, fundamentally, possessions of the individual. Rather, they are organic, jointly constructed products of social interchange. "We are born into relationships and come to our individual identity while resting upon social connectivity" (Cozolino 2010, 178). In fact, connectivity and the storying that maintains it are so integral to our lives that our neural-physiological development reflects their process: our brains develop socially, in relationship.

Storying the Brain

Neurocognitive research acknowledges that "the evolution of the human brain is inextricably interwoven with the expansion of culture and the emergence of language" (Cozolino 2010, 163). Throughout the course of known human history, the formation of society and the creation of culture have centered around sharing stories. Recounting tragedies, heroics, the hunt, or exploits of ancestors or telling of good fortune, bad luck, or mysterious (evil?) happenings is a shared social activity, one that integrates and reproduces group identity through the construction of a shared history. The process of telling and retelling transmits both practical and social knowledge, reinforcing values and norms. The shared cache of tales, continually massaged, reworked, and expanded, formulates relationship roles, identifying appropriate behavioral (and emotional) responses to actions, interactions, and events. Experiences are distilled through this growing store of narratives that come to define a group or a culture. Common knowledge is a sieve woven of stories that filter the world. They frame and establish society, connecting parts, linking past to present and future.

In addition to connecting individuals and forming community, shared stories "prop up our often fragile identities, and *keep our brains regulated*" (Cozolino 2010, 163; emphasis added). Stories facilitate the integration of neural networks that are responsible for producing homeostatic balance in our brains (an internal state necessary for effective functioning). Louis Cozolino's seminal work, *The Neuroscience of Psychotherapy: Healing the Social Brain*, lays bare the ability of stories to prompt interrelating between hemispheres in the brain, a process as important as (and that may be contingent on) a story's—or storyteller's—ability to interweave relationships, constructing social networks and assimilating cultural knowledge. In fact, "it is likely that our brains have been able to become as complex as they are precisely because [of] the power of narratives and the group to support neural integration. . . . An inclusive narrative structure provides the executive brain with the best template and strategy for the oversight and coordination of the functions of mind" (164).* In other words, the interhemispheric connectivity that knits together and coordinates different areas of the brain, facilitating the processing of diverse sensory input, may owe its complexity to narrative's ability to integrate information. A "story well told, containing conflicts and resolutions, gestures and expressions, and thoughts flavored with emotion, connects people *and* integrates neural networks" (164; emphasis added). Thus, storying, often a dialectical process, informs the structure and functioning of society *and* coordinates our nerve center: our brain.

The habit of storying is rooted in languaging emotions and linking them to experiences. This begins in earliest infancy, when caregivers assign words to a child's expressions, creating neural pathways between different hemispheres in the brain. This blending of affect with cognition, which prompts feelings about thoughts and thoughts about feelings, is contingent on a caregiver's ability to translate a child's emotions into language—what psychologists call affect labeling. "When the parents' inability to verbalize internal and external experiences leaves the child in silence, the child does not develop a capacity to understand and manage his or her own inner and outer world. The ability of language to integrate neural structures and organize experience at a conscious level is left unutilized" (Cozolino 2010, 208–209). What, we must ask, becomes of emotions, such as shame, if they are not languaged? Is the individual unable to manage her inner and outer world when in the throes of a relatively unarticulated emotion?

As the child grows, feelings paired with words are situated in stories, furthering the integration of the biological-social self. Of particular interest is the space where this occurs. Cozolino compares humans to neurons, with the space between individuals likened to social synapses. This synaptic space is

---

* The *executive brain*, which separates domain-specific areas in the brain and links them to various functional specializations, refers to the frontal lobes responsible for higher cognitive functions, such as language, reasoning, and behavior. "Much of neural integration takes place in the association areas of the frontal, temporal, and parietal lobes, which serve to coordinate, regulate, and direct multiple neural circuits. They are our conscious switchboard operators, able to use language and stories to link the functioning of systems throughout the brain and body" (Cozolino 2010, 164).

the medium through which we are linked together into larger organ-isms such as families, tribes and societies. When we smile, wave, and say hello, these behaviors are sent through the space between us via sights, sounds, odors and words. These electrical and mechanical messages received by our senses are converted into electrochemical impulses within our brains. These signals stimulate new behaviors, which, in turn, transmit messages back across the social synapse. From the moment we are born, our very survival depends upon connecting to those around us. (2010, 179–180)

It is in this space that meaning is constructed, begotten by and in turn fos-tering a dynamic interdependence. This interdependence, a fundamental as-pect of social life, is transcribed in the brain and is integral to our existence as social animals. (Social connectivity is responsible for the ideas we formulate of others' perceptions of our own actions and our perceptions of their responses. These reciprocities mediate meaning.) Shame and pride are encoded in the neurofunctioning of our brains, incorporating the values of society into neural networks. They are, Cozolino argues, preverbal, psychologically based orga-nizing principles that reflect our primal need for connectedness and belong-ing. Because shame arises preverbally and if unacknowledged remains mute, it lives in and often finds expression through the body. We story shame in our posture, in our investments in the world (or lack thereof), and in other embed-ded, preconscious dispositions that have incomplete cultural stories and inad-equate verbal expressions. Generated across social space, shame and rejection strengthen or weaken attachments, imprinting (or impairing) brain function-ing, stimulating communication across synapses, and embodying response.

If stories create culture and tend society no less than integrate brain func-tioning, the act of sharing an experience can be seen as the mortar that builds relationships. What, then, can be said of experiences that cannot be shared, that are refused an audience because they are barely languaged? The short-hand that flows back and forth between social synapses, the "ready-made in-telligibilities" (Gergen and Gergen 1988, 28) embedded in cultural narratives, are nonexistent. Should this not be expected, though, since shame involves severance? With whom would one be communicating?

To be denied language is, at the same time, to be denied narratives, to be denied a story that frames the experience, allowing it to cohere to self. This absence—or rather, omission—can be linked to the disappearance of atone-ment paradigms, as well as psychology's war on guilt. Unacknowledged, shame festers, only furthering the likelihood of cognitive deconstruction. Onlookers leave a victim to negotiate its consequences as best she can, reduc-ing her humiliations to little more than a sidebar in others' stories.[1] This is tan-tamount to a dismissal of traumatic experience. Culture's silent invalidation of confusion and pain opens a gap in her self-narrative—one she often falls through. Suffering in the face of negative social feedback is not valorized; nor is a confession of her particular inadequacies the foundation of a bridge back to community.

Expressive writing initiates a process that challenges cultural as well as individual inarticulateness, laying the groundwork for the normative story-ing of bullying. Templates appropriated from models of grief and loss allow experiences to be reconstructed in terms of a coherent, legitimate cultural nar-rative, one lending shame dialogues for social and personal resolution. Florin Dolcos and Gregory McCarthy claim that "journaling about emotional issues likely increases prefrontal activation, downregulating the negative emotional activation of the amygdala" (Cozolino 2010, 169, citing Dolcos and McCarthy 2006). It seems clear that expressive writing is an emotion-regulation strategy that facilitates reappraisal, through which—in both adaptive and maladap-tive ways—the unfolding emotional trajectory of an event is altered. This al-teration can, in turn, influence cognitive functioning as well as rumination. Routinizing expressive writing as a response to victimization gives a person the tools and the potential to begin (re)connecting the dots in her own stories. Languaging stressful, traumatic experiences and exploring their fringes, their affects, and their implications allow her to shape, negotiate, and even trans-form her shame, rejection, and victimization—in short, to (re)story her self.

Expressive Writing: Integrating the Neural, the Social, and the Psychological

Storying traumatic events has, for decades, been at the center of research con-ducted by a diverse group of scholars, including James Pennebaker, Robert Neimeyer, and Arthur Frank. Their work sheds light on multiple aspects of trauma, loss, and the negotiation of social pain and explores various ways that society might prompt and sponsor the processing of these experiences. They have all contributed to the mounting evidence that individuals who are re-quired to *confront* stressful life experiences reap physical and psychological benefits. Each has choreographed his own dances of process, variously em-phasizing the expression of trauma, its cognitive restructuring, and narrative elements that tacitly inform the restorying of individual and cultural self. Ac-cording to all three researchers, traumatic experiences invite us to restructure our self stories by owning pain, chaos, and change and mapping their rela-tionship to core identity constructs. When coaxed beyond the account giving of low-level thinking, experiential writing fosters the cognitive functioning associated with the (re)emergence of voice, without which the person loses the potential to become (re)invested in the world.

Confronting trauma begins with languaging experience. Languaging, which places a shared cognitive framework around experience, *contains* emotions, interpreting their boundaries and allowing their expression. Attempts to verbalize internal feeling states and physiological responses to bullying, to bundle and identify their interface, will help a victim, those around her, and society itself bridge the void in which she embodies her shame, the negative space that separates bodily experiences from social constructions of being.[2] Expressive writing positions her in this space and allows her to challenge the social pain inscribed *in* her body. It helps construct a site of resistance, reclaiming the void (denying it a space in which she can be readily co-opted) and allowing her to assume—or retain—ownership over her outcome. In objectifying accounts through writing, in acknowledging and describing emotions, pain, and chaos, she begins filling negative space with her voice, controlling the narration of her experiences. In this, she moves beyond being a cipher in other's stories, determined by voices other than her own.

Chapter 4 argues that the language games most amenable to the coherent structuring of experiences of bullying, and able to facilitate it, are those linked to grieving and grief work. Despite their suitedness, the appropriation of grief paradigms is challenged by the inability to articulate varied aspects of bullying. To the extent these aspects are not languaged, any meaning making that positions an individual in relation to trauma and grief or *any* response to shame and shaming is categorically questionable. These experiences have been denied significance, repressed, and emotionally locked down for so long that *no* response *is* the legitimate or even productive response. (In this absence of script, society might have capitalized on analgesic reactions, interpreting a deadened affect as a lack of upset, a reflection of her ability to ignore the abuse and simply walk away. In other words, neurophysical responses have been co-opted to support cultural denial.) How can she be asked to reflectively write about an incongruous, Kafkaesque world, where her needs and expectations are uncommunicable, unmet, or responded to in nonsensical ways? A world that seems increasingly un-narratable, because it is filled with unintegrated memory fragments, unreconciled emotional responses, and bytes of humiliating interaction that intrude on consciousness.[3]

Incomplete stories often have dangling aspects: "Stressful experiences that cannot be integrated with other experiences or with the self schema perpetuate the fragmentary and disorganized representations of the experience (Fivush 1998)" (Klein 2002, 142). This disorganization is extremely taxing. Fragments erupt into the conscious flow of daily life, looking to link to larger knowledge schemas (and, it seems, would be articulated as low-level descriptive accounts that defy assimilation). Her experiences, overrun by forces beyond her ability to adequately conceptualize, let alone negotiate, appear to be beyond her control.

More than one interviewee described being at a loss as to why he or she was ostracized or how to stop it:

> *If I could have figured out what was wrong, I would have changed it—or tried to. I just couldn't figure out what it was about me—I mean, if I had stopped doing those things [speaking British English], it wouldn't have made me popular, so I just didn't really know how to [pauses], you know, change. (Dan)*

> *I grew up in an integrated neighborhood [pauses], and I actually remember being singled out by black kids more than anybody else. . . . But the other piece that concerned me very much is [that] I was usually brutalized by women—black women, girls. Horrible things. I bothered them, and I couldn't figure out why. I don't understand it. That's why I said that piece about different with no meaning. Is red hair a meaning? (Anonymous)*

> *It's hard to try and convince yourself that there isn't something wrong with you. I mean, even if you don't think there's something wrong, if everyone else thinks there is, then there is. What's wrong is you can't be part of all the laughing and chatter in the hallway, which means there is something wrong, even if what's wrong is totally normal—like you're helpful or like reading or sewing, or whatever. It's wrong, because it doesn't get you invited out or get notes passed to you in class. But it was, somehow, [pauses] more than those things. (Caroline)*

Pennebaker's research (beginning in the mid-1980s) blazed a trail in establishing the physical toll that avoidance, refusal, or an inability to confront traumatic experiences takes on bodily functioning. Blood pressure, skin conductivity levels, and immune system functioning were among the measures shown to be significantly, negatively influenced by an inability or refusal to confront and engage events that were emotionally charged. Put differently, the inhibition of thoughts and feelings associated with traumas appeared to undermine the body's defense mechanisms.[4] (I asked Caroline, "Would you describe yourself as having gotten angry at any point, even if you didn't express it aggressively?" She responded, "No, but I think the anger came by damaging my health. That's why I think I was ill so often.")

Intrigued by psychosomatic responses that resulted from the stress of avoidance or denial, Pennebaker began attempting to manipulate inarticulateness. He asked research participants to write about disturbing life events. To his surprise, the exercise of writing about trauma (and rewriting about it daily) unpacked pent-up emotions and in many instances facilitated productive reflection on embodied response (Pennebaker 1997). That is, writing exercises often engaged higher-level cognitive functioning, allowing individuals to elaborate on and analyze traumatic experiences (in addition to revealing and facilitating a critique of the power structures of society). The psychological benefit of working through difficult experiences was enhanced by measureable health benefits, which accrued to many participants.

That benefit *would* accrue to Pennebaker's subjects should not be altogether unexpected. Ever since Freud, it has been believed that expressing one's emotions—especially troubling emotions—is constructive. Pain and trauma need to be teased out, coaxed into the open, and analyzed, thereby dispersing any hidden investment of psychic energy in the event.[5] Expressive writing is a powerful tool advancing that end: "In reprocessing a past stressor more slowly and completely, the person may become aware of dimensions of the experience not previously realized and come to see it in a different way" (Rice and Greenberg 1984, quoted in Ullrich and Lutgendorf 2002a, 178). Transforming experience into written artifact allows the sufferer to turn her pain over in her hands, examine it, and address it.

Again though, how, if she has no language? Although a potential stumbling block, the absence of language or cultural narratives that speak to various aspects of her struggle for intelligibility is not an insurmountable obstacle. The process of writing itself, of creating an artifact, prompts her to reprocess experiences by objectifying them. She is required, as narrator, to organize the telling, often inserting additional, qualifying information to produce a coherent story. Even if the end product is not offered to others, the process of objectifying the experiences in a written format prompts emplotment by generating details that fill in such things as context, motivations, and prior history. Organizing details into a coherent narrative requires cognitive functioning, which may facilitate the introduction of new pieces to the puzzle, illuminating new potential alignments, giving pause to her confused, unresolved, judgmental, and even self-deprecating conclusions.[6]

First steps in this process can rely on situational structures within experiences themselves. For example, recounting begins from a less-than-random starting point in anticipation of an end point. Guided reflection might ask her to specify what considerations determine where and how she begins. What is the temporal frame around the sequence of events? Is the account linear? Is the frame significant? Why does the account break off; does it bring the audience up to date? Is its final tone matter-of-fact, despairing, future or past oriented? Are motives and intentions important, and do they shape the telling? How are relationships positioned? From this, language itself might be examined: What word choices does she make—negative? oblique? attributive? What tense dominates the telling? Or is it all a present, barely contained chaotic "and then . . . and then . . . and then . . ."? What are the relative number of

I-statements and the amount of control linked to those statements in the account? Additional features that are revealing in all narrative accounts include voice (standpoint) and style of narration. Does a first- or third-person perspective organize and interpret the story (or does perspective switch)? Is it a monologue or a dialogue? If the latter, is it a private, internal dialogue or a dialogue with a public? (See Weber 1992; Moffett and McElheny 1966; Neimeyer 2000b.)

Clearly, these aspects, once objectified, can be shown to organize and bundle experiences, highlighting aspects that passed unnoticed, filling in gaps, habituating individuals to both experiencing and analyzing negative emotions, and providing a toehold into the framing and reframing of disturbing, traumatic events or self-defining memories.* Expressive writing allows her to begin asserting control. Her bundling of the experiences—selecting events, linking them, writing beginnings and endings (perhaps from multiple perspectives)—creates an artifact capable of looking back on itself, allowing her to begin actively editing identity, even as she reflects on—and confronts—her loss and pain. What will it mean to triumph? What are the moral issues to be faced and the questions to be resolved? What range of choices are legitimated (for protagonists as well as audience- or bystanders-turned-supporting-cast), and what consequences are linked to them? Even if narrations are confused and reflection is jumbled and inconsistent, the process of writing itself puts distance between the experience and its construction. Pennebaker notes that when subjects are required to *repeatedly* write about the same trauma the exercise causes "a gradual change in perspective. Over time, individuals . . . tend to become more and more detached" (Pennebaker 1997, 95).[7]

Were these narrations assisted by cultural accounts, were bullying embedded in traditionally structured narratives, it might be clear that character is being tested, even forged, and suspense over its outcome might be underpinned by a very real hope that she will be up to the challenge (or even supported in it). But there is no clear sense of what, if any, possibilities for action are open to those cast as victims (or as bystanders) or what will lead to resolution and growth. While the action identifies and situates protagonists, antagonists, and an audience, it appears that the antagonists are the only players who have scripts. Protagonists may or may not be deserving victims, may or may not have been betrayed, may or may not be required to take some unspecified action.[8] Bystanders do not know if, how, when, or why the victim—or they—are expected to act or respond. This story seems predestined to be a tragedy because neither the protagonist/victim nor the audience/bystanders has any

---

* Thomas Langens and Julia Schüler, after Jefferson Singer and Peter Salovey (1993), understand self-defining memories to be "vivid, repetitive memories that focus on enduring concerns or unresolved conflicts, are highly charged emotionally, and help to explain to an individual how she came to be the person she is" (2005, 825).

sense of outcome or what is needed, by whom, to arrive at or avert it. (How does one narratively embody hope, sympathy, and courage?) Despite her best efforts and attempts at cognitive restructuring, the result may still be an anti-story—an unemplotted situation or an outline that does not acknowledge the trouble central to the plot, let alone suggest what the victim must do to come to terms with it.

Understood in these terms, even the most articulate rendering of victimization experiences would seemingly produce little more than well-structured *accounts* in search of a narrative. When others are unable or refuse to play supporting roles, they inhibit the (productive) storying of the experience. To be caught up in depressed culpability, no less than rage, is to be, at best, a player in bullies' stories, a character in culturally unfinished scripts. Neither the protagonist nor her audience have story lines to maintain or are invested in the outcome. They are disenfranchised from and underestimate the narrative potentials inhering in shame. Without norms promoting expressive writing exercises, even the potential of creating *personal* narratives is left to chance. The victim is left crouching in fragments of story lines that go nowhere, with no hope of resolution, and, with greater and greater frequency, explode into improv blame endings. Blaming others provides answers—even if they result in violence. Blaming self provides them as well, the difference being the focus: the substitution of other-directed rage for self-directed violence.[9]

Despite the limitations that a paucity of cultural narratives about shame, pain, and grief predicts, research exploring the dynamics of expressive writing has turned up, time and again, positive expectancy. Across such variables as sex, race, age, and depression, findings have documented a *hope* that expressive writing as a strategy will be of benefit.[10] This hope is often instrumental in it being of benefit: "Writing about upsetting events *induces* high positive affect regulation expectancies and . . . , in turn, these expectancies may lead to improvements in emotional well-being and physical health (Langens and Schüler 2007, 175; emphasis added).[11] In other words, researchers have found that optimism, or hope, not only is of benefit to the process but may emerge from the process itself, becoming a self-fulfilling prophecy. This further complicates inquiries as to exactly *why* expressive writing is beneficial to individuals (see Appendix E for a summary of assessments from differing theoretical perspectives). Regardless of rationale, increased expectation of a positive outcome ("positive affect regulation expectancies"), whether pre- or postprocess, diminishes the physical *and* emotional effects associated with the trauma, suggesting that this active strategy, with its potential to become a self-fulfilling prophecy, should be privileged in the arsenal of responses to bullying. Hope keeps a victim invested in connection, in her own outcome.

These impressive results should not, however, foster the expectation that expressive writing is a panacea. Unproductive, low-level accounts populate the writing samples that researchers have collected over the decades. That is, high and low levels of *cognitive functioning* have been *consistently documented* in writing samples that span not only decades but a variety protocols and controls. (Interestingly, these accounts do not fall across a continuum. By and large, the test pool produced bifurcated results: expressive writing facilitated a productive process, or it did not. Few accounts fell in between.) Low-level thinking is often characterized by responses that are primarily descriptive—for example, "this happened, and that happened, and . . ." Analysis of these samples indicates that "when people don't have control over a stressor, they move to a lower level of thinking. . . . Low-level thinking helps people to avoid thinking about the stressor as well as their own feelings about lack of control" (Pennebaker 1997, 63).[12] Might this be what we can expect from victims of bullying, even if they do engage in writing exercises? As long as victims are able to shut down and escape from the torment of negative, judgmental self-evaluations—through high-risk behaviors (that enable them to feel) or through books, movies, blogs, video games, and the web—why move beyond them? Caroline, one of my interviewees, was quite clear about this:

> I read books because I was lonely and I couldn't—I wanted to immerse myself in stories and fantasy worlds, really, because I didn't have friends. And the books I was reading only separated me from them even further.

Laurie also had an escape:

> I had Spock. Star Trek *came on the same week that we moved from Marblehead to Schenectady, and it wasn't on in Schenectady, and we were staying in this hotel, and I remember trying to get the reception, get the station. And there was one instant when the show almost came in, and [pauses] you know, this is the second episode, and this stuff is already there—the loner, the half-breed, the only one on a spaceship full of humans—and it was just one instant, and I just looked at him, and I only knew I loved the show.*

Today it is video games, whether simple or complex, that distract victims from thinking about larger stressors over which they have no control, deflecting intrusive thoughts. Low-level cognitive processing—simplistic, repetitive tasks—keeps the threat of chaos at bay. (Many parents I have spoken with report that their children are "almost obsessed" with playing "inane" video games.) It is important to stress that low-level functioning, in response to rejection, humiliation, exclusion, or changes in social status, is an *adaptive coping strategy* and may even be temporarily beneficial. But to move beyond the stuck, isolated space that the victim inhabits, where she controls anger and/or despair (however inadequately), she must do the work. She must engage the social ruptures, the pain or numbness, and especially the confusion and chaos—or at the very least, open herself to chaos's possibility.[13]

Storying Experiences: Writing, Chaos, and the Reclamation of Voice

> Let mine adversaries be clothed with shame, and let them
> cover themselves with their own confusion, as with a mantle.
> —Psalms 109:29

Becoming inarticulate to herself and mute to others ("Like I care," "As if—!" "So?" "Whatever"), an individual rejects the risk of connectedness, denies investment, and reinforces emotional numbness. These responses shield her, curling in on and attempting to protect any nub of self that remains.

Her collusion in the silencing of voice begins with a denial of bullying's significance: "It was nothing," "It doesn't matter," "It's just so-and-so's drama." Unfortunately, however, the "difficulty of regaining one's voice, one's subjectivity, after one has been reduced to silence, to the status of an object, or worse, made into someone else's speech, an instrument of another's agency" is well documented (Brison 2002, 55). Society, complicit in this silencing, has not only turned a blind eye but proposed responses ("Just ignore them") that share characteristics with bullying: they colonize experience, invalidate response, rob her of voice, and disenfranchise self. As the gap between self and others' narratives widens and grows treacherous, she becomes increasingly intent on avoiding its edge, lest she slip into a void. She may withdraw (i.e., choose to be disinvested) to keep her psyche intact or allow herself to be defined and determined by forces external to her, acceding to, even owning, others' narratives, becoming a coherent, if disaffected, character in *their* stories. *The cost of coherence is inarticulable, incalculable even, a self-inflicted wound that cannot heal and can at best be cauterized.*

Expressive writing rejects this cost and the stories of others by enabling the exploration of the void, the deconstructed self, and the chaos it portends.

Chaos is an antinarrative. It is Alice through the looking glass:

> Those who are truly *living* chaos cannot tell in words. To turn the chaos into a verbal story is to have some reflective grasp of it. The chaos that can be told in story is already taking place at a distance and is being reflected on retrospectively. For a person to gain such a reflective grasp of her own life, distance is a prerequisite. In telling the events of one's life, events are mediated by the telling. But in the lived chaos there is no mediation, only immediacy. The body is imprisoned in the

frustrated needs of the moment. The person living the chaos story has no distance from her life and no reflective grasp on it. Lived chaos makes reflection, and consequently storytelling, impossible. (Frank 1995, 98; emphasis in original)

Chaos is thus an unintegrated *now*,

told in the silences that speech cannot penetrate or illuminate. . . . Chaos is what can never be told; it is the hole in the telling. . . . [It] is the ultimate muteness that forces speech to go faster and faster, trying to catch the suffering in words. (Frank 1995, 101–102)

Often terrifying, chaos is the threatened end result of cognitive deconstruction. It goes beyond identity disruption and subordination to others' stories, dismantling coherence, shattering control. At best it involves account giving, because, severed from the connective fibers that orient perspective and interpret stimuli, she cannot manage more. Even a sequential ordering of events represents a minimum of control over the telling and is not always possible. Fragments intrude, demand recognition, press for integration, and explode (or gradually erode) ontologically secure narratives. Self is jumbled, disoriented, breaking apart. Swept along by currents of daily life, she is often unable to do more than moor herself in routines.

Chaos, when articulated, cannot but present as low-level account giving. (Though, to be clear, not all low-level accounting reflects chaos). It exposes a breakdown of boundaries, structures, and expectations of how the world works. Attempts at accounting, in such a deconstructed state, may themselves be an achievement, the articulation of a profound struggle. Or these low-level accounts may be an attempt to resist chaos, reflecting numbness and a shutting down in the face of threatened turmoil. Their achievement is the walling off of nonsensical experiencing (at the cost of creative reassessment and meaningful integration of events). In refusing to engage the trauma, they hold the threat of the void—of breakdown—at bay. Whether psychic feats or merely disengaged reporting of events, low-level accounts provide few, if any, meaningful connections between events, responses, and outcomes.

Interestingly, once chaos is engaged and a nonnarrative state prevails, similarities between it and *play* can be observed. Both are unintegrated states in which self is lost, released from expectations and social structures that bind thoughts and actions. Boundaries are dissolved; interrelating is unstructured and unregulated. The key difference between the two lies in play's voluntary engagement with indeterminacy, its positioning in what D. W. Winnicott (1971) refers to as a potential space, where the dissolution of boundaries is normative and indeterminate relating and relationships are nonthreatening.[14]

Play, as Winnicott conceives it, is integral to the development of selfhood as well as emotional and psychological well-being. It is characterized by the interplay between "personal psychic reality and the experience of control of actual objects" (1971, 47). The manipulation of external artifacts or phenomena in the service of an inner, personal reality occurs in an arena in which the subjective and objective overlap and are indistinguishable. (Think here of a child's imagination, translated into playing house, pirates, and the like. She physically moves self and objects through space, constructing relationships and imagining scenarios, which unfold according to their own logic). Children and adults are often caught up in the ebb and flow between boundaries and states of boundarylessness, imaginatively creating new potentialities that allow them to lose self, only to rediscover it, to become lost, only to be found.

In contrast to this, chaos is an involuntary falling through the treacherous cracks between self and other-constructed reality. Self is similarly lost, but it is not given over willingly. It is stripped away or forfeited, through attempts to gain love and acceptance. Whereas in play it is safe to relinquish boundaries, in chaos an individual is cut adrift. In playing, she *trusts* the space in which she plays. The environment itself and those within it are reliable, allowing her to relinquish self without fear of rejection, refutation, or ridicule. In letting go, she cannot know her outcome but is eager to explore its possibilities, giving herself over to creative integrations between her inner, subjectively perceived world and objects and relationships external to her.

In the chaos precipitated by bullying, an individual may lose herself and likewise cannot know her outcome. However, she fights this loss of control, refusing to relinquish self, resisting the letting go. A breakdown of boundaries (between what is real and what is subjectively conceived of) is forced on her. Stripped of certainty in knowing how the world works, she is faced with a threatening, incoherent, uncontrollable environment in which she becomes lost. To forestall cognitive deconstruction (i.e., to safeguard her mental functioning), she may relinquish identity to the determinations of others. In exchange, she retains coherence and perhaps even gains acceptance.

If this sacrifice of self is rejected or still not good enough, she is broken. Indeterminacy, the condition of play, precipitates a terrifying free fall. Should she give herself over to this free fall, the experience of chaos becomes less threatening, perhaps opening on the potential harbored by all such boundaryless states. The dissolution of borders invites a re-visioning of narrative and enables transformation of self as well as of relationships. (As Mark Matousek's aptly titled 2011 book instructs, when you're falling, dive; turn the loss of stability into an opportunity to explore—if not to play.)

To attempt this psychic feat, individuals grieving the loss of a significant bond need a safe space, one in which norms and expectations are held in abeyance as they attempt to reconfigure self. Victims of bullying must have claim to this space, as well as to sympathy credit and the social courtesies that promote grief work. This is precisely what they are denied. Rejected and untethered from community, they are refused a social shelter in which to reconfigure relationships to self, other, and the world, denied the supportive conditions that foster a *capacity* to re-vision, and perhaps redeem, self-narrative.

Environmental instability is especially threatening during adolescence. At this juncture, social realities are integrated into the individual's own personal development and factored into her identity project. As young people create the foundations of being in the world, victims come to drive these pylons into shifting sands, constructing a self whose position in the world (and ability to navigate it) will always be tenuous. Should she find a source of stability during this period, prompted by or residing within a gaze that connects to her (the wink of a bystander, a shrug and an eye roll, a friendly nod in the hallway), or a safe space in which to renegotiate relationships, she may become capable of productively storying her experiences, including her pain. The gestures of others indicate social support, which may lessen her fear of rejection. They sustain the precarious connection between objective possibilities for belonging and inner, subjective hope of inclusion, either forestalling free fall or sponsoring her ability to tolerate chaos—to ally herself with disorganization and antinarratives and explore multiple outcomes. This is the way *through* shame, bullying, and ruptured connection.

While bystanders (who are, at best, *barely* invested in her identity project) cannot be fully charged with responsibility for her remediation, they can acknowledge her distress and leave her in peace to negotiate it. Her process itself—her negotiation of loss, pain, numbness, and rejection—can begin within the confines of expressive writing exercises. This space, a surrogate, safe holding environment, provides a place for the confrontation of chaos, trauma, and the pain of loss. Expressive writing exposes individuals to fear-provoking stimuli in a safe way (see Lepore and Greenberg 2002). Gestures that imply even a modicum of support[15] can, in myriad nuanced ways, moor her to community as she *writes herself.* Generating an artifact whose objective reality tacitly constructs the interest, belief, and acceptance of an audience allows her to become an active agent in her own experiencing.[16] This, in turn, can become a stepping-stone in the narrative reclamation of self. Small, token signs of connection foster this project, forestalling the foreclosure of her ability to be and to be found. Forays into dark confusion, explorations of her capacity to *be* in a boundaryless space, begin the process of regaining control. This is not, of course, to suggest that professional help may not be warranted. But many of the more significant ebbs in the flow of life—notably illness, divorce, and death—benefit from engaging turmoil in informal, even random, in-the-moment spaces. Norms of tolerance complement formal staging areas, allowing chaos's daily incursions to lay claim while offering support in the form of a safe environment in which she is able to explore their potential.

In *The Wounded Storyteller* Arthur Frank argues that the worst thing that can be done to someone grappling with chaos is "rush [her] to move on. Moving on is desirable; chaos is the pit of narrative wreckage. But attempting to push the person out of this wreckage only denies what is being experienced and compounds the chaos" (1995, 110).[17] This is not to suggest that we callously leave an individual to the throes of her confusion but that we stand guard as she falters, perhaps even breaks apart, fending off bullies as she (aided by the prompts and new cultural narratives) negotiates incoherence. This, in itself, is an act that signals belonging and connection. Far short of this, it is to be hoped, disruptions to her self-story can be acknowledged and addressed. But if not, society can stabilize her environment, so that she might give herself over to transformation. Cultural narratives can legitimate her standing outside the flow, exempt from normative expectations, free to discover her possibilities. It is here, in a space identical to that provisioned for loss and grieving, that she is permitted—even encouraged—to creatively reconstruct relationships and forge new connections to self and to others.

Frank further argues that "the way out of narrative wreckage is telling stories. . . . The self-story is not told for the sake of description, though description may be its ostensible content. The self is being *formed* in what is told" (1995, 55; emphasis in original). She grows and changes by participating in the narration of her vulnerability. Her process (including grief work) requires nothing short of her relearning the world and in so doing relearning and reclaiming the self. Because "the narrative becomes part of individuals' cognitive representation of the experience, thereby broadening their perspective . . . expressive tasks can potentially change the content of trauma-related thoughts and memories" (Lepore, Ragan, and Jones 2000, 501).

Susan Brison (2002) contends that the articulation of trauma does something to it. Authentic telling is no longer a performance of others' scripts, moving the victim away from being the object of others' speech to being the subject of her own. Bearing witness to pain, to raw silences, and/or to rage facilitates a shift from mere account giving to ownership in the chronicling of *her* stories. Reinserting *her* voice into accounts, she begins to see herself differently, to overcome numbness and encounter humiliation and social agony, and through this, to reconstruct both stories and identity. Expanding what happened by articulating and owning internal responses, regrets, frustrations, and re-visionings sets the stage for reflective analysis, for higher-level cognitive functioning, while simultaneously privileging the perspective of the narrator. At the very least, (re)writing potentially "positions the author as someone whose experiences are worth recounting and reading; someone whose interpretations give meaning to mere events; someone who deserves a response; someone who is preserved into the future through written artifacts" (Daiute and Buteau 2002, 57).

Engaging *process* (as opposed to orienting toward outcome) and languaging trauma "enables persons to separate from the dominant stories that have been the shaping of their lives and relationships. In so doing, persons are able to identify previously neglected but vital aspects of lived experience—aspects that could not have been predicted from a reading of the dominant story" (White 2003, 165). Rather than borrow the frameworks of others or focus on end results—a redacted artifact—a victim chronicles her struggle: her rejection *by*, as well as her rejection *of*. The possibilities that inhere in this process bear restating: writing objectifies the attending thoughts and details that shape and situate memories, refashioning them as artifacts to be turned over, examined, and manipulated. Self-defining memories that inform the main plot line organizing her life (e.g., loser) might be revised or even abandoned as twists, turns, and subplots emerge, taking the narrative in unexpected directions. In writing, she is free to imagine an audience for her experiences, not just for her words. She *plays* with the possibilities, losing herself in re-creations of the trauma that she is able to manipulate. The upshot of this exercise, a written artifact, allows her to continue to process her experiences but from a new perspective—from the outside looking in. She may pose anticipatory questions to herself, ones it would not occur to her to pose otherwise, ones whose answers might surprise her. And she will have to defend her answers to herself. Her ability to do this and gain insight into her experience begins the process of editing and rewriting the blame-the-victim story in which she has been cast and trapped. The editing, performing, redrafting, and modifying that go into the *reorganization* of self confirm that "writing is her struggle for coherence; its truth is her achievement" (Frank 1995, 65).[18]

[Even] children can use it [narrative writing] to perform their identities or to reflect on them. Young persons can craft self-representations in narrative writing—trying on and revising identities and creating motivations for engagement in social life. With adequate support children can, thus, use writing to create healthy orientations to life. Writing about stressful events can, therefore, be a self-regulative process, in which writers represent themselves handling challenging experiences, and, over time, crafting effective selves that, whether true or not, are the basis for ongoing self-reflection and motivation. (Daiute and Buteau 2002, 56)[19]

But what if her truth, bathed in culpability, *is* their story? What if she cannot escape the humiliating scenes from last week, the ones branded into her psyche and impossible to simply revise because they are an accurate accounting? Some stories reflect facts that, at bottom, witness ugly self-truths (and to that extent owning them, even coauthoring them, is not submission to others' narratives). Coloring in these stories, elaborating experiences, may be an interesting exercise, but what of their unalterable core? If those facts cannot be changed, especially if, through her process, she comes face to face with her liability, can memory and identity be renarrated in any significant way? Perhaps hived in retrospect? Or does blameworthiness fix the account—and its owner—in a personal and social story from which there appears no redemption? Does verity chain body and psyche to memories steeped in legitimate shame, hindering productive restructuring and repositioning of trauma? If there is truth in the negative stories recounted by her peers, are narratives fixed, memories indelible? Will expressive writing exercises only bear further witness to her flaws, inadequacies, and unworthiness?

The potentials attributed to expressive writing exercises, as presented here, all assume the malleability of self-narrative and, surreptitiously, of memory. But to what degree—if any—is there elasticity around stories grounded in facts? What potential is there for movement in tales of transgression for which she has been rightly held accountable and penalized? Does the overlap in self- and other-narratives preclude a potential to edit stories and reposition self? That is, do corroborations of culpability lock in negative articulations of identity? Arthur Frank contends that "finding voice becomes the problem of taking responsibility for memory" (1995, 132). Actively owning one's perspective, including one's shame and incoherence related to an experience, engages memories. And remembering, despite appearances to the contrary, is an organic process.

Memory

> The past is not simply there in memory, but it must be articulated
> to become memory. The fissure that opens up between experiencing
> an event and remembering it in representation is unavoidable.
> —ANDREAS HUYSSEN, *Twilight Memories*

What determines recall? Or how the past is articulated?
How is the relation between memory and self-narrative arbitrated?
Can unacknowledged shame be remembered, and if so, how?
All shared experiences are perceived, narrated, and remembered by different individuals in different ways. More than this, differing versions of the same event are reconstructed by the same individual for different audiences, at different times, for different reasons, and from different moods or perspectives.

The conditions under which issues of self-memory become focal are either directly (or indirectly) social in character. They occur within such processes as conversing about the past, answering questions about personal history, justifying actions, entertaining one's children, setting the record straight, demonstrating how certain tasks were accomplished or goals obtained, or documenting events for the public record. (Bruner 1994, 88–89)

Each experience, in its recall, is reconstituted by the motives and context that prompted its remembering. When we remember, we reconstruct events in our past in terms of our present, because we are recalling them—perhaps actively reperceiving and reunderstanding them—from the perspective of our current knowledge, beliefs, and self-narratives. Inevitably, the motives, intentions, beliefs, and agency we attach to the event—motives, intentions, and beliefs that *exist in the present*—imbue it (and actions surrounding it) with significance. Put differently, memories are not a fixed mental photo album. They are organic, ever-changing, and their recollection is an activity that people often do together.

This intersubjective nature suggests that there is no single, individually constructed memory and no need for an ineradicable calcification of meaning (or affect) linked to the recall of an experience. Instead, it can be claimed that *all* acts of remembering involve acts of re-*creation* (Bartlett 1934; Neisser 1981; Barclay 1986, 1994; Linton 1986; Bruner 1994; Gergen 1994). Experiences course around a person—around all of us—like water flowing along its way. Remembering dips into the eddies of our mind, yet (as Heraclitus famously noted) it is impossible to step into the same river twice. Other waters continually replace those once there. Streams of new experiences and modifications affected by time, place, and new information (all of which are integrated into ever-evolving social and personal frames of reference) constantly transform the past. Information is integrated into, and events re-remembered in terms of, self-narrative *at the time of recall.*

More often than not, our repositioning of memories shifts in slow, imperceptible ways—ways not consciously noted, as new pieces of information are quietly massaged and fitted into autobiography. These in turn influence the appropriation of subsequent events—though indiscernable modifications are not the only formula for change (*Yes, Keisha did hook up with Sara's dates at prom, and yes, that was definitely not cool, but her older sister was right to ask why she—not he—was publicly crucified*). Our memories, whether of a past that is an hour ago or many decades gone, are organic, informed by and reflecting adjustments in perspective and intent (*Yes, Keisha did hook up with Sara's date at prom, and yes, that was definitely not cool, but the STD she was diagnosed with—and the car accident her sister was involved in—diminished the castiga-*

tions of peers). Remembering is little more than a present reconstruction of subjectively perceived past events, a cognitive process that involves a subjective positioning and repositioning of self (*Yes, Keisha did hook up with Sara's date at prom, and yes, that was definitely not cool, but they got together again when they were both in college and have been married for years*).[20] The fact of hooking up has not changed, but subsequent frames of reference position the memory differently and incorporate it into autobiography in ways that may well lend support to different self-narratives. Because "the plots and themes constituting the interpretive networks of our daily lives are relatively stable or mutate only slowly, our remembered selves are experienced as stable or as changing only gradually" (Barclay 1994, 59). Anchored in personal biography (see Appendix A), memories and the remembered self are emergent, occasionally "punctuated by some transformational event(s), for example, loss of job, birth of child, divorce, war" (59). Remembering is an unfolding, interpretive process that informs being and becoming.

If self is an ongoing process, the site of identity construction, then autobiographical memory (the interpretation of links between experiences) actively creates coherence between past, present, and future events.[21] How the event is perceived and incorporated ("They're right" vs. "I am a victim" vs. "I am a loser" vs. "I have bad luck") largely determines what else is selected, tagged, linked, and stored as meaningful (thereby supporting and furthering current narratives). "As we forge notions of our 'selves,' we shape and frame the nature of our later recollections. Our identities and memories are two sides of the same coin" (Greenwald and Banaji 1989, 47). And what is relevant to us today—both personally and as a culture—is directly related to what has already been selected, tagged, and stored as significant.[22] As Michael White notes, "Not only do the stories that persons [and cultures] have about their lives determine the meaning that they ascribe to experience, but *these stories also determine which aspects of lived experience are selected out for the ascription of meaning*" (2003, 164; emphasis added). What and how we recall are functions of what and how we perceive (what is selected and privileged) and what and how we come to articulate and (again) understand that experience.[23]

This does not necessarily bode well for culpable victims, whose personal incriminations and self-indictments position them to tag negative experiences as significant and perceive the event and themselves through story lines that others write, creating an autobiographical self rooted in a spoiled identity. The likelihood of becoming a character in others' narratives is fostered by gossip, as events *"gain their meaning through their usage, not within the mind nor within the text, but within social relationships"* (Gergen 1994, 89; emphasis added). When the responses of others repeatedly confirm the repugnance of a victim's actions, rejoinders, and *being* and endorse her contemptuous self-judgments, what narrative recourse has she?

In the face of this threat to growth and change, expressive writing exercises employ devices to guide reflection, prompts tailored to challenge fixity and/or reposition the experience in self-narrative, broadening the context of event recall and even revising the emotionality associated with it (see Lutgendorf and Ullrich 2002). (*What if* he *had been publicly crucified? What if everyone found out* he *had an STD? What if, at the same time the gossip broke, you learned that your sister was in a car accident? What if the future validated seemingly poor judgments in the present?*) Such exercises are not likely to immediately realign self-concepts, revise perceptions and the tagging of information, or overhaul memories. But the possibility of movement, the potential for fresh perspectives to challenge the self-judgments that tether memory, is planted.[24] Ian Rivers claims that "the process of recovering from traumatic events is the transformation from being a victim to being a survivor" (2004, 170). Expressive writing can help facilitate such a shift.[25] Engineered re-remembering has the potential to sponsor the reinterpretation of experiences, narrative threads, and self-concepts (perhaps by selecting and highlighting other aspects of experience). Whether deliberately prompted (through therapy, expressive writing, *or bullying*) or left to its own devices, the self is relentlessly constructed and reconstructed,

> a perpetually rewritten story. What we remember from the past is what is necessary to keep that story satisfactorily well formed. When new circumstances make the maintenance of that well-formedness sufficiently difficult, we undergo turning points that clarify or "debug" the narrative in an effort to achieve clear meaning. Sometimes these changes or their prospect become so difficult that we even go to the doctor or priest for help. More often, the culture has a sufficiently rich store of prescriptions so that we can make out on our own. (Bruner 1994, 53)

If meaning, as well as coherence, is an interdependent weave, constructed *with* community through sociation, the question that again arises is what can be made of experiences that have been denied articulation, incidents that are not even acknowledged, let alone privileged or creatively storied? If society has no narratives around which to construct experiences (leaving an individual with self-blame), then the potential for multiple coherences (through a variety of coauthorships) is all but nonexistent. On what basis might the correctness of well-formed derogatory self-characterizations be challenged? (In addition, what of the emotional aspect of remembering? If analgesic responses deaden the experiencing of bullying, do such events stand out in autobiography? How are they recalled?)

The cultural stories that have begun to emerge around social abuse unfortunately skirt experiences of shame—whether such self-feeling is deserved or socially machinated. Unacknowledged, unshared, ungrieved, and unresolved, shame remains raw and isolating and may quietly come to dominate and organize autobiography. Inscribed on the body and seared into the psyche, inadequacies become etched into neurocognitive functioning—especially if the target is culpable and believes the social policing justified. Derogatory self-concepts cohere, unchallenged and unchallengeable. How are they to be re-remembered? As one anonymous interviewee put it:

> The thing that concerns me more than anything, even though I say you can't figure it out, is what I don't remember. Because at least if I remember it, I know what's driving me. I think there's a lot I don't remember because it was so painful that I blocked it out. And I think that to some degree that's the stuff that's automatic—that's living in the body.

Of the utmost significance for bullying, in this brief consideration of memory, is that *every act of (re)remembering is pregnant with the potential for transformation and change*. Remembering is a re-collecting of all aspects of the experience in terms of the present. Background considerations can be teased to the fore and linked in new ways to create new narrative coherences. Reinterpretations and realignments, especially if furthered by revised cultural stories, reconfigure the weave of autobiography itself (even allowing for new *co*constructions). If memories are personal reconstructions grounded in and organized by cultural narratives, expanded stories (that highlight alternate aspects of experience) can facilitate radically different *re*productions of memory, fostering high-level cognitive functioning and cognitive reconstruction. (An example of realignment can be found in Calhoun 2011.)[26] "Remembrances that become selves are pregnant with meanings: Meanings are bound together by the emotional life of individuals interconnected with the lives of others" (Barclay 1994, 61). Whatever the past might have been, its rendering in the present must nonetheless occur within a broader context, supported by narratives that organize both cognitive and affective elements. Bullying and shame, re-remembered along different trajectories, reinterpret personal and social *practices* (which are responsible for constructing reality).

Even without expanded, multifaceted bullying stories, expressive writing is an invaluable exercise, a crucible in which memories are forged, shaped, and (re-)created. Its *process* facilitates a person's struggle for sovereignty over the past. Self, in this, is little more than a consequence of remembering, a by-product of *what* particulars she recalls and *how* she—and we—recall and integrate them. Writing exercises prompt reflection, changing the conditions under which re-remembrances are elicited, challenging the emotional and mental status of experiences, and actively promoting the reconfiguration of social trauma. They encourage adjustments to perspective and may even facilitate hiving, cordoning off the memory's ability to influence and determine autobiography. The ability to satisfactorily reposition one's experiences in a narrative that challenges self-blame, or global indictments of being, may well be handicapped by judgmental, one-sided, or incomplete social accounts of bullying. But this need not be the end of the story. There are, even now, alternative cultural narratives that can be appropriated, even if they do an end run around many of the issues involved in abusive situations. The mythic lone rebel, the phoenix rising from the ashes, and the ugly duckling transforming into a swan all support personal triumph and a rejection of dominant narratives.

Narrating an Audience and Defining a Victim: The Paradox of Social Stories

Culture and society can most readily support the reconfiguration of memories and restorying of self by scripting active roles for its members. Through cultural prescriptions that *sponsor* grief work, which may include small gestures that imply a degree of social support, bystanders become more like the audience a victim imagines or writes for. Their subtle, barely perceptible indications of connection sponsor change (helping re-emplot her experiences). Every member of society is a gatekeeper of hope and positive expectancies and, in fully acknowledging this responsibility, becomes part of an audience *invested* in her outcome.

Whether this audience ever actually materializes is less important than the storying of its possibility (not unlike the ever-elusive Prince Charming). This gives her full license to imagine a sympathetic, *engaged* outsider witnessing her struggles and to write for that hypothetical someone, who encourages, and wants to hear, her voice. Even if this interested other remains little more than a cultural plot device, its availability is significant to her restorying. Research confirms this assertion, finding that "written emotional expression is an intentional strategy which may serve to compensate for a lack of perceived social support"—especially, it would seem, if that support, that chance to connect, was legitimated by cultural narratives (Langens and Schüler 2005, 23).

However, even optimal narratives and well-constructed plot devices (campaigned for throughout this book) have drawbacks. Imagining a receptive audience, while productive, scripts bystanders as two-dimensional sympathetic caricatures. Bystander lack of definition (like that of Prince Charming) is both serviceable and detrimental. Consider that *someone telling someone else that something happened* [is] a social interaction—actual or imagined or anticipated or remembered—in which what gets told is shaped by the (perceived) interests of the listeners, by what the listeners want to know and also by what they cannot or will not hear. (Brison 2002, 102; emphasis in original)

Recall that we tell particular stories to particular audiences. Narrations are jointly constructed products of social interchange. "Whether a given narrative can be maintained depends importantly on the individual's ability to negotiate successfully with others concerning the meaning of events in relationship with each other" (Gergen and Gergen 1988, 30). The particular audience a victim writes for is composed of wise, benign, nonjudgmental listeners who are willing and *able* to hear her chaotic first drafts and re-visions without expecting they—and she—will achieve one or another particular outcome.

An ability to *receive* her futilities, despair, intent, need, and desire and an investment in doing so turns bystanders into more than bystanders. It turns these onlookers into individuals with whom she has a fairy-tale personal relationship. This, of course, is precisely where bystander intervention breaks down. Bystanders are not benign, nonjudgmental listeners who are interested in negotiating the meaning of events with her. While imaginary listeners encourage her to play at response options, allowing her control over the interface between subjective and objective, this is something that only the best of therapists cede victims (parents and others invested in her well-being usually orient support around one or another particular outcome). Bystanders, even those willing to commit to small gestures, may nonetheless perceive victims as needy. Or as possessing unappealing qualities. Or lacking social skills. Or they are, in teen parlance, "just annoying." In the face of this, bystanders will *need* to remain two-dimensional, diminishing the victim's expectation of friendship while policing the perceptions of others (the attribution of such a friendship by bullies might stigmatize a bystander). What more can be expected when victims are relatively unknown to these onlookers or when distance and rejection sends a legitimate social message: "Your behavior *is* inappropriate, and it needs to change"?

Social scripts involving bullying also type victims and victimization (creating roles, affects, expectations, and ready intelligibilities around abusive experiences). This typification tacitly limits any actual claims that can be made on bystanders. Once *stereotyped*, a victim's behaviors begin to fall into an expected, narrow range, delineating and depersonalizing any sympathetic response directed toward her. Bystanders, relatively uninterested in the nuances of her pain (or incapable of bearing witness to it), respond in ways that tether her to (revised) cultural story lines.[27] These ground her, yet even while they sustain inclusivity in the community, they limit her outcome. Insofar as "people need to first interpret the situations they act in, [they use] common definitions of the situation and understandings of how to act" (McCall 1990, 159). Legitimating social victimization culture creates circumscribed story lines for victims—roles that, paradoxically, can be enacted correctly or incorrectly. *Belonging in the victim category is ultimately on another's terms* (see, for example, *Seventeen* magazine's column "Traumarama!" For a significant analysis of the specific and limiting victim roles this column illustrates, see Appendix F). Once others begin to offer platitudes and token gestures of inclusion, they have caricatured a victim's status. Further, in defining her responses, they risk overemplotting *her* story.

This, then, is the catch-22 for victims. To be intelligible and capable of being shared, personal experience has to be translated into prefab narratives that interpret a victim's trauma to others no less than to herself. However, this overwriting has an important secondary function: liability. The greater range society gives her voice on a personal level—that is, the less it scripts her story—the more difficulty it has in assessing and redressing violations. Claims need to fit templates that help establish victimization in ways that outsiders, especially courts of law, find plausible, tangible, and prosecutable.

These limitations and drawbacks to storying victim and bystander roles do not undermine the need to narrate social aggression. The victim's *hope for* and even *belief in* (re)connection, as anticipated by the very existence of sympathetic stories, will help (re)invest her in her outcome. Her faith in the prospect of others out there who are capable of hearing, authenticating, and investing in her is of crucial import. Small, insignificant gestures support this hope. These (scripted) affirmations, coupled with expressive writing, hold great promise.

A Final Note

The task, for both society and the individual, is to define and story boundaries in social relating and to understand when and why they are violated. In the rush to *do* something, school authorities and politicians have instead defined tangible objective offenses in the name of zero tolerance (some of which threaten a host of civil liberties and have already provoked a backlash against antibullying campaigns). Despite the general consensus that bullying involves *repetitive* and *chronic* behavior (as opposed to a mean-spirited, even cruel, incident), the *what* of "repetitive and chronic" is not readily identifiable or able to be operationalized. Bullies, like terrorists, are often at pains to blend into the culture, to operate under the radar, undetected. Victims often desperately try to assimilate as well, craving social affirmation, unwilling to admit rejection or abuse. Who, then, gets caught in these dragnets? Consider offenders like

Zachary Christie, a six-year-old who brought a Cub Scout camping utensil—a fork, knife, and spoon in one—to school (see Urbina 2009). Turning schools into panopticon police states is not the answer, and embracing zero-tolerance solutions—in effect, witch hunts for bullies via objective artifacts that betray them (today's penknife or single, unkind tweet is yesterday's wart or broomstick)—compromises the moral integrity underlying truly comprehensive antibullying initiatives: the mitigation and mediation of the social destruction of selves. Such overzealous campaigns threaten to turn *us* into bullies, modeling intolerance.

Even if authorities were successful in operationalizing a clear definition of bullying (i.e., of unacceptable *behaviors*), their isolating decontextualization of interactions interrupts the ebb and flow of social relationships, crippling our children's ability to repair bonds and negotiate negative feedback. The perils of continued silence and the limitations of overdefined response suggest the need for a middle-of-the-road action plan. Perhaps it is most productive to envision responses to bullying that take, as a model, the improvisations of jazz.[28] Norms provide a bass line (baseline) that supports social tunes (e.g., bullying is not okay, shaming requires the possibility of redemption, grief paradigms of support can facilitate a person's process, expressive writing allows her to renarrate self), and bystanders interpret the situation and riff on these story lines. Given this unfinished score, bystanders can accompany her efforts to cultivate voice, negotiate pain, and more fully realize herself. Limited, even tenuous, grace notes (gestures) support and enrich the melody. The safe social space (provided for in the bass line) allows pain, anger, shame, and loss to be taken out, examined, and negotiated. Creating this space—embedding it in the rhythm so that it courses through daily life (where it is safeguarded by minimally involved bystanders)—is a social responsibility, one that devolves on each and every member of the community.

It might well be argued that "there's no place to be in the world outside of stories" (Haraway 1999, 107). Ultimately, however, "WHAT a story is about is a question of HOW it is told. You cannot separate the tale from the telling. Beneath the content of every message is intent. And form embodies that intent" (Moffett and McElheny 1966, 567; emphasis in original). How are we couching and phrasing this story? What definitions, values, and beliefs are becoming privileged in this telling, and how are we positioning ourselves to solve the problem? How well will the stories we tell mesh with the needs of both bystanders and victims?

6

TYING UP LOOSE ENDS

Challenges to Bystanders, Challenges of Cyberspace

Culturally storying bullying (recasting it as a social problem, scripting new norms and roles, and repackaging behaviors and expectations) is an extensive undertaking that is well under way. The redrawing of behavioral boundaries, the development of responses for bystanders, victims, and authorities, and the (re)narrating of individual experiences are all evolving apace. These changes will mitigate stark experiences of social cruelty and help reposition the subtle social malices that still haunt many life stories—for example, those recounted to me by Caroline and Ken. Caroline recalled:

> So the worst moment was when one girl—I'll call her Vanessa—she was with her sister, I think, and her mother [pauses] and their car broke down on the roadway, and these girls were pushing the car on the hard shoulder of the [road], but they turned the lights off in the car, and another car crashed into them, and Vanessa was killed. And what happened to me was, at school the next day, the girls in the class knew of this, they knew the girl in our class had been killed, but didn't tell me, so that I was caught. I was sort of acting normally, you know, laughing and joking and talking about things, and they condemned me for not being sad, but they hadn't told me about the fact that one of our classmates had just died. [Pauses] So that kind of summarized for me how isolating it was and how they deliberately excluded and made it hard for me.

Stories like Caroline's were often prefaced by statements that indicated their unresolved status: "I still don't get why . . . ," "I just don't understand how everyone stood around and . . . ," or "I still cannot believe that even teachers—who knew what was going on—allowed . . ." Years later, these experiences continue to resist meaning making and integration, especially if they involved teachers and authority figures who ignored—or even furthered—the humiliation.[1] Ken, today a senior manager, is still disturbed by one such incident:

> *Most of the bullying that was directed at me came in the form of unprovoked insults and mocking laughter. One incident, however, remains vivid in my memory to this day—some thirty-five years later—because it was condoned by the Catholic teaching staff.*
>
> *It happened during my junior year's religion class. For whatever reason the priest leading the class—for some unfathomable reason—separated our class into groups of five. Like he just picked people randomly, and we had to go to different tables, and the people at each table would have to vote off one person. [Pauses] Right away they looked at me, because unfortunately, the table I was at was all full of these people who were in the dominant circle, and I still remember one of them gleefully encouraging the others to vote me out. He said, "Let's get rid of Smith." And so, in short work, I was left at a table with the other losers who were voted off from other tables. And to this day I still have no idea what the point of that exercise was. I still don't know what it was all about. I was cast off to a table with the other "losers," where we sat, morosely and silently, for the rest of the period. The teacher gave no explanation for this—this institutional ostracism—and to this day I have no better understanding of it myself. It was just a humiliating experience. [Pauses] Even more humiliating was the fact that it was initiated by the teacher.*

Unfortunately, new social norms cannot preclude such intentional or unintentional cruelties. But it can be hoped that the pain, grief, and trauma that such incidents call out will increasingly be viewed as legitimate and negotiable. That the heightened intrapsychic reverberations and the shame associated with them (that add a secondary level of humiliation) will lessen.

Should such optimistic hopes begin to be realized, the social narrative of bullying, as outlined in the preceding chapters, would still be far from complete. At no point does it fully address the social forces linked to bystander passivity or even broach the dynamics of cyberspace. (To have fully explored either in a preceding chapter would have sidetracked or fragmented the larger unfolding story into which arguments were organized.) It therefore seems appropriate to conclude by briefly addressing these aspects of interaction, offering insights that not only deserve fuller consideration but suggest directions for further inquiry.

Bullying, as the term has been used throughout this book, involves pervasive ill treatment that may or may not culminate in a climactic event. Interviewees spoke of daily, ongoing slights—comments, "accidents," nicknames, mockery, and laughter. More significant than the cruelty, however, was their incessant anxiety over its next occurrence—their exhausting anticipatory dread. Harassment did not occur every day, in every post or tweet, or always after math class. Random and sporadic, it had the potential to erupt anytime, anywhere. This kept bullying alive in the minds of victims, languaging their bodies, searing the threat of inadequacy deep into the core of their being. One anonymous interviewee explained:

> If it wasn't daily, it felt daily [pauses] because if it didn't happen, I was waiting for it to happen. See, what happens is that you're always thinking about it. So I walked around with a tension in my body, because I always thought it would happen.

And it goes almost without saying that rarely did a bystander intervene.

Everyone Else: A Breakdown of Bystander Responsibility

In the interviews conducted for this book, participants repeatedly shared remembrances of primary antagonists, charged interactions, climactic incidents, and a *differentiated* cohort of bystanders. In addition to speaking of primary aggressors, they often outlined secondary relationships and a variety of subtle roles *within* the category of "everyone else." When I began pressing interviewees to more closely break down amorphous audiences, it became clear that many onlookers were connected to victims and their tormentors in nuanced ways (e.g., friends of friends of the bully, associates of the victim such as former lab partners, or onlookers who had a relationship with a sibling of the perpetrator or the victim). Others *were* members of a general population who hardly knew either party and whose allegiances and alliances shifted. Chapter 2 touches on the neurological limits of information processing in out-group relationships and the significance of in-group versus out-group status for positioning self and passing judgments. While this breakdown of social dynamics is useful, it does not fully capture the complexity of daily interactions or the fluidity of affiliations modified by multiple, overlapping reference groups. Onlookers exist along an organic continuum of investments that are relative to innumerable aspects of any social situation, including once-removed connection to one or another participant. Indirect, complex social accounting positions them to social spectacles in nuanced ways. Multiple facets of connection suggest the potential for a range of (mediating) responses (for example, consider their potential in terms of the complex codes governing sympathy etiquette that Candace Clark [1987] documents). Allegiances are fluid, multidimensional, and even intertextual, making for protean responses.[2]

Bystanders who are, in some capacity, connected to one or another participant are better able to sort significant social slights and devastating public rejections from the routine ups and downs of everyday life. Capable of contextualizing exchanges, they are better positioned to judge the level of loss and potential for repair caught up in the situation (and communicate that information to others).[3] Although they have been conceptualized as two-dimensional, these onlookers embody a variety of response potentials. These fluctuate as a function of relationship to the parties involved, personal strengths and weaknesses, situational factors, the personality of the victim as well as the aggressor, and the density of support networks (the victim's as well as that of the antagonist) (see Eckenrode and Wethington 1990, 91).[4]

In addition are those bystanders not known to either party, who watch but rarely become involved. Not only do they believe it none of their business; they have no reason to suspect that they might be capable of effecting change. Why get involved? Why go out on a limb? How, even, would they strategically interrupt unfolding events? For what reason? Most individuals are not only unprepared to risk their own social acceptance for the sake of a relative stranger (who may deserve at least some of the abuse she receives) but have no basis from which to challenge the aggression linked to the negative social feedback a victim is receiving, no proactive norms in which to ground and position themselves.

As suggested in preceding chapters, bystanders need a range of options, including nominally risky acts that follow up on the personal fallout from public humiliations. Rather than arbitrators of spectacles (which may occur around legitimate grievances), they are better positioned as facilitators of the recovery of face, purveyors of personal, if not social, redemption. Gestures oriented toward subsequent support—even from relative strangers—reconnect targets to community and spark a different cognitive and emotional processing of the experience.

ABC's series *What Would You Do?* models a variety of interventions they might choose from. Staging inappropriate, abusive, and even illegal situations, the show focuses on bystander responses (giving a new twist to the earlier TV series *Candid Camera*). TV audiences, themselves bystanders, root for bystanders on camera to disrupt spectacles of abuse or to privately counsel or console victims. Their support of bystanders gives them to understand that other bystanders might feel or act similarly toward them should they intervene on behalf of a victim. ABC cannot be praised enough for programming that sponsors and promotes the sea change that is called for.

It is worthy of note, however, that bystanders in the staged vignettes have absolutely no relationship to either party or to each other. Anonymity and lack of connection seemingly embolden them to act. Precisely because they are not invested in either party, they have less to lose than others. A want of anonymity may limit bystander intervention in school hallways, where even if actors are unknown to each other, they circulate in the same small community. This makes it all the more important that, alongside low-risk support of victims, we model and encourage *bystander support of other bystanders*.

Responsive, interbystander connections begin to marshal crowd potential and address the so-called bystander effect. This concept, related to what Bibb Latané and John Darley identify as a "diffusion of responsibility" (Darley and Latané 1968; Latané and Darley 1970), emerged in the late 1960s in response to the apparent indifference of *thirty-eight witnesses* to Kitty Genovese's murder.[5] Lack of response (to three separate attacks on the victim) pricked the country's collective conscience, sparking outrage and intense public debate. The flurry of social theorizing that followed included the "unresponsive bystander" hypothesis.[6] In brief, it posited that bystanders' lack of involvement was not mere apathy but rather related to the belief that someone else—perhaps someone more qualified—would do (or perhaps already had done) something to help. In *The Unresponsive Bystander* Latané and Darley contend that people look to the reactions of others around them to determine what to believe and how to behave (1970, 33–34). If no one is reacting, inaction would appear to be the appropriate response: someone else has already done something, or it is not a situation in which one should get involved. Cued by the nonresponse of others, concerned about the investment that involvement might suggest, they wait and watch, *gazing and being gazed upon*, perhaps hoping for a sign legitimating some—any—response.

Subsequent research not only confirms a diffusion of responsibility among bystanders but adds that bystander involvement may be influenced by personal (physiological?) reaction to the ill treatment and humiliation witnessed. Recent studies have documented heightened response in onlookers who are watching harassment and humiliation unfold—*response similar to that of the victim* (Janson and Hazler 2004). (Protocols, it should be noted, measured response at a distance from aggressive incidents themselves and documented heightened response to hypothetical scenarios and to the recall of repeated personal victimization or the witnessing of repeated victimization of another person.) These findings are in line with a phenomenon that sociologists, after George Herbert Mead, have observed for years: the response of the first party will call out and cue the same response in the second party.[7] Whether distress, as opposed to a numb, analgesic response, was found in victims because the abuse was repeated over time, because measurement was taken at a temporal distance from the aggression, or because of some other factor is unclear. However, as noted in a previous chapter, the responses of victims—or lack thereof—are not unanimous in the research, and further study is called for.[8] These considerations aside, heightened levels of distress in bystanders (whether a function of victim response or not) raises the question of how *they* have been handling reverberations in their own bodies (have they been repressing their own deep responses, numbing themselves to their own internal, witnessing-provoked reactions?). Will new social scripts proactively influence the way they negotiate their own agitation?

In minimizing and overlooking bystanders' felt witnessing, culture smothers what may be its greatest resource.* The norms that silence bystander discomfort result in two uninspired cultural scripts: denial (of connection and response) and noninvolvement, which is tacit support of aggressors (quashing their own response). It would not be surprising to find that their own unease quietly echoed shame-rage cycles, eliciting strong reactions to empathetically experienced humiliation. Aggressive response that follows these once-removed reverberations may be directed at the victim. (*She is responsible for my discomfort, and in helping annihilate her—even by tacitly siding with her tormentors— I will regain control and squash this feeling.*) Roy Baumeister, Arlene Stillwell, and Todd Heatherton speculate that if aggressive bystander response is not linked to echoed shame, it may be prompted by guilt: "Derogating a victim [is] an effective way of minimizing guilt. . . . Such derogation may accomplish the result of making one's relationship to the victim trivial, expendable, or undesirable" (1995, 260). By diminishing, if not severing, the social bond, bystanders negate responsibility for what they have done or failed to do. And once the potential that bystanders represent to victims is removed, the possibility for hope or gestures of inclusion—that is, for salvation from shame—fades.

Were bystanders themselves supported by other bystanders, effective social response would be closer at hand. It would not rely on individual willingness to go out on a limb to support victims or on the needy appeals of victims themselves. This latter point cannot be overlooked: "Seeking help from others often carries psychological costs in terms of feelings of vulnerability, weakness, or failure . . . and is more threatening to one's self-concept than accepting help that is offered without asking" (Eckenrode and Wethington 1990, 92). Admitting stress, strain, and depression may be stigmatizing, may call out uncomfortable feelings about the self, and may even affirm inadequacies. Unsolicited gestures address the unfairness of the interaction, as opposed to tacitly reinforcing the victim's incapacity to negotiate it. Recognition of her struggle—even merely offering an acknowledgment of cruelty—legitimates pain and grief response, potentially interrupting ruminations and shame's embodiment.[9]

---

* Note that *empathy* is often, and erroneously, used as a synonym of *compassion*. If we could but put ourselves in the shoes of the other, we would, it is believed, sympathize with her plight. Putting oneself in the shoes of another may well *foster* compassion, but empathy is the experience of imagining and feeling what the other is feeling, not compassion for her feeling.

Support, solicited or otherwise, is invaluable to victims because lack of support—ostracization and loss of social network—is itself the crux of the stressor. *Relational aggression*—sabotaging a victim's friendships and social network—is cruelly effective because it disrupts present relationships and damages future ones. If attempts to isolate the target and cause her to lose face fail, the primary stressor has been removed. While the ability of bystanders to intervene and disrupt social cruelties varies as a function of their own characteristics and coping resources, cultural norms that recommend their support of each other (as well as of victims) will only augment that ability.

Cyberspace: New Dynamics, New Challenges, New Potentials

In recent years, cyberdynamics have created new shaming configurations as well as new modes of bystander witnessing, and these must frame future inquiries.[10] Nancy Williard (2007) identifies seven formats of abuse: *harassment* (repeatedly sending insulting, even nasty, messages), *flaming* (online fights that involve rude, angry, or vulgar messaging), *outing* (forwarding private messages or posting material that contains private information), *trickery* (eliciting secrets or embarrassing information to share it online), *denigration* (relational aggression online: posting or forwarding gossip, rumors, or cruel, even false, information to damage relationships), *impersonation* (pretending to be someone to make that person look bad or get her in trouble), and *exclusion* (intentionally, maliciously blocking someone from an online group). *Stalking*, or repeatedly sending intimidating, threatening messages, must be added to this set of behaviors.

With the exception of flaming, all these bullying behaviors are well known. Yet in their transposition to cyberspace, they come to configure audiences and the potential for response differently, resulting in increased anxiety, distress, and emotional impact. Respondents to research conducted by Robert Slonje and Peter Smith (2008) consistently rated all forms of cyberbullying as more harmful than traditional bullying. Undoubtedly, this is related to their bypassing the nuances of face work and the dialogues of bodies.

To the extent that cyber interaction is limited to wordplay in a vacuum, in no place, participants are released from social constraints, free to machinate all manner of self-posturings, to provoke disruptions, and to explore risky behaviors. Both the actor and any consequence to her actions exist in a virtual reality, one that is removed from gaze of others, as well as the emotions and affects that tether, constrain, and orient further (social) action. In taking up different semantic (and ideological) space, expressions of self are able to skirt the limitations and liabilities that circumscribe face-to-face interacting, redefining the parameters of intersubjectivity. *Seemingly* cut off from real-world ramifications or tangible emotional fallout (not least of all because the integrity of the real world—its coherence as well as its reality—has been challenged by reality TV), interactants in cyberspace stand in need of normative guideposts.[11] The lines between experience and fantasy have softened and blurred, leaving the social media with little more than entertainment value to rudder the course of interaction.

In addition, computer-mediated communications (CMCs) preclude any significant emotional contagion to bystanders or to the aggressors themselves. Participants in online exchanges are distanced from victim response, itself capable of eliciting unease in perpetrators' and witnesses' bodies. Since the impact of the bullying is not seen (or felt) by those who are privy to or perpetrate it, cyberaggression precludes any visceral response on their part, further eroding restraint, as well as the potential to co-opt mirror responses in the service of nuanced prosocial gestures (see Metts 1992). The absence of mediating face work not only negates the potential for bystander discomfort but deprives all parties of incidental cues used to check claims being made, responses being affected, and impact being gauged.

Compounding this is the reach of the social media. Streaming into a victim's home at all hours of the day and night, it ensures that *no place is safe*. Individuals cannot retreat to the haven of their bedroom to get away from the torment at school, because the torment follows them there. With the advent of the smartphone, it follows them *everywhere*.

More than this omnipresence is the seeming omnipotence lent it by the objectification of interactions, the freeze-framing of spontaneity. CMCs decontextualize intimate, intersubjective constructions (of self and other), turning personal and social intercourse into artifacts or even data objects. Frozen, disembodied texts are circulated outside space-time limitations, allowing them to be inserted into a variety of social frameworks that service personal agendas (including predatory social practices that trade on humiliation as entertainment). Words and images are cut, pasted, or retweeted, dropped into various social media formats, where they modify and link to other relationships in unanticipated ways. New meanings are created and circulated by a variety of others, who produce the *victim's* identity by appropriating texts and photos in terms of *their* needs and interests. This intertextual editing and resending has tremendous implications for the molding of subjectivities, as well as for the dynamics of sociation itself. At the very least, the pastiche identities that are created by this process, fashioned in one or another capacity mediated by social media, illustrate the need for new forms of information management. When *anyone* can construct information and manipulate reality, who or what is to be believed, and how is that to be determined?[12]

The potential inhering in CMCs gives performativity (and Goffman's front stage) a whole new meaning. Because cyberrelating takes place outside the immediate, watchful gaze of others, with no physical cues to contextualize it, it relies solely on posturing, posing, and even masquerading to forge and

reproduce identities. Self is cut, pasted, and enacted within intertextual practices, as opposed to interpersonally. In this cutting and pasting, cyberspace
effectively obscures the boundaries between subjective and objective realities,
opening new potentialities to social actors.

Virtual reality might be looked at, quite literally, as a large Winnicottian
playground, a potential space between the individual and her environment,
in which she feels secure enough to act out fantasies. Cyberspace is indeterminate, an intermediate arena in which the actor can negotiate the strain of
relating inner realities to external experience. D. W. Winnicott argues that
such indeterminate arenas are potentially *creative* spaces, ones in which "the
child gathers objects or phenomena from external reality and uses these in the
services of . . . inner or personal reality" (1971, 51).[13] Simply put, cyberspace
affords individuals new, ongoing opportunities for self to transcend its own
boundaries, to explore the interface between inner psychic realities and the
world external to them, to probe and test the extent to which each can influence or, conversely, withstand the other—for better or worse.[14] The space
of play is an amoral no-place, where boundaries separating internal from
external, self from other, and right from wrong have collapsed. (And, according to Winnicott, it is only through a loss of self in the exploration of such a
space that the individual is able to creatively recover self and be found.)

Playing is productive when the arena in which it occurs is safe, when players feel free to let go and explore the interface between what is and what is
possible. However, when narcissistic posturings and predatory impulses are
given free rein, with only personal gain and entertainment values to guide
them, "virtual" activity becomes ominous. Insidious, even. Anonymity (and
the invisibility of consequences) only furthers a feeling of invincibility, of
safety. Victims, on the other hand, become trapped in this fun house. Not
only are they uncertain who has seen, or been sent, damaging information (or
how many people in the future will be able to access their degradations and
defamations), but they are also unsure *who is responsible* for starting rumors
or leaking information. Perhaps a friend or someone they have no reason to
mistrust? Cyberbullying makes its targets anxious, worried about who has
seen damaging information and thinks differently of them, not knowing what
relationships are safe.

These uncertainties have been linked with hopelessness, with the sense
that emotional and psychological violences are inescapable. Cornering and
tormenting a victim like prey (behaviors that flirt with sociopathic designa-
tions and are discouraged even toward war criminals) *is* the central dynamic
of cyberbullying, giving the call for a socially protected space (see Chapter 4)
a greater urgency.

Feelings of hopelessness are significantly related to suicidal ideation
among adolescents . . . and are a better predictor of suicide . . . than de-

pression. . . . Furthermore, students who are victimized by cyber means are less likely to report it and seek help than teens who were victimized by more traditional means . . . , which may decrease students' levels of perceived social support. (Bonanno and Hymel 2013, 694)

Such hopelessness is compounded by the new ways the social media reconstruct the practice of memory. In converting the organic fluidity of *interacting* into an exchange of written artifacts—or bytes of data—performances are objectified and archived. Not only can they be recycled into new texts; they can be viewed and creatively reappropriated into the foreseeable future.

Lev Manovich (2001) conceptualized digitization as a shift from narrative culture to database culture, which represents the world as a database (unordered lists and search mechanisms) rather than causal narratives. . . . IM protocols (like photos . . .) do not represent a certain narrative concerning the past, but a raw extension of the past into the future, an accessible past that may also be used as raw material for the production of future narratives. (Schwarz 2011, 74)[15]

The preservation of past (humiliating) data bytes continues to exist alongside the new pieces of information, so that one can forever cringe at revelations, suppositions, and cruelties, which will not be shifted and eroded by the moving stream of re-remembering:

If an individual is bullied in a face-to-face situation, when s/he recalls the incident later s/he can emphasize or de-emphasize aspects of the interactions selectively. The narrative of the incident can be personally tailored to allow the victim to cope with it. (Wingate, Minney, and Guadagno 2013, 94; see also Bollmer et al. 2005)

This indelibility might be countered by the proactive reuse, counteruse, and recontextualizations of CMCs. Through deliberate digitized reconstructions (re-remembering) data can be creatively renarrated, reconstructing self, other, and relationship. (Victims, given the right support—which, ironically, might be found online—can play as well.)

Admittedly, the cyber age is still in its infancy, and the possibilities that inhere in it raise more questions than they answer—for example, does this creativity parallel the organic creativity associated with all forms of re-remembering? Are textual cues and identity markers becoming nuanced, perhaps beginning to parallel many of those offered by face work and linguistic gestures? Can indelibility be offset by the creative potentials for renarrating self that are contained in expressive writing (especially if communications outside and around the text are malleable and able to be manipulated)? These, as well as questions regarding the effect that negative *artifacts* of sociation will have on processes of grief work, are all deserving of much further study.

Alongside these questions is the reality that cyberspace is an ever-expanding rapid-fire arena—one in which the onslaught of information itself might come to mediate shame. Most indelible CMCs are tumbled and buried by new conversations almost instantly. In fact, the ability to remain in the memory of others—even if disreputably—may become a (narcissistic?) feat that is aspired to. Even if shameful data bytes remain readily accessible and are thus kept alive in a victim's mind, they can be counterbalanced (and recontextualized) by the overabundance of voluntarily posted shameful information. Privacy, and the infrastructure that supported and maintained it, is challenged by digital capacities. New norms (and expectations) are emerging. Voluntary exposure seemingly contravenes many of the dynamics discussed in Chapter 3, but it may, instead, move beyond them, suggesting that new modalities are in play in the cyber age. Francis Broucek argues that publishing shame allows individuals to assert control over the facts of their lives and bodies by displaying and owning them before others produce them as artifacts in their own narratives. In our narcissistic, documented, media-mediated society, shame is reconfigured: "Exhibitionism defies taste and dignity and redeems them. . . . [T]he only aspects of their lives that they control they control by saying them first. What we give you can't take" (1991, 146).[16]

There is, as yet, no way to assess the costs and benefits of these new modalities. Those born into a cyber-mediated society read, write, and construct self in ways that are foreign to those who were not born into it. Technosociation is producing new dances of intersubjectivity, as identities continue to be shaped by (and shape) what counts as knowledge:

> When technology becomes "normal" in this way it is no longer . . . notable to its users. It is a fact of life, a way of being in the world, a producer of social subjects that find it unremarkable—so unremarkable that it seems "everybody does it." (Lewis and Fabos 2005, 470)

The social subject that emerges in the midst of and in relation to this technology has vastly different expectations of privacy, information sharing, intimacy, and spatial-temporal configurations, all of which create new patterns in the production of identity.[17] This shift does not imply that we have moved from a narrative to a database culture but that we author self and narrate culture in new ways, developing new modalities for interconnectivity between lists, data, and personal information. Conversation, objectified as experience, constructs (inter)articulations as actions. (Does this add to, or challenge their status as simulacra?) At the same time a new fluidity collapses dichotomies of past and future, subject and object, providing new techniques for being, for becoming, for authoring, renarrating, and costorying selves. Online iterations of identity may take on a life of their own, but that does not stabilize them across the digital divide. Identity still depends on the mirroring of others, and gestures in real time offer a way out of the cyber fun house, offer hope, and affirm the value of self and its belonging.

In sum, whether a person is victimized in real time or in cyberspace, new cultural stories provide her with the means by which to interrupt her suffering. They require a redefinition of her relationship to experiences of exclusion, pain, and humiliation. A victim, in assuming responsibility for the voice that narrates her self stories, for the reconfiguration of memory, and possibly for the ongoing production of self-as-artifact in cyberspace, takes on responsibility for her redemption. Rewriting her self-story allows her to construct vastly different intra- and intersubjective positions. This potential is *inherent* in whatever process we call grief work, in restorying events and reconfiguring personal and social identity, though it is not publicly held out as such. Online forums have begun to part the shrouds that have isolated grief work. They represent just one of the resources of the cyber age, allowing trauma, loss, and confusion to be supported twenty-four/seven, even anonymously supported.

If a victim believes that such a reconfiguration, though painful, is possible, if she has hope and positive expectations—for example, those who have had their hearts broken often believe they will, someday, love again—and if society and bystanders support this process in concrete ways, she will be better able to confront and negotiate social trauma. Unexplored connections between mind, body, and other, the basis of alternative responses to trauma, are gaining currency and may be of support to her negotiation of shame. Post-traumatic stress disorder treatments (such as rapid-eye-movement therapy), so-called Emotional Freedom Technique (EFT, also known as tapping), and a variety of energy-healing practices linked to cognitive-behavioral reorganizations of experience (e.g., biofeedback) are gradually moving into the mainstream of response to trauma and might further support her processing of social cruelty. At the same time, cultural narratives are beginning to reflect hope, beginning to suggest that shame and rejection do not necessarily signal a bottomless social abyss but rather a tunnel, and there is light at the end of it. The norms that support and cultivate such beliefs, including searching for a silver lining, actively create the expectation that positive benefits can come from negative experiences (positive affect-regulation expectations). This is not a promise of happily ever after as much as it is a recognition of the radical potential inhering in events that have disrupted a victim's life, including shame, rejection, and social abuse. Their negotiation has significant bearing on her future and on her *being* in the world. Less bound by the opinions (and expectations) of others, she is in a position to reconstruct intersubjective realities and the stories that have been authored—and are able to be authored—around them. Society must partner with her in this effort.

POSTSCRIPT

Practical Suggestions

Bystanders can employ a variety of gestures and verbal cues (many of which are suggested in Chapter 2) to interrupt bullying or combat its effects. For example:

1. If emotional and psychological abuse is undeniable, make eye contact with the victim. Shrug your shoulders, roll your eyes, arch your eyebrows, smile apologetically, shake your head, and walk away.
2. If the incident or the victim is the topic of gossip, do not further it. Change the subject.
3. If the target has transgressed and been publicly shamed and her torment is ongoing, say, "Yeah, but I feel bad for her." It is not threatening and could curtail gossip while introducing empathy and generating sympathy.
4. Make eye contact beyond the spectacle of shaming—in the halls, in the cafeteria, on the bus.
5. Redirect the attention of aggressors to a more preferable activity (skateboarding, streaming videos, etc.). "Yeah, yeah, we know; now let's go and . . ." is a safe intervention because it neither challenges the aggressor nor appears to sympathize with the target.
6. Risk telling an aggressor to "chill." The incident is not worth getting so worked up over.
7. Connect with other bystanders through body language, and support those looking to be proactive. Bystanders look for backing from those who are watching. Catch someone's gaze. Allow yours to be caught.

8. Film the interaction.
9. Take screenshots.
10. Avoid contributing to any abuse through the social media.
11. Turn laughter back on itself, defusing the situation. Young people do this every day, in hallways, in cafeterias, and on social media. "Yo—why you still violatin' *x*?" "Dude, [chuckle] that's pathetic." Or "*Seriously?* You're still bothering with this drama [laugh]?" (These expressions will undoubtedly be obsolete by the time this book is in print, but their rephrasings will reference the same sentiment.) Generated by the peer cohort, these politically incorrect checks on behavior are effective. They tease, suggesting that aggressive behavior might begin to reflect negatively on its perpetrator. Not everyone has a relationship with an aggressor that allows this banter. But someone does. Bystanders can back such nonthreatening remarks by nodding; by adding, "Yeah, it's time"; or by dispersing.

Teachers and guidance counselors can also obliquely support an individual being tormented by peers:

1. Integrate expressive writing exercises into your curriculum, or ask a colleague in the humanities or social sciences to do so. Be sure to construct nonjudgmental writing prompts. Rubrics for the analysis of student writing at any grade level can even be generated—see, for example, the suggestions offered in the Chapter 5 section "Expressive Writing: Integrating the Neural, the Social, and the Psychological" and Weber 1992.
2. Integrate opinion exercises, which affirm the likes, dislikes, and points of view of all students, into the curriculum. Require that they be argued, not asserted: *explanations* for musical preferences, *calculations* of ethnic pride, concrete suggestions for bettering movie plots. Endorse the "I," and help sustain its coherence. See DeWall 2009, 219, for further suggestions.
3. Role-play in the classroom.
4. Create lesson plans around perspective. Websites that feature optical illusions are extremely useful points of departure for discussions of the legitimacy of multiple points of view.
5. Create lesson plans around shame. Shame is little discussed in the literature, but much of the fiction that is assigned will include instances when the protagonist or antagonist feels humiliated. This is often seen as secondary to the action. Focus on it.
6. Turn victims—and bullies—into mentors for children in younger grades. Make them the experts on bullying, and enlist their

energies—formally (for example, through joint art projects) or informally, as a big brother or big sister.

7. Plaster public areas in and around schools with a multitude of anti-bullying and "cyberbullying will not be tolerated" messages—even broadcast them over morning news channels in classrooms. While each of these, in itself, might be considered namby-pamby or even ridiculous by the intended audience and on that basis dismissed, an onslaught of such messages begins to change the climate of an institution and begins the process of institutionalizing new norms.

8. Create safe, anonymous ways for students to alert adults to emotional and psychological violence, *and* have a clear, up-to-date action plan for the handling of such information (see http://www.relationalaggression.com for a list of resources).

9. Creatively, proactively employ t.he social media as a resource for victims and bystanders.

APPENDIX A

The Uniqueness of Self and Personal Biography

In the face of prepackaged experiencing, freeze-dried individualism, and an army of talking heads is the fragile, and perhaps ultimately narcissistic, belief in the *uniqueness* of self. This uniqueness emerges from sequences of experiencing, which a person patterns into an organized *autobiographical* self. The order and appropriation of life events, even if significantly influenced by the opinions of others, arrays itself *as the basis of* distinct, individual identities.

Different experiences (no less than difference in experiences), in addition to variations in sequencing and interpretation, coupled with an unshakable belief in options and self-determination, cohere in terms of, and anchor self in, personal biography.

Although biography derives a sense of direction and purpose, even, from its situatedness in class, race, society (no less than from neurofunctioning), this sense of direction, filtered through a unique series of experiences and relationships, "becomes the *property* of the individual. It is something taken on from community and culture, but once acquired it begins to have a life of its own" (Hewitt 1989, 182; emphasis in original). Biographical narratives, replete with commodified ClubMed experiences, accommodate many of the paradoxes of modernity, not the least of which is the tension between norms of individualism and the yearning for community. Biographies come to articulate unique similarities, illustrating how "the desire to be oneself does not mean the desire to be fundamentally different from everyone else, but rather to situate individual differences with communal allegiance" (Fiske 1989, 3).

Should this delicate balance fail to be struck, for whatever reason, personal biography is at risk, imprinted by experiences of rejection, pain, and isolation that are difficult to narrate. The likelihood of damage to identity increases in a narcissistic society that refuses to narrate its own Machiavellian aspects and thus temper the swath of destruction that potentially follows from the urgency of its needs.

APPENDIX B

The Re-visioning of Liberation and Womanist Theologies

Many who have suffered ongoing oppression (the poor in Latin America, blacks in the United States, or women in Christian cultures) have turned back to religion and in so doing have rewritten its salvation story, offering an alternative reading of Christ's suffering, death, and return. Liberation theology and womanist and feminist theologies have adopted a social-relational, Christological perspective in understanding the suffering of the Redeemer, Jesus Christ. In these (re)interpretations, oppression results from the sins of the rich and powerful, those who Christ confronted in his teachings. Confrontation, rather than submission, becomes the leitmotif, and Christ's active crusade against inequality is pivotal in his crucifixion. Put differently, the re-visioned salvation story does not center around Christ's freely chosen surrender to the will of his father, his acceptance of a shameful, degrading death on a Roman cross. Such interpretations resulted in admonitions (to the disenfranchised) to be more Christ-like, to more willingly shoulder and quietly suffer oppression and humiliation. In liberationist reinterpretations, it is not the death on the cross (e.g., suffering) but its cause—confrontation with the symbols and sources of inequality (e.g., agency)—that is valorized.

These alternative theologies do not exalt or pay homage to a Christ who came to earth to die in order to atone for original sin. The "suffering on the cross could not have been the goal of his mission, but was instead the predictable result of a confrontation with the powers that be—confrontation aimed at relieving the world of the cross of suffering and injustice" (Kotsko 2010, 37). In this rereading, Christ's crucifixion centered around resistance to social injustice, with no hint that such injustices (suffering) are to be bowed to (submission) or construed as integral to redemption. Hope lies in reclaiming the right to resist evil (however that be defined), in refusing to acquiesce to their oppression, in modeling their God on an all-powerful iconoclast rather than a silently suffering martyr. Adam Kotsko contends that this interpretation constructs the life and death of Jesus in concrete, relational terms. African Americans, for example, focus on "strong parallels between Christ's own situation as a Jewish peasant living under Roman rule and that of blacks in America and therefore perceive Jesus as a liberatory figure bringing hope to the oppressed in *both* those contexts" (36).[1]

If the founding gesture is not God's sacrifice of his only son or the freely chosen obedience Christ models in accepting his shameful death but instead his rising up, then the foundational narrative is fundamentally realigned. In this retelling, oppression and death are the cost of resistance to injustice, and the authority by which Jesus was put to death (and that oppresses and bullies others) is akin to a mob mentality that must be challenged. To be more like Christ is to confront suffering born of inequality, scapegoating, and cruelty and to be purified by endurance and resistance. Repentance does not dominate this rereading, because social suffering has cleansed and will redeem them. Acceding to suffering, acceptance of their lot, endorses exploitation from which Christ looked to free men (despite assertions that his kingdom was not of this world). Oppression is not God's will, and Christ did not model passivity in the face of it. "This bespeaks a view of Jesus and the martyrs as empowered, *sacramental* witnesses, not as victims who passively acquiesced to evil" (Terrell 2005, 142; emphasis in original).

Undeniably, this resistance, this rewriting of sacred stories that decenters unconditional obedience, reintroduces the problem of shame and redemption: what is right (and deserving of pride), what is wrong (and deserving of shame), and who mediates the two (and holds out the possibility of redemption)? Are all resistances to be lauded, or must some be decried?[2] More importantly, can this model be secularized? Can the sacred scripts of our culture—independence and self-determination—be renarrated? If so, in whom is hope vested, and what are the terms of redemption?

APPENDIX C

Scheff and Retzinger: The Redemptive Role of Communication

Undoubtedly, communication, centrally positioned, is able to reciprocally affect the nature of social bonds (secure vs. insecure), the emotion associated with them (pride vs. shame), and the behavior (cooperative and productive vs. conflicted and alienated) caught up in the whole. As the arbiter between the *overall state of the individual* and *social behavior*, communication becomes pivotal in determining the functionality (or dysfunctionality) of relating (to self and other). The challenge Thomas Scheff and Suzanne Retzinger (1991) have put themselves is to rescue vestiges of normal shame from the pathological individualism that denies a need for connection and the capacity for secure social bonds. Respectful, open communication, which is attuned to the potential for destructive alienation, is key in this. It promotes a safe self-awareness, because ties are not severed and the healthy shame that follows such communication can be addressed and negotiated.

Aside from such issues as (1) the necessary (unstated) correlation between open (interpersonal) communication and self-aware (intrapsychic) communication and (2) the assumption that respectful communication can effectively come between humiliating content and maladaptive responses, Scheff and Retzinger's model seems to rest on an inherent contradiction. According to the dynamic they establish, the *overall state* of the individual is reciprocally linked, via communication, to the state of social relations between the parties. That is to say, communication, in creating a context of respect, maintains secure social bonds on an interpersonal level and a secure bond with oneself on an intrapsychic level. If this condition for ongoing interdependency is met, shame can be focused on behaviors.[1] But at this point *shame no longer augurs or reflects broken social bonds, its own defining characteristic.* Instead, the shamer is charged with the maintenance of connection—in short, with constructive criticism. Shaming, by definition, stands in opposition to this. It does not create insecure social bonds; it denies social bonds. *In that moment* (and perhaps beyond) reciprocity and affirmation are revoked, and when they are not, as in the socialization of young children, there is an investment in relationship that transcends the threat or damage to bonds. In addition, this model presupposes that shamers are, themselves, in full control of their behavior, that *it* is not driven by some psychic wound or reactive anger.

Perhaps more troublesome is that Scheff and Retzinger do not consider the reintegrative model popularized by Braithwaite (e.g., 1989) to have made a dent in the repressive mandates of culture. Nor do they suggest motivations for culture at large to adopt such practices. Might this failure be linked to the infrastructure of competition within society?

To norms that allot secrecy an important role in impression management, so critical to social success? Open, full communication may involve a level of disclosure that is *not* functional for *social* relationships and does not lead to cooperation and solidarity, and by the same token, indirect and inadequate communication may not always be dysfunctional or lead to conflict and maladaptive anger responses. Each individual juggles a variety of social roles, many standing in conflict with others. Open, full communication (for example, to narcissistic individuals who are not a person's highest priority) may exponentially expand unintentional shame.

This aside, Scheff and Retzinger have made tremendous contributions to both social and personal action plans, not the least of which is a model that emphasizes *connection*. The social isolation that follows shaming must be mitigated by hope of bridging the void that opens between offenders and others. This potential is lacking in the silence surrounding bullying, which endorses—even magnifies—the *intent* of the aggressors to strip the target of relationship possibilities. Scheff and Retzinger shift the onus of responsibility to shamers and insist on the continuation of secure bonds. Instead, I argue that shame breaks bonds—in bullying, it deliberately annihilates them—and it is the responsibility of bystanders to hold out hope for potential, eventual forgiveness and reintegration, not necessarily at their hands.

Reintegration must be made a possibility—one that has no guarantee of realization but nonetheless exists as a potential. Victims must remain invested in the possibility of redemption, and to do so, they must continue to be capable of *feeling*—and caring.

APPENDIX D

Lyn Lofland's "Threads of Social Connectedness"

It might reasonably be expected that the *type* of bond will affect the nature of a person's grief and perhaps her ruminations. Lyn Lofland's multidimensional "threads of social connectedness" (1985, 175) typify these bonds:

1. *Role partnerships*—a bond or connection with another person based on complementary role performances and their specific enactments (e.g., wife and husband)
2. *Mundane assistance*—a bond or connection with another person based on concrete, often day-to-day services that the other provides
3. *Linkage to social network*—a bond or connection with another person based on the various forms of access to important associates and friendships that she provides
4. *Self-confirmation*—an intersubjective bond or connection with another person that constructs and affirms character and other cherished and preferred self-images
5. *Comforting myths*—a bond or connection with another person based on the cocreation of myths and architectural stories useful in coping with life's challenges and catastrophes
6. *Reality maintenance*—an intersubjective bond or connection with another person that creates, validates, or supports the reality of the social world, including basic assumptions about its nature and functioning
7. *Shared futures*—a bond or connection with another person based on possible futures, which involve complementary roles, common goals, and mutually coordinated efforts

APPENDIX E

The Dynamics Underlying Expressive Writing: Why Does It Work?

An array of theoretical perspectives attempts to explain *why*, exactly, *expressive writing* shows physiological and emotional benefits in all manner of protocols. How does it function intrapsychically, as opposed to what variables stimulate its positive outcomes?

Attempts to answer this question include the following: (1) Expressive writing promotes catharsis, or physiological release, reducing the physical and psychological strains associated with inhibition. (2) Expressive writing promotes habituation to or builds up tolerance for uncomfortable emotional states. Prolonged exposure to a traumatic, psychologically threatening stimulus desensitizes victims, preventing them from feeling (and negotiating) their own pain. Expressive writing repeatedly calls out and confronts the stressor, challenging its positioning and the response to it, priming it for reappraisal. (3) Expressive writing augments the perception of control over stressful stimuli or over a person's own response to it. Meditation and mindfulness, as suggested by Stephanie Rude, Kacey Little Maestas, and Kristin Neff (2007), seek to separate out self-judgments, enhancing self-concept and self-regulation. (4) Expressive writing facilitates cognitive reorganization, which has repercussions on a variety of levels. Reprocessing a stressor more slowly and completely "can lead to insight or a change in perspective (reorganization of the schema), decreased distress . . . , and decreased bodily tension" (Lutgendorf and Ullrich 2002a, 178). Cognitive reorganization reconceptualizes distressing trauma-related fragments that intrude on consciousness, reconciling them within a coherent story, one that does not necessarily blame and indict the victim.

For a variety of reasons and from a number of perspectives, "expressive writing can help people to feel more connected with their own selves and to experience and accept their emotional reactions" (Lepore et al. 2002, 110).

APPENDIX F

Traumarama!, Seventeen *Magazine, and Prepackaged Shame*

One of the most cogent articulations of the dilemma posed by ready intelligibilities appears in an article by Carley Moore titled "Invasion of the Everygirl: *Seventeen* Magazine, 'Traumarama!' and the Girl Writer" (2011). "Traumarama!" is a monthly column that chronicles the "I could have died of shame" experiences of teens.[1] Limited to 75–150 words per entry (and clearly edited by the staff), these stories share one after another humiliating scenario. Moore admits that the column creates a support for girls, providing them with real stories of the gaffes and inadequacies of others, legitimating and giving voice to shame. Yet she laments that it prescribes an etiquette for these situations—one, she argues, that subtly reiterates to girls that "it's *never* okay to be real or imperfect" (1251; emphasis in original).

While Moore is certainly correct in this, I am not sure that I fully agree with the way she assesses the cost of the column's formulaic format. Acknowledging and languaging humiliating experiences, even connecting them with "omg!!!" reflective humor or beginning to script stories around them, is itself an important *first step* in negotiating shame, despite the cookie-cutter rearticulations. The column, which is the epitome of prepackaged narrations, *normalizes* social shame, makes it commonplace, and this service must be weighed against the unfortunate fact that the cost of learning that there is life after painful social indignities, public degradations, and shame—that others have lived to tell—is voice. That is, the others who tell are not those who have survived the experience but the editors of the column. Survivors are required to surrender their experiences in exchange for the experiences' publication and circulation. These are rewritten into templates that overly homogenize *accounts*, predigesting humiliations into situational adventures and aligning them with embarrassment, which is easier to recover from than shame.

It is regrettable that the column merely narrates circumstances. It

> never offers any interpretation or analysis of why teenage life is the way it is, or at least why girls have chosen to represent it this way. Girls are invited to give voice to their experience and to see a connection between their lives and those of other girls, but they remain solitary individuals, unorganized and unpoliticized. . . . In "Traumarama!" there is no authority, expert or guide to help girls think about and question their stories. There is just the "everygirl," and the

"everygirl" is an embarrassed, isolated, self-conscious, occasionally funny, rarely angry consumer. (Moore 2011, 1262)

This overwriting of voice is far from innocuous (appropriating another's story rarely is). Moore argues that the column creates a complicated partnership with feminism "because rather than have the magazine and advertisers represent the teenage girl as insecure and obsessed with her body, the 'everygirl' writer represents *herself* as insecure and out of control, which fulfils the magazine's obligation to its advertisers who know that an insecure girl will buy more products" (1250; emphasis in original). This everygirl situates herself within well-worn narratives of awkwardness, inadequacy, and desire. Yet these familiar narratives are subtly purloined and repositioned by others, inserted into alternative (capitalist) metanarratives (the raison d'être of the magazine).

Indeed, this subtext certainly exists, and it could even be argued that humiliating experiences are put on the table and acknowledged in order to tap the vulnerabilities of readers (bystanders) who will empathize with the teller's story (and perhaps be more susceptible to purchasing products themselves). Worse yet, it might be argued that the short, formulaic accounts communicate little more than "you ought to be able to just get over it" to readers. Not only is this problematic in itself, but it has broader, subversive implications: "Because the everygirl always moves on, there is no time or space for girls to envision themselves as potential political agents capable of empowering themselves or changing the world they inhabit" (Moore 2011, 1263). The cost of normalizing shame (or more correctly, embarrassment) is that experiences are reported as low-level "and then . . . and then . . . and then" accounts that magically skirt the pitfalls discussed in Chapter 4. There is no room for reflection and no interest in encouraging it. Rather, the reader turns the page and becomes armed with up-to-date knowledge circulating in the teen cultural economy, currency that, it is intimated, allows her readmittance to the tribe of teenage girls, allowing her to get on with her life. Humiliations happen all the time, and they are survivable—in fact, the message she may ultimately take away is that consumption can never fail as an effective restoration-coping strategy.

This, then, is the trade-off. For now, unreflective cultural scripts serve an important cultural function, not unlike the adaptiveness of inane video games. "Traumarama!" brings embarrassment and shame into the light, acknowledging its ubiquitousness, if not its potential, illustrating that there is life after social disgrace. In addition, it begins the process of creating ready intelligibilities capable of bonding her to others, connecting her, and beginning to enfranchise her losses. The survivability of social pain is being patterned into the language games of youth culture: a group of supportive readers (bystanders) empathize and laugh *with* her (reintegrative shaming), and often a redemption coda ties the whole together. That the patterning models moving forward at the cost of a subtle, individualistic renarrating of experience is, unarguably, problematic. Yet even while reinforcing *expectations* that she can readily recover from trauma, somehow negotiating rumination, depression, and aggressions, it illustrates and normalizes humiliating ebbs in the flow of life. It may, arguably, promote hiving. The column's seeming authenticity *does* belie its theft of voice in the promotion of lemming-like consumption, as well as its tacit disenfranchisement of any pain associated with a failure to get over it. Nonetheless, it serves crucial functions in the evolution of bully-victim stories. "Traumarama!" assures her that, no matter what she has suffered, readers will feel for her—she still belongs and is entitled to support and compassion.

Backlash is to be expected from those genuinely suffering social shame, the innumerable young people attempting to negotiate indictments of self that are trivialized by these absurd, preresolved scenarios. While "Traumarama!" cannot speak to their experiences, it has the potential to communicate the importance of sharing humiliations and the possibility of support in doing so—everygirl does not deny connection. This mediated connectedness can, in the future, mature into participation in social networking sites that encourage her to write her own story, to articulate her reality in her own voice. In this rereading, "Traumarama!" is a first, rough draft of social pain, a low-level unreflective account that gets the experience on the table. Where is the line between narrating that social pain is recoverable and imposing scripts that rob her of voice? It is to be hoped that these formulaic vignettes do not preclude her ability to rewrite memories, that they are a start, not a final version that is (yet again) storied by the voice and agenda of others.

NOTES

INTRODUCTION

1. This list does not include shootings that were not rampages. For a more comprehensive list of teen violence during this period, see http://sitemaker.umich.edu/356.dolan/list_of_school_shooters.

2. Possible exceptions are Eric Harris and Andrew Golden, who both appear, in retrospect (after all the information has been compiled), to have suffered from psychopathologies.

3. Katherine Newman, then a professor at Harvard, was recruited by the National Academy of Sciences to explore school tragedies.

4. It is important to note, as Michael Kimmel does, that if the shooters had been other than white middle-class boys—black girls from poor families, for example—the response would have been very different: "Would not the media focus entirely on race, class, and gender? Of course it would: We'd hear about the culture of poverty; about how life in the city breeds crime and violence; about some putative natural tendency among blacks towards violence. Someone would probably even blame feminism for causing girls to become violent in vain imitation of boys. *Yet the obvious fact that these school killers were all middle-class white boys seems to have escaped the media's notice, in part because race, class, or gender are only visible when speaking of those who are not privileged by race, class and gender, but invisible when speaking of those who are privileged by them*" (Kimmel 2005, 146–147; emphasis added). In other words, the assessment would fall more squarely on social forces. Because the shooters shared a trifecta of privileged social attributes (white, middle-class, male), the focus has been much more psychological, for it is assumed that these social forces linked to these attributes could not have destructive motivating power.

5. Notably, these voices include Dave Cullen and Peter Langman. However, even Cullen, who spent a decade exploring the Columbine tragedy (and remains unconvinced by the bullying motive explanation), admits that while "there's no evidence that bullying led to murder, [there is] considerable evidence it was a problem at Columbine High" (2009, 158).

6. Bullying narratives are situated in comfortably coherent social stories (as opposed to those suggested in *A Clockwork Orange* or *Natural Born Killers*). These stories have begun to caricature victimization, elevating it to epidemic proportions that threaten to trivialize experiences. Oversimplified overexposure leads to "a new trap to watch for: being too quick to slap the label of bully onto some kids and the label of victim onto others. It is kind of crying wolf, and it does damage. For one thing, calling every mean comment or hallway clash bullying breeds cynicism" (Bazelon 2013, 298).

7. Although instances of savage cyberbullying (addressed in Chapter 6) *seem* clear-cut and readily identifiable, it would be a mistake to simplistically link derogatory texts to victimization. The cyberspeak of teens is fluid and ever changing. A rushing torrent of wordplay, it exploits ambiguities and reconfigures significances, manipulating and subverting linguistic structures of power. Challenges to established usage are a counterbid for control and entirely normative, in addition to being a favorite tactic of those who are disenfranchised in the cultural economy. Authority figures who hold up tweets and comments left on Facebook walls as tangible proof of bullying must tread cautiously and keep this fact in mind. Does the exchange say what we think it says, have the connotations we believe it to have, and imply the social responses we expect it to? It might, or it might not.

8. Value-oriented voluntary communities continue to coexist alongside more or less compulsory social communities (e.g., the school or workplace), which may claim a different, often lesser, psychic investment from an individual. Communities have endured and continue to function *within* culture (as opposed to embodying overarching cultural norms). Their diminishing purview and curtailed capacity to make claims on the population at large should not cause us to lose sight of their ongoing functioning and potential influence.

CHAPTER 1

1. "Individualism was influenced not only by the *absence* of religion and stability but also by the *presence* of the various interests and forces that socially constructed a certain type of individual with certain kinds of wishes, urges, ambitions and proclivities" (Cushman 1995, 11).

2. The psychologistic view, as it came to be articulated by Sigmund Freud (1963), was rational and sufficiently scientific to simultaneously encompass the irrational, emotional depths of romantic culture. The iconoclastic mental healer Franz Anton Mesmer, whose cure (mesmerism) for ennui, morbid introspection, and psychic imbalances was developed well over a century before Freud's theories of the mind, also integrated rational and irrational forces into his overview of human nature and its *being* in the world (see Buranelli 1975).

3. Though of course the expanding economic order relied on the cultivation of desire—on the instincts—for its success, thwarting the impetus toward pursuit of rational choice.

4. Free will, it was believed, had been vouchsafed by Jesus's freely chosen violent death. Importantly, his sacrifice also atoned for original sin, ordaining the practice of daily forgiveness and social redemption.

5. The self became "a box without content because the content has been thrown out and what is left is a set of psychological descriptions with no referent. There is no referent because, in order to substantiate the ideas, one requires an explanatory cosmology that makes sense of the individual's place in the world and not a market brand name or a set of abstract ideas extracted from older traditions" (Carrette and King 2005, 73).

6. Vesting authority in new experiences also became a favorite orientation, but it raised the question of how, and on what basis, these experiences were to be appropriated—a dilemma that loomed large when experiences were bad and individuals were faced with making sense of them.

7. When published in 1950, Riesman's book received critical acclaim. Yet it became and remains one of, if not the, best-selling sociological treatises of all time. For this reason alone it cannot be sidelined and dismissed. Whether correct or incorrect in its analysis of social types, the book's popularity and the common misinterpretation of its thesis as an indictment of conformity (a threat linked to the fears this raised at the onset of the Cold War) are themselves significant.

8. Riesman notes that this inner-directed individual is integral to Max Weber's Protestant ethic thesis (Riesman 1950, 18).

9. "The American frontiersman, as [Alexis de] Tocqueville encountered him in Michigan, was, though hospitable, uninterested in people. He found physical nature problematical enough: to alter and adapt it required that he become hard and self-reliant" (Riesman 1950, 112).

10. Christopher Lasch was under no illusions about the aggressive side of this rugged individualism: "In the heat of the struggle to win the West, the American pioneer gave full vent to his rapacity and murderous cruelty, but he always envisioned the result . . . as a peaceful, respectable, churchgoing community safe for his women and children. He imagined that his offspring, raised under the morally refining influence of feminine 'culture,' would grow up to be sober, law-abiding, domesticated American citizens" (1979, 10–11).

11. Attuned and malleable, this individual constructed a self that was increasingly *derived from others' objectifications of her*. Their characterizations, culled from patterns of acting and responding that emerged over time and across a series of diverse situations, coalesced as more than *social* identity. Motivations and values, ascribed to social behaviors, were folded into a social identity that was taken up by the individual and, as John Hewitt argues, came "in its own turn *to shape the person's responses to . . . situations and roles*" (1989, 175; emphasis added). Put differently, a person's social identity, established by others' articulations of her, their representations and expectations, was internalized and came to order experience, subsequent behavior, and *personal* identity. Importantly, the self-principles that emerged through this process were, more than ever, linked to the gaze and opinions of others, suggesting that identity might increasingly be characterized as that which emerges from a dialogue between internalized social identity and the ongoing opinions of others.

12. The affluence accruing to successful salesmanship produced a double-edged sword. The authentic experiences it could buy, no less than leisure, quickly eroded the rules, regulations, and norms the company man had imported to manage his economic success. In addition, almost as soon as he was established, the company man began to be undermined from within. Corporate structures evolved increasingly efficient, rational divisions of labor, making his capacity for independent judgment, self-reliance, and self-discipline obsolete. Don Draper, protagonist of the popular series *Mad Men*, epitomizes this personality type and all its fracture points.

13. Conversely, efforts to fit in provided others with a basis for assessing the extent of an individual's commitment to their group. Yet this commitment had to be weighed against new social threats. The literature of the post–World War II period, especially the emerging genre of science fiction, reflected the paranoia of a society well versed in the perils of social determinism, which translated in the United States as a risk of becoming automatons. And automatons—other-directed conformists—were linked, through

this mind-set, to communism. *Copycat* became a pejorative term referring to those who had no inner core, hollowly imitating the trends, opinions, and judgments endorsed by others.

14. In terms of relational aggression and bullying, this analysis illuminates why telling victims to just walk away and forget about it or make other friends is an inadequate, inept response.

15. "In 'Egocentrism: Is the American Character Changing?' (*Encounter*, August–September, 1980), Riesman conceded that, alongside genuine social activism, aggressive egoism was alive and well. The 'rather timid . . . corporate civil servants'—so strongly featured in *The Lonely Crowd*—had never been more than just one species in the business zoo" (Wilkinson 2010).

16 "As a form of information, style creates a consciousness that is seductively at war with much of our experience. That is part of the point; style addresses deep-seated desires, it promises to release people from the subjective conditions of their experience" (Ewen 1988, 263).

17. Further continuities between other-directed individuals and narcissists "reside in a pattern of personal flexibility that was only superficially, and not yet comfortably, adopted in the 1950s. The other-directed person clung to his institutional self despite the discomforts involved, whereas the narcissist embraces the new identity" (Thomson 1985, 278).

18. "We are educated, from infancy, to *look*, we are not encouraged to see and interpret simultaneously. Our eyes imbibe images, with little critical resistance, as if they offer an ordained glimpse of some distant, yet accessible *reality*. It rarely occurs to us, as we pass through the perpetual corridors of visual representation, that (to borrow a phrase from Helen Merrell Lynd) 'every way of seeing is also a way of not seeing'" (Ewen 1988, 156; emphasis in original).

19. The specific behaviors that call forth shaming practices change rapidly, and what is permissible one day is often punishable the next. But can we really compare the sexual license of ancient Pompeii, d'Medici Florence, or our own flapper era with what appear to be more comprehensive changes to shame today? Nick Serpe, writing for *Dissent* magazine, elaborates on the extent of shamelessness in contemporary culture through a series of examples: "Tom is going to repo her car, but if she can answer three of five trivia questions right, the car will be hers, and fully paid off. The tow rig lifts the back of the car when she gets answers wrong and brings it down when she gets them right. With six family members watching on, [she] prevails. She dances with Tom and then boasts in the postgame interview, 'I ain't going to even fucking look for a job now.' The next contestant, a skinny, shirtless stoner living at his mom's, has a similar message when he wins: 'Guess what I learned, America: if you don't pay your bill, somebody else will'" (Serpe 2013). Shame is not only uncoupled from sexuality, as it has been in countless periods throughout history; it is removed from considerations of dignity.

20. The trials and tribulations of this-worldly life were but a reflection of "divine conflict and victory [in which] Christ—Christus victor—fights against and triumphs over the evil powers of the world, the 'tyrants' under which mankind is in bondage and suffering" (Aulén 1931, 4). (Wo)man must model her behavior on that of Jesus, looking to imitate his acceptance of suffering and his triumph over Satan.

21. See, for example, the prints of Daniel Defoe in the stocks at http://www.google.com/search?q=daniel+defoe+in+the+pillory&hl=en&authuser=0&tbm=isch&tbo=u&source=univ&sa=X&ei=MD6SUob_OsPckQeir4GoAQ&ved=0CDIQsAQ&biw=842&bih=368. Although the spectacle did not occur in colonial America, it suggests that

the audience to such events could actively participate in—or resist—the shaming that was intended (for example, by throwing flowers). In smaller communities, members might pass the stocks with their eyes cast downward, looking away from a victim's pain, not adding to it, or they might actively sneer, hurling taunts and rotten produce at the sinner.

22. Mayberry is the iconic, friendly community that is the fictional setting for *The Andy Griffith Show*, and River City is the fictional small-town setting of *The Music Man*.

23. Harold Hill is the protagonist of *The Music Man* who is reformed by love.

24. Humans continued to consider themselves fundamentally flawed, but the doctrine of original sin gave way to secular psychological disorders resulting from early childhood traumas.

25. Francis Broucek notes that "Freud's failure, and the failure of later psychoanalysts, to recognize shame's healthy functions led to the culturally disastrous notion that freedom from shame is the mark of the healthy personality" (1991, 135).

26. These opposing tendencies have been variously construed by cultural scholars. Hewitt emphasizes the impulse to participate in society's strivings, to accept and embrace obligations to others and seek belonging, as well as the impulse to differentiate self, perhaps by leaving community, moving on in search of new experiences, or simply by creating distance from and Othering those who have disparate tastes, backgrounds, and points of view. He claims that "American culture is best characterized not as relentlessly individualistic or as lacking in the capacity to conceive of or discuss community, but as torn between individualism and communitarianism, thus creating serious, felt difficulties of social adjustment and personal meaning" (1989, vii). Michael Sandel (2009) construes the tension in terms of cultural ethics, as a straining between the values of individual freedom, on which its laws are grounded, and those of virtue, which animate relationship and community. T. J. Jackson Lears traces the roots of a dichotomous tension in culture to the post–Civil War era, when what he calls "anti-modernism," or a longing for meaning, authenticity, and morality, emerged in reaction to the impoverishment of secularizing tendencies. In his view, "Europeans and Americans alike began to recognize that the triumph of modern culture had not produced a greater autonomy (which was the official claim) but rather had promoted a spreading sense of moral impotence and spiritual sterility—a feeling that life had become not only overcivilized but also curiously unreal" (1981, 4–5).

27. Secular prejudices helped the disenfranchised reappropriate Christian narratives: "The relationship between God the Father and his Son who saves the world through his obedience even to the point of death maps out onto asymmetrical intimate relationships—the abused woman or child identifies with the obediently suffering son" (Kotsko 2010, 27). So too did blacks, who were infantilized by white, patriarchal society.

28. Attempting to move beyond deviant constructions of self brings an individual face to face with culture's valuation of control over her body. This responsibility "seems central to a Western understanding of human agency" (French and Brown 2011, 2). To assume control over her body (i.e., agency), she must admit inadequacy and endorse her subsequent humiliation. According to Sandra French and Sonya Brown, this may lead to self-injury—Kenneth Burke's (1965) very particular conceptualizations of "mortification"—as well as shame (French and Brown 2011, 12).

29. For a comprehensive review of the development of social emotions, especially shame and pride, see Barrett and Nelson-Goens 1997.

30. William Damon argues that "our heightened concern with children's internal mental states has combined with the increased child-centeredness of modern times to

create crippling imbalances in children's views of themselves and the world. When we tell children that their first goal is self-love, we are suggesting to them that they are the center of the universe. By contributing further to the already child-centered orientation of modern culture, this emphasis can push a child toward a *narcissistic insensitivity* to the needs of others" (quoted in Ryan, Bednar, and Sweeder 1999, 116; emphasis added; see also Ryan 1997).

31. The options that a polycultural world opens to adults are not necessarily available to schoolchildren, who often cannot change schools, move from the area, or even successfully trade reference groups within the fishbowl of their learning institution. This, of course, limits self-determination and agency.

32. Schools have increasingly limited authority over, and responsibility for, the content of the cultural economies that circulate in their institution, which leaves them constantly negotiating the interface between norms and laws, mediating behaviors intent on testing that boundary. Many of the behaviors that disrupt a school's functioning must now either be criminalized, medicalized, or accommodated (allowing bullying to fly below the radar).

33. *What* is left of this person? Nothing (so he or she commits suicide) or overwhelming shame (which compels him or her to use weapons to *make* others see him or her as worthy of respect, if not inclusion). These responses are precisely those that Kenneth Burke outlines in his understanding of the dynamics of oppression (1953). His conceptualization includes *victimization* (whereby the injustice is addressed homicidally) and what he calls *mortification* (whereby the injustice is addressed suicidally).

34. There is, of course, a third option, the deliberate rejection of social norms, which often entails transformation (discussed in Chapter 5).

35. School shootings have, in the main, been carried out by white, middle-class males whose parents have access to the media and are able to influence the redefinition of norms and the construction of social problems. Defined as representative of American society and culture, behaviors threatening this social demographic were immediately put on the cultural radar. Authorities and specialists instantly emerged and socially positioned the tragedies by identifying and labeling a causal factor: bullying. Responsibility was shifted to the behaviors of *others*, which were problematized.

36. Certainly more than harassment and humiliation led to atrocities, and these factors must also inform the shaping of bullying as a social problem. Variables including neurological wiring and the availability of semiautomatic weapons are equally significant to rampages, but an exploration of their role in recent tragedies is beyond the purview of this book.

37. While teachers, supervisors, and behavioral specialists may certainly note a depressed affect or changes in dress, grades, or friendships, peers are often better able to assess what distress level has been triggered. This may be because many of the so-called warning signs of distress are normative at an age when children are trying on, and growing into, young adult identities and negotiating (many for the first time) interpersonal setbacks. Couple this with awareness that bullied youth are desperately *trying* to hold it together, to convince themselves and others that they fit in, and it is easy to understand why their pain goes undetected by professionals—and even by peers.

38. Perhaps, following Wittgenstein ([1953] 2009), a hybrid incorporating behaviors, responses, and contexts can be created. It may be possible to construct a model of bullying that rests on *criteria* that are an admixture of contingent relationships and conceptual attributes, each of which partially defines, and thus contributes to, a more accurate account of bullying. Outlining such a project is beyond the scope of this book. See Lehtinen 1998.

39. Note that, on the basis of what we have concluded in retrospect, an ability to answer any or all of these questions would not have prevented the school tragedies that spurred national focus on bullying. These rampages hinged on additional elements, but this should hardly dissuade us from working out terms for the mitigation of emotional violence and psychological abuse.

40. Note that this degradation is willingly suffered in the hopes of winning—that is, gaining salvation and redemption from a life of obscurity and its workaday requirements.

41. A number of contestants who have been sent home from game shows, having been shown to be losers on national television, have committed suicide. This is downplayed, and support for their felt experiences of inadequacy remains elusive.

CHAPTER 2

1. This nonverbal communication is so important that we now have complex FaceReader software and elaborate facial-expression coding systems.

2. Foucault argues that power is more than a repressive force: it "traverses and produces things, it induces pleasure, forms knowledge, produces discourse. It needs to be considered as a productive network which runs through the whole social body, much more than as a negative instance whose function is repression" (1980, 119).

3. See Winnicott 1971. According to D. W. Winnicott, play is a losing of self to find it. Gossip's trilling along topics allows its form to mimic play, yet its content, situated and tied by the world of immediate concerns, may—unlike play—be grounded by distinct concerns and boundaries.

4. Whether the description of events can be separated from the event itself is a question that is beyond the scope of this book, though I am inclined to believe, with Norman Denzin (2007), that it cannot.

5. The "social construction of reality" refers to a specific concept within social theory (see Schutz 1967; Berger and Luckmann 1967). Briefly, it states that individuals and groups who interact establish over time characterizations of each other's actions and reciprocal roles. Their social identities become embedded in larger networks and are soon institutionalized, *becoming reality*. A less entrenched conceptualization of key aspects of this process is the Thomas theorem (named for its author, W. I. Thomas), which states, "If men define situations as real, they are real in their consequences" (Thomas and Thomas 1928, 571–572).

6. Gossipers are, themselves, situated in group infrastructures and relationships of power that circumscribe what they are allowed to say and to whom. Sociograms (graphic, quantitative measures of social relationships) bare these infrastructures.

7. Even by suggesting interpretations and speculating about, if not asserting, motives, "gossipers contribute to the psychological reality of what they are watching or talking about" (G. Taylor 1994, 41).

8. Laurence Thomas (1994) argues that the intention behind the judgment determines whether one is gossiping or engaging in some other form of information exchange. In his view, a discussion of a third party's behavior by a group of individuals would not necessarily constitute gossip if this group were a handful of friends discussing something potentially harmful to their friend. In this instance, the aim of the conversation, its underlying motives, removes it from the realm of gossip and places it squarely in the realm of friendship and support. Their friend's personal affairs are discussed with concern for her well-being. This requires the speakers to put themselves aside and relate information to how it might affect the subject, as opposed to relating it to their own

position in the social matrix. However, this does not change the fact that group speculation about an absent party, for whatever reason, is still the sharing of social information. Altruistic intent is, in this instance, the gossiper's backstage.

9. Roz Dixon contends that scapegoating occurs only at particular junctures in the life of a group—namely, when it is developing or perhaps fractioning into another group. "During the early stages of dependency, the group defends against anxieties about rejection and abandonment through conformity: Conformity with the leader's supposed wishes and conformity with each other—to stand out from the crowd seems risky. The scapegoat is the only person besides the leader who is differentiated" (2007, 85).

10. Laughter is subversive to the extent that it bonds individuals in a shared "pleasure at the idea of disrupting the social order" (Billig 2001, 38). Such enjoyment over token challenges to authority is familiar to adolescents, who are often limited in the extent to which they are able to challenge official orderings of reality.

11. Laughter's contagion can best be seen in videos of babies laughing. We often have no idea why they find ordinary objects humorous, even hysterical, but are readily induced to laugh along with them. See, for example, the video at http://www.youtube.com/watch?v=RP4abiHdQpc.

12. This sets the stage, it would appear, for self-degrading laughter later in life, as it too, though at much greater cost, retains connection.

13. Young people who readily comply with adult norms may be particularly susceptible to ridicule by their peers. Laughter at them is a thinly veiled challenge to authority through the mockery of its young purveyors. These covert challenges disrupt the status quo and have high entertainment value for subordinate groups (e.g., adolescents).

14. Michael Pickering notes that the term *stereotype* was "taken metaphorically from the trade vocabulary of printing and typography, where it referred to text cast into rigid form for the purposes of repetitive use" (2001, 9).

15. See, for example, the "cafeteria tribes" scene in *Mean Girls* at https://www.youtube.com/watch?v=gZ_qXmxdgGM.

16. This tendency leads to what psychologists call correspondence bias.

17. José Marques and colleagues (1988) hypothesize that members of an in-group (broadly defined as either a group sharing a characteristic or a coterie of friends) are subject to more extreme judgments (for both likable and unlikable behavior) by their in-group peers. The researchers theorize that this is because the behavior in question has greater relevance, and potential threat, to members of the in-group's social identity, causing it to be more weighted than behaviors of out-group members.

18. Developmental psychologists soon added particularly strong evidence demonstrating that "children acquire and use stereotypes before they can appropriately distinguish groups on the basis of the cues thought to be crucial to such a task" (Mackie et al. 1996, 62). This means that children internalize the specific characteristics informing stereotypes before they are fully capable of applying that information and sorting the world on the basis of it.

19. It must be emphatically noted that several academic subspecialties acknowledge the subjective, social construction of stereotypes, and research is even focused on how it might be possible to interrupt the connection between sorting and stereotyping.

20. The Thomas theorem is as true for gossip as it is for stereotyping.

21. Stereotypes that highlight the aesthetic sensibilities of gay men (as modeled in such shows as *Queer Eye for the Straight Guy*) do not diminish the two-dimensional caricaturing that characterizes all stereotypes, but they counterbalance the derogatory overlay with positive attributes.

22. Today, most scientists agree that genetics and environmental factors contribute to the behavioral traits in humans, but which of the two dominates and is foundational is still a contested issue.

23. Carol Gilligan contends that "boys' games appeared to last longer because . . . when disputes arose in the course of a game, boys were able to resolve the disputes more effectively than girls. . . . In the gravest of debates, the final word was always to 'repeat the play.' . . . In contrast, the eruption of disputes among girls tended to end the game" (1982, 9).

24. Numerous researchers have noted that talk is the substance of female relating and relationships, while engagement in activities is the substance of male relating and relationships.

25. See Carol Gilligan's classic *In a Different Voice*, in which she argues that women "try to change the rules in order to preserve relationships, [while] men, in abiding by these rules, depict relationships as easily replaced" (1982, 44).

26. More than three decades ago, Carol Gilligan persuasively argued that women, in "illuminating life as a web rather than a succession of relationships, portray autonomy rather than attachment as the illusory and dangerous quest" (1982, 48). If women define self in relationship, competition is doubly threatening, because it entails the inevitability of standing separate, as either winner or loser. It is unlikely that success can be defined as victory if it means standing alone. Conversely, if men define self in terms of separation and independence, competition has the potential to enhance masculinity.

27. Resources, power, and prestige do not publicly accrue to girls for feats and accomplishments that parallel those of boys. Although we have female athletes, no event that women participate in has either the salary or the visibility of male sports. Although women are successful financially, only three of the top twenty billionaires are women (Dolan and Kroll 2014). More to the point might be a comparison of inherited wealth versus entrepreneurial wealth along gender lines.

28. This is in no way intended to suggest that boys do not avail themselves of these covert forms of competition—even to the extent that girls do. However, they have not been limited to these formats.

29. For a comprehensive review of this literature, see Bateup et al. 2002.

30. John McMurtry notes that "arguments for and against competition have raged since Heraclitus's condemnation of Homer in Fragment LXXXI for lamenting the 'conflict among gods and men'" (1991, 201).

31. Muzafer Sherif and colleagues ([1954] 1961) set out to probe the origins of prejudice and discrimination, both of which ultimately pit one individual or group against another. Their experiment divided twenty-four white, middle-class boys attending a sleepaway camp into two teams and observed how each group formed relationships and how infrastructures of leadership, power, and status emerged. Initially, the existence of another team was not known by either group, and the construction of internal social hierarchies proceeded without reference to clear definition of group boundaries or even group identity. The experiment then moved to a second phase, when each group became aware of the other, and friction, in the form of athletic competitions, was introduced. Researchers noted that in-group and out-group identities strengthened almost immediately, and hostilities between the two groups quickly escalated. Rivalries became so intense that within days this phase of the experiment was halted and a third phase begun that introduced superordinate tasks requiring cooperation between the groups. The necessary collaborations forced the hostilities to subside. Researchers were stunned at the rapidity with which in-group and out-group antagonisms, prejudices, and discriminatory behavior arose, especially in light of the two groups having no substantial difference between them.

32. The classic study of competition and cooperation was done by James Julian and Franklyn Perry in 1967. Researchers examined productivity in terms of (1) competition between individuals, (2) competition between groups, and (3) cooperation between individuals in groups. Groups were composed of both men and women and were generalized across gender lines.

33. Of course, these findings are not unanimous, and additional variables must be controlled for. The initial observation, made by Norman Triplett in 1898, documenting a link between cyclists racing against each other (as opposed to solo) and improved task performance, has been substantiated by other researchers (see, e.g., Mulvey and Ribbens 1999; Tauer and Harackiewicz 1999, 2004; Brown, Cron, and Slocum 1998). Still other researchers (e.g., Hammond and Goldman 1961) have found support for cooperation, demonstrating that competition results in reduced motivation and productivity.

34. Studies have unpacked these dynamics, modifying replications of this research. Manipulation of such variables as structure of the competition (zero-sum gain vs. winner takes all), what is at stake in the competition (personal development vs. winning a desired object), the relationship between competitors (friends, opposing teammates, strangers), personality traits of competitors, risk aversion and gender, and single-sex versus mixed-group dynamics. This research has yielded results and conclusions that defy generalization and complicate claims about the nature and value of competition.

35. "Evolutionary psychologists have proposed two theories to explain why men may have evolved to enjoy competition; both are tied to the reproductive strategies of the two sexes. One theory is that, because men can have many more children than women, the potential gain in reproductive success from winning a competition is much greater for men. . . . The second theory focuses on one gender being responsible for parental care. While a man's death does not diminish his current reproductive success, a woman's death may cause the loss of her current offspring . . . , increasing the cost associated with competitive behavior" (Niederle and Vesterlund 2008, 448–449).

36. The suicide (and attempted suicide) rate for losers of competitions on reality-TV shows is not well publicized or socially analyzed. It remains a statistic, available to those who look for it.

37. Although we narrate all the hard work that our Olympic athletes have put in for even a chance at a medal, those stories are aired before competitions, and follow-up with those who do not medal is rare. On the other hand, personal respect for everyday people who train and compete in marathons—and who finish, no matter in what place—is growing and is a hopeful sign, a behavior to be promoted and modeled in other arenas.

CHAPTER 3

1. For further research and insight into school shootings, see Langman 2009, Newman et al. 2004, Cullen 2009, and Bazelon 2013.

2. Etymologically, *shame* appears to derive from a Proto-Indo-European word meaning "to cover." It is linked, at its earliest, to "exposure" and the risks of being uncovered or unprotected and may allude, in its broadest sense, to the aspect of self that we go to great lengths to keep others from seeing.

3. As Erving Goffman noted, "An individual may recognize extreme embarrassment in others and even in himself by the objective signs of emotional disturbance: blushing, fumbling, stuttering, an unusually low- or high-pitched voice, quavering speech or breaking of the voice, sweating, blanching, blinking, tremor of the hand, hesitating or

vacillating movement, absentmindedness, and malapropisms. . . . There are also symptoms of a subjective kind: constriction of the diaphragm, a feeling of wobbliness, consciousness of strained and unnatural gestures, a dazed sensation, dryness of the mouth, and tenseness of the muscles. In cases of mild discomfiture, these visible and invisible flusterings occur but in less perceptible form" (1967, 97).

4. A discussion of the interface between cognition and affect is beyond the scope of this book. However, as David Franks noted more than two decades ago, "The linguistic dimension of affect is so much a part of the assumptive order that cognitive processes are taken for granted and left unaware of their influence" (1989, 97–98).

5. Note that Agnes Heller (2003) uses shame and guilt interchangeably, although many scholars separate these emotions. The significance of this is discussed later in the chapter.

6. A sense of failure is predicated on the ability to take her own behavior (perhaps her entire self) as an object, one *she* is able to review, assess, and critique. As Charles Horton Cooley put it, "In imagination we perceive in another's mind some thought of our appearance, manners, aims, deeds, character, friends, and so on, and we are variously affected by it. A self-idea of this sort seems to have three principal elements: the imagination of our appearance to the other person; the imagination of his judgment of that appearance, and some sort of self-feeling, such as pride or mortification" ([1902] 1922, 184).

7. Hence the well-worn response to victims, "Why do you care what she thinks?" This may lead to double shame, as the victim is being urged to confront the fact that she cares what her socially ruthless peers think, even though she cannot articulate why and knows she probably should not care.

8. It is worth noting that this interpretive aspect is equally present with an actual looking glass, or mirror. Consider a one-hundred-pound young woman who, in gazing at her reflection, clearly sees how fat she is and *is concerned because of the social implication of being fat.*

9. This holds true even in a consideration of embarrassing self-revelations and humiliating pictures posted on the Internet. What would be truly compromising would be the discovery that these stories and images were fabricated—that is, other than what they seem. As long as they are *self*-posts (or friendly posts), they are scripted transgressions aimed at a reference group that understands, supports, and lauds such candid revelations—*however shameful they may seem to mainstream proprieties.* (A competition of sorts over who has debased herself most frequently or degradingly may even be in play.) The embarrassment that Goffman, Scheff, and others refer to is not content specific and emerges in relation to a violation of the norms held by the reference group *in which the individual is invested* (whatever those norms may be).

10. Typically, we are not aware of these demands—what they are or having made them—until they go unmet or are unfulfilled. Whether we are aware of it or not, "society is organized on the principle that any individual who possesses certain social characteristics has a moral right to expect that others will value and treat him in an appropriate way. Connected with this principle is a second, namely that an individual who implicitly or explicitly signifies that he has certain social characteristics ought in fact to be what he claims he is. In consequence, when an individual projects definition of the situation and thereby makes an implicit or explicit claim to be a person of a particular kind, he automatically exerts a moral demand upon the others, obliging them to value and treat him in the manner that persons of his kind have a right to expect. He also implicitly forgoes all claims to be things he does not appear to be" (Goffman 1959, 13).

11. In this conceptualization, embarrassment falls at the opposite end of a continuum from shame. It is linked to particular situations and circumstances that do not threaten social relationships, even if felt acutely. Scholars debate as to whether this continuum model is valid, though Silvan Tomkins, Helen Lewis, Norbert Elias, and Thomas Scheff, among others, have found it compelling. It appears to have merit insofar as both are negative, self-conscious emotions; both concern behaviors attributed to the individual; and both have similar interpersonal origins. However, significant phenomenological differences between the two feeling states suggest, to some scholars, that shame and embarrassment are two distinct emotions. In his 1996 *Embarrassment: Poise and Peril in Everyday Life*, Roland Miller gathers, groups, and analyzes variants of either model. Of particular usefulness is his analysis of the possible causes of embarrassment linked to one or the other model.

12. Other psychologists who have found shame to be a central component include Erik Erickson, Alfred Adler, Abraham Kardiner, and Karen Horney.

13. Durkheim's classic treatise, the first scientific study of suicide, found a relationship between it and a lack of belonging—anomie—offering the first proof of the significance of social bonds.

14. Research has found that even "people's memories of past rejections are tainted with anxiety . . . , and just imagining social rejection increases physiological arousal" (Baumeister and Leary 1995, 506).

15. William James, in his influential *Principles of Psychology* ([1890] 1983), suggests a relation between rejection (in itself shameful) and rage: "If no one turned round when we entered, answered when we spoke, or minded what we did, but if every person we met 'cut us dead,' and acted as if we were non-existing things, a kind of rage and impotent despair would ere long well up in us, from which the cruelest bodily torture would be a relief" (281).

16. Feeling traps other than shame and rage were documented, but the cycling of these two emotions arose most frequently in her data.

17. Interestingly, a growing body of research suggests that a reactive anger response does little to alleviate feelings of shame, which perhaps resurface over the outburst itself.

18. James Gilligan argues that "people resort to violence when they feel that they can wipe out shame only by shaming those who they feel shamed them. The most powerful way to shame anyone is by means of violence, just as the most powerful way to provoke anyone into committing violence is by shaming him" (2003, 1163).

19. The fuller series of studies conducted by Mark Leary and his associates (Leary et al. 2003; MacDonald and Leary 2005), as well as those by Twenge and colleagues (Twenge et al. 2001; Twenge and Campbell 2003; Twenge, Catanese, and Baumeister 2003), lend support to this contention.

20. "In videotapes made before the incident, the two Columbine shooters made several statements that were remarkably similar to items on the Narcissistic Personality Inventory [NPI; Twenge and Campbell 2003]. For example, Eric Harris said 'Isn't it fun to get the respect that we're going to deserve?', which is very similar to NPI Item 14, 'I insist upon getting the respect that is due me.' Harris also said, 'I could convince them that I'm going to climb Mount Everest, or I have a twin brother growing out of my back. I can make you believe anything,' which is strikingly similar to NPI Item 35, 'I can make anyone believe anything I want them to'" (Leary, Twenge, and Quinlivan 2006, 119).

21. In 2001, the surgeon general's report on youth violence found that weak social ties (e.g., rejection and exclusion) were the most significant risk factor for adolescent violence (U.S. Department of Health and Human Services 2001). This finding merely confirms Durkheim's research published in *Suicide* ([1897] 1997) over a century ago.

22. In keeping with violent impression management, Gilligan also reports that "one of the most common fantasies I have heard from many of the most violent prison inmates is the scenario of going to their deaths in a hail of gunfire while killing as many people as possible before they themselves die" (2003, 1150–1151).

23. In his 2011 article "Social-Emotional Origins of Violence: A Theory of Multiple Killing," Scheff elaborates this theory, connecting the dots between school shootings and unacknowledged shame. Importantly, he posits two kinds of recursive loops: a *social* loop of rejection and isolation, which goes hand in hand with Helen Lewis's (1971) *personal* loop of cycling feelings. Insofar as Scheff considers rejection and isolation to be intertwined with and critical to shame-rage feeling traps, his thinking is crucial to contemporary culture, which fosters these recursive (read, unredeemable) conditions and responses.

24. This is contrary to neurological findings discussed in Chapter 4 that contend that repeated exposure to social pain diminishes the capacity to feel, producing numbness.

25. Scheff is at pains to address pair killers such as Klebold and Harris. He does this by recourse to the writings of Murray Bowen (1978) and Norbert Elias (1978), who both speak to two types of alienation: that which results from isolation and the self-annihilation that comes with overidentification with another. This latter (engulfment) involves a comprehensive other-directedness, one that is invested solely in one other individual to whom one subordinates her own thoughts.

26. Should an individual be unable to preclude social exclusion following shaming, it might further impair an (already diminished) ability to make coherent choices. See Chapter 4; DeWall 2009; Twenge et al. 2007; DeWall and Baumeister 2006.

27. After extensive research (see Cullen 2009; Langman 2009), it appears that Harris met the clinical definition of a psychopath (or sociopath), as did Drew Golden. These personality disorders might have been aggravated by shame and humiliation.

28. Shaming in any formal fashion rarely occurs in contemporary society. Voluntary participation in AA meetings and rehab, which have clear affirmation of a higher (unspecified, moral) authority, as well as (voluntary) legal allocutions, are two clear instances in which humiliating, self-abasing public confession remains integral to participation in the program. Beyond this voluntary basis, it is worth noting that judges have begun to hand down public-shaming sentences, requiring offenders to make spectacles of themselves by publicly owning and advertising their misdemeanors (see, e.g., Matt Berman 2013).

29. While Suzanne Retzinger and Michael Lewis do not distinguish anger from aggression (allowing them to contend that "anger is a simple bodily response, whereas rage is a process, moving from shame to rage in alternative spiral fashion"), they do make additional distinctions that are quite significant: "Anger feels justified, whereas in rage one feels powerless. Injury is recognized in anger, but injury is denied in rage. Anger is conscious, whereas rage, based on shame substitution, is pushed from awareness. While anger may be easily resolved, rage, initiated by shame, sets up a feeling trap. . . . Anger is not displaced, whereas rage is. Anger focuses on the actual cause, whereas rage is a generalized response. Anger is an individual phenomenon, rage is a social phenomenon. Anger results in a few negative consequences, and rage results in many" (Lewis 1992, 153, paraphrasing Retzinger 1987). School shooters recognized injury, felt justified in their responses, and might or might not have been conscious of their shame, implying that this dichotomous, mutually exclusive ordering of definitions of anger and rage may be, in large part, a heuristic device.

30. This strength may also be linked to other factors. Research protocols support nine "possible explanations for the link between rejection and aggression: rejection as a source of pain, rejection as a source of frustration, rejection as a threat to self-esteem, mood improvement following aggression, aggression as social influence, aggression as a means of reestablishing efficacy and control, retribution, disinhibition, and loss of self-control. Most of these explanations have both conceptual and empirical support, and the current literature is inadequate to eliminate any of them. At present, it seems likely that rejection may lead to aggression via a number of independent routes, which may explain why the effect is so robust" (Leary, Twenge, and Quinlivan 2006, 124).

31. This rage may seem a bit puzzling in a world in which individuals establish their own reference groups. Not accepted by one? Find a better cohort online. Even with this potential, rage (e.g., road rage) seems chronic. Can it be explained in terms of a sense of entitlement (which unconditional love engenders)? When others do not acknowledge our entitlement they disrespect us. Perhaps because exclusion and shame interfere with higher-order cognitive functioning, there may be "a bias toward more automatic processing under [socially painful] circumstances. Thus, one response to social or physical pain appears to be a heavier reliance on more automatic cognitive processing, suggesting that both types of pain are treated as highly threatening, requiring a quick response" (MacDonald and Leary 2005, 214).

32. Barbara Herman and Jaak Panksepp first proposed such a conflation while studying separation distress in animals: "It is conceivable that brain circuits for 'separation distress' represent an evolutionary elaboration of an endorphin-based pain network" (1978, 219). In more recent studies using functional magnetic resonance imaging (MRI), "results revealed that social exclusion, compared to social inclusion, increased activation in the dorsal anterior cingulate cortex (dACC). The dACC is a region of the brain that functions to warn organisms of potential predators or other environmental factors that thwart their goals. . . . [Other studies] also demonstrated that social exclusion increased activation in the right ventral prefrontal cortex (rvPFC), which is a brain area that functions to regulate distress associated with physical pain and negative affect. Additional support for common neural overlap between social and physical pain systems can be found in neuroscience research on the periaqueductal grey (PAG) brain structures" (DeWall 2009, 206–207).

33. It is worth noting that in a study looking at gender and pain, distinct differences between men and women could be pointed to. "Although researchers found some overlapping areas of brain activation in men and women, several areas of male and female brains reacted differently when given the same pain stimulus. The female brain showed greater activity in limbic regions, which are emotion-based centers. In men, the cognitive regions, or analytical centers, showed greater activity" ("Gender Differences" 2003).

34. If chronic pain is defined as ongoing pain in the absence of tissue damage, might it not have social correlates (perhaps linked to stockpiled shame)? Although it is tempting to speculate on this, even preliminary research suggests that the overlap between sensory and psychological pain will have highly contested boundaries.

35. In conditions of exclusion, either future social isolation was predicted to subjects (on the basis of pseudo-surveys they completed) or they experienced rejection in some immediate capacity.

36. These protocols suggest that even the threat of pain calls out an analgesic response. Such findings may lead researchers to revise their hypothesis, perhaps correlating a freeze response to (threatened) social trauma. This would translate as a shutting down of the organism, a deadening and numbness, which may present as depression. Although the freeze response is also a hardwired, it has no direct bearing on the shame-

rage cycle that I am looking to interrupt (and may itself be addressed by the interruption of rumination—see Chapter 4).

37. This finding is the opposite of what would be predicted on the basis of extensive research on recurring physical pain. Literature on nociception and on chronic pain documents that pain thresholds *decrease*, not increase, in response to nociceptive activity and to central nervous system activity associated with persistent pain states. That is, endorphin release does not lead to the deadening that DeWall, Baumeister, and their colleagues associate with an increased pain threshold (itself a new steady state). Rather, over time, the central nervous system (CNS) situation that led to the increase in endorphin release changes, and endorphin release changes correspondingly. Even if endorphin release were maintained, the endorphin receptor receptivity for the endorphin molecule changes, and it becomes less receptive, which is referred to as adaptation. This is why people increase their dosage of opiate drugs to have the same level of analgesia: the receptors adapt to the current level of opiate medication (an extrinsic endorphin), and so the medication has to be increased.

In short, even though social pain has been shown to activate the same circuits as physical pain, it appears that the way the other CNS circuits continue to act on that pain experience are different from the way somatic circuits continue to act on physical pain. This is indicated in findings in which repeated social damage appears to decrease sensitivity, while exactly the opposite, an increase in sensitivity, holds for repeated experience of physical pain. (I am indebted to Richard Ohrbach for alerting me to this literature and for discussing pain and chronic pain with me.)

38. In addition to these studies' innumerable variables, keep in mind that analyses of these dynamics are linked to professionals' varying perspectives, biases, and emphases: "Neuroscientists have stressed the importance of emotional insensitivity as a predictor of irrational and self-defeating decision-making. . . . [P]eople with lesions to the ventromedial prefrontal cortex (vmPFC) appear unable to make rational decisions and to learn from their mistakes. . . . Clinical psychologists have focused on the role of emotional insensitivity as a predictor of suboptimal responding, namely aggressive behavior. People who have deficits in emotional reactivity tend to engage in more frequent and severe acts of violence" (DeWall 2009, 215).

39. A. W. Crescioni and Roy Baumeister further clarify, noting that common sense tells us that rejected individuals should show *increased* attempts at self-regulation to reestablish connections and prevent further rejection. "The observed drop in self-regulation therefore seems maladaptive. The explanation for [this] finding lies in rejection's effect on self-awareness. Self-awareness is an important prerequisite of conscious self-control" (2009, 266).

40. Even Hester Prynne, who was certainly guilty of a heinous transgression in her society, was not cut off and excommunicated. Daily acknowledgement of her shame, her *A*, was itself the *condition of her continued connection to the community*. She lived on the fringes, taking in piecework, and those who condemned her were compelled, by her daily act of repentance, to acknowledge her and perhaps even forgive her.

41. Shame has been a hot topic in psychology for over three decades, and understandably, the hypotheses that have emerged and research that has been produced are somewhat inconsistent in both their definitions and their findings. The base distinction I employ, rooted in Helen Lewis's work, is fundamental to much of this research and dominant in the discipline.

42. Tangney and Dearing (2003) argue that an individual tends to be prone to either shame *or* guilt and that such proneness is an identifiable character trait.

43. Tangney and Dearing argue that "people's implicit theories of the self seem especially relevant to the experience of shame or guilt" (2003, 66). That is, the authors separate individuals into categories (using scales they developed to determine shame proneness vs. guilt proneness) and consider one or the other a reflection of the flexibility of self.

44. Considered in this light, guilt seems more aligned with Goffman's (1959) concept of impression management and the social self, while shame appears to relate more closely to backstage, or personal, even ontological, self.

45. The authors even argue that "guilt causes people to act in ways that will be beneficial to relationships, such as expressing affection, paying attention, and refraining from transgressions. . . . [An additional] function of guilt is as an influence technique. One person may get his or her way by making the other feel guilty. . . . The third function of guilt is to redistribute emotional distress. . . . [T]he transgressor's guilt may make the victim feel better" (1994, 256–257).

46. This shame is hidden despite civilizing tendencies requiring a thousandfold increase in shame-driven behaviors. Consider Norbert Elias's historical analysis of the civilizing process, which Scheff and Retzinger cite to uphold their claim: "By examining instance after instance of advice concerning etiquette—especially table manners, body functions, sexuality, and anger—[Elias] suggests that a key aspect of modernity involves a veritable explosion of shame" (1991, 9). Thus, even as the potential for shame increases, shame acknowledgement and, concomitantly, thresholds have decreased.

47. Restorative justice focuses on the personal needs of the victims and the offenders, as well as the broader needs of the community. A dialogue between victims and offenders, in which reparation is negotiated, is central to this process. Offenders are encouraged to assume responsibility for their actions, offer apologies, and make attempts at reparation, thereby enabling the community, if not victims, to extend terms of forgiveness.

48. Braithwaite, a distinguished criminologist at Australian National University, gives special attention to the terms of shame management (1989). Harry Blagg (1997) has challenged his critique of the criminal justice system on several fronts, most notably its claim for universalism and its foundation in an assumed consensus.

49. Note that an acknowledgement of shame need not include an acknowledgement of culpability on the part of the victim or entail forgiveness on the part of the bystander. It affirms an experience of humiliation, of having others believe one is culpable, of suffering a scornful and perhaps wrongful gaze. Although Scheff and Retzinger argue that "for shame to occur, one must place at least part of the blame on oneself" (1991, 44), it seems that the process of publicly accusing and derogating an individual in instances of bullying, which manipulate information—or promulgate misinformation—can itself be humiliating. The experience can be more readily recovered from if there is no culpability, but to have character indictments and questions of integrity raised in the minds of others—doubts that may be given credence—can be shameful. Acknowledging shame to bystanders risks their conflating humiliation with an admission of culpability, of having shame itself brandished as certification of an individual's guilt and an additional weapon turned on her, the victim. When culpability is involved, this may seem just consequence, suffering through it seem an attempt to restore connection by submitting to penance, which will allow one to be redeemed.

50. This quotation comes from the foreword, which is by Braithwaite, but it is his summation of Scheff and Retzinger's project. To attribute the quotation to him here would misleadingly appear to credit him with their particular re-visioning.

51. With the exception of Francis Broucek, none of the authors cited in this chapter attempt to account for the "cultur[al] heroes offered the young—. . . [who] are mostly

noteworthy for their pride in their aggressiveness, crudity, narcissism, and general boor-ishness—traits that would have been cause for shame in former times" (Broucek 1991, 135). This trend seems to be about more than denied shame or its current availability in language games, and Broucek goes on to argue that "hypocritically, we as a society fail to acknowledge the *economic reasons* for not cleaning up our act and pretend that it is only our great respect for the constitutional right of free speech and aversion to censorship that make us tolerate the rot eating away at the core of our culture" (1991, 139; emphasis added).

52. Interestingly, the twelfth season of *Project Runway* featured two rage-aholic contestants, who pitched frightening, violent tantrums at the perception of disrespect from judges or fellow contestants. Was the airing of this behavior meant to entertain us? Caution us? Or was it just the irresponsibility that can be claimed by reality TV? On the other side of the spectrum, the NFL penalizes players for taunting, publicly denouncing any team member who attempts to humiliate and enrage an opponent, leveling a consequence at the entire team.

CHAPTER 4

1. In an article titled "Grief, Bonds, and Relationships" (2001), Robert Weiss argues that bonds underlying primary relationships are "attachment bonds," while those underlying other, secondary relationships are "affiliative bonds." Attachment bonds are irreplaceable, while affiliative bonds are multiple and interchangeable and often can be interrupted without great suffering and loss. In other words, the nature of these bonds is qualitatively different. Weiss argues that the loss of an attachment bond will call out grief, while the loss of an affiliative bond will produce only distress and sadness. While the qualitative differences Weiss posits may be valid, the conclusions that he arrives at are overly simplified and do not necessarily follow from these differences.

2. Even the added investment to be found in rivalries should not call out the confused sense of loss incurred by death or divorce (see Kilduff, Elfenbein, and Staw 2010).

3. As June Tangney and Rhonda Dearing note, "The shamed individual is [often] still left with the problem of a hopelessly defective self" (2002, 92).

4. Interestingly, more than one scholar has contended that, as Lyn Lofland put it, "the decline of well-developed death rituals has pathologically extended grief's 'normal course'" (Lofland 1985, 173).

5. "Feeling rules" are derived from Arlie Hochschild's seminal work on the culture of emotions (1979, 1983). They are culturally normative indicators of the appropriate experience and expression of an emotion. Hochschild also argues for "framing rules" to be considered part of our "emotion culture." Through these, culture informs us of the meanings we should give to situations.

6. See the seminal articles by Steven Gordon, "The Sociology of Sentiments and Emotion" (1981), and Arlie Hochschild, "Emotion Work, Feeling Rules, and Social Structure" (1979).

7. Freud understood the pain of loss in terms of an "unsatisfiable cathexis" ([1926] 1959, 172), whereby what was released in relationship with the individual must find other outlets. Until this can be done, the energy will press on the individual's psyche, causing pain (grief). The bereaved may initially introject the lost object and identify with it in an attempt to preserve the bond, but this is ultimately unsatisfactory and will need to be overcome.

8. Note the ready parallels to illness narratives, remissions, and their aim of getting well.

9. Darcy Harris argues that the market economy places great pressure on individuals to "make a quick return to functionality" and that such expectations oppress those who are suffering loss (2009–2010, 249). However, they do not want to be further cut off from relationships by failing to conform to cultural expectations regarding expression of grief or the time it takes to negotiate the loss.

10. In response to such charges, scholars have countered that, fully understood, stage theories are descriptive but have been decontextualized and treated as prescriptive, often in service of an oversimplified, medicalized template (Samarel 1995). John Steiner furthers this position, arguing that stage theories are not a prescription to "come to terms with the reality of the loss" by systematically letting go but instead reflect a recognition of the interdependent boundaries that require renegotiation. "As reality is applied to each of the memories of the lost object what has to be faced is the painful recognition of what belongs to the object and what belongs to the self. It is through the detailed work of mourning that these differentiations are made and in the process the lost object is seen more realistically and the previously disowned parts of the self are gradually acknowledged as belonging to the self" (1996, 1077).

11. Dennis Klass, Phyllis Silverman, and Steven Nickman (1996) note that even Freud was unwilling (or unable) to put the loss of his daughter at age twenty-seven or his grandson at age four behind him. Neil Small (2001) takes issue with their argument on the grounds that the authors privilege a reading of Freud's personal correspondence, elevating "the letters to the status of 'truth' apparently on the grounds that they encompass the subjective" (24). This critique may be more telling of theories of postmodernity than merely of Klass and colleagues' critique.

12. For a chilling description of this process, see Margaret Atwood's *Cat's Eye* (1989).

13. Note that reconceptualizations of grief and grieving hardly preclude the possibility of bereaved individuals becoming stuck in their processing or negotiating loss in maladaptive ways.

14. However, as Lou Taylor (1983) and Tony Walter (2007) have noted, this process began significantly earlier than Stroebe and Schut's dual process model (2001) and can be linked to the emancipation of women. In fact, "the requirements of mourning were one way in which Victorian women had been kept in their place by a patriarchal society. If the modern woman is to grieve not as dictated by society but as she personally feels, then she needs not to be under external surveillance; hence her grief needs to be private" (Walter 2007, 126).

15. As numerous authors have noted, there is a dual meaning to meaning: meaning as sense making and meaning as significance. The two are not unrelated.

16. "I worry about what I've said today, the expression on my face, how I walk, what I wear, because all of these things need improvement. I am not normal, I am not like other girls. Cordelia tells me so, but she will help me, Grace and Carol will help me too. It will take hard work and a long time" (Atwood 1989, 125).

17. For the emotional violence and loss associated with bullying behavior to be identified and acknowledged, there must remain some part of the self that is not defined by the incident, that can do the witnessing and acknowledging. Her voice is the site of resistance, echoed and reinforced through expressive writing.

18. Girls and women are particularly susceptible to this downward cycle, not only because social arrangements leave them few other options but because women experience less control of their environment than men and are responsible for fewer activities that afford a sense of mastery. They frequently work in support positions for lower wages, simultaneously overseeing household chores, child care, sick care, and elder

care. Numerous sites for potential failure increase her opportunities to feel inadequate, familiarizing her with the dynamics of self-doubt and rumination. Unseen interrelated stressors do more than "contribute additively to women's greater vulnerability to depressive symptoms. Chronic strain, low mastery, and rumination *contribute to each other* as well, keeping women bound in a cycle of low control over their environments and frequent experiences of depressive symptoms" (Nolen-Hoeksema, Larson, and Grayson 1999, 1061–1072; emphasis added). Interrelated stressors expose women to increased opportunities to become overwhelmed and break down. Perhaps this chronic condition and social expectations of femininity (maintaining connection) contribute to responses that include more frequent advice seeking in their attempts at coping (see Orbuch 1992, 198). Because of their greater susceptibility, they have developed support structures to assist in the processing of negativities associated with helplessness and threats to self.

19. For a discussion of links between empathy and helping behavior, see Decety and Ickes 2009 and Batson 1991. More recently, the *Smithsonian* ran an article on recent findings that suggest empathy, long believed to be a learned, social emotion, may have distinct biological roots (Tucker 2013).

20. See J. Gilligan 1996. Once self is lost, or deadened, any number of sociopathic responses become possible.

21. Alcohol and drug use are often related to pain management, no less than promiscuity may be related to coping with belongingness needs, belying the pain of rejection. And as long as these behaviors are in the service of pain negotiation, Just Say No programs and calls for sexual abstinence cannot possibly be effective.

22. New, pragmatic role tasks do not fall to victims of changed social status within schools. The distraction of immediate demands (moving, paying bills, sorting belongings) and the support of others that facilitates coping strategies are not available to those navigating fun house mirrors in cafeterias, hallways, and buses.

23. Noting that the scale "has been criticised for the fact that many of the items confound rumination with reports of depression symptoms," researchers argue that, in conflating the two, cause and effect became muddled and led to findings that could not clearly assess distinctions between self-reflective and passive aspects of rumination. In particular, numerous items on the scale contained "fairly striking self-critical or judgmental statements—e.g., 'Why do I always react this way?'; 'Why do I have problems others don't have?'" (Rude, Maestas, and Neff 2007, 845).

24. By sorting items on the scale in terms of phrasing (implied self-criticism leading to brooding or detached contemplation leading to reflection), the researchers confirmed a pattern that allowed them to characterize responses on the basis of the way the question itself was formulated and framed. A second phase of the experiment reworded the questions, neutralizing the wording of the RRS, and again assessed responses. The researchers found that if the degree of self-judgment implied by the questions was reduced and respondents were encouraged to distance themselves from evaluative judgments and assumptions that often cloak events associated with unhappiness, the productive aspects of rumination—reflection and the ability to cognitively and emotionally process the event—were enhanced.

25. Note that the *ongoing* nature of trauma that results from bullying may mitigate the extent to which reconfiguring and cognitive reorganization is possible.

26. Because these global responses appear unreflective, common wisdom would suggest that a victim's employment of them is linked to denial and suppression—not grieving and not acknowledging or processing her pain. However, recent research suggests

otherwise. Individuals who do not preoccupy themselves with *why* questions do not necessarily suffer the consequences of denial or become psychically overextended by suppression. This is a startling, radical idea that emerged in studies of bereavement coping (Davis et al. 2000). Researchers noticed that a minority of bereaved individuals did not seek meaning for their loss (instead ascribing it to God's will or simply accepting loss as part of life). Surprisingly, "those persons who sought answers to no avail fared worse in their adjustment to the loss than did those who never sought answers in the first place (14% of sample)" (Neimeyer 2000c, 549).

27. On a larger scale, Elspeth Probyn notes that "any politics not interested in those placed beyond its ken [e.g., victims of bullying] will continue to be a politics of shaming: a bastion of moral reproach. And that is shameful" (2005, 106). This echoes Kenneth Doka's disenfranchised grief (1989, 2002).

CHAPTER 5

1. This cultural blindness is also reflected in the invisibility of oppressed *groups*. These unseen races, classes, or social aggregates have often sidestepped their experiences of shame, focusing instead on the identification of other ready intelligibilities, such as rage at their common oppressors, or they have, like Alcoholics Anonymous, developed their own language, through which they build community. Even the experience of being cut off from society, the pain of severed bonds (or the numbness that replaces it), requires integration in the self and brain.

2. This recalls one of the positive functions attributed to stage theories in Chapter 4.

3. See Dan Wegner's well-known book *White Bears and Other Unwanted Thoughts* (1994). Also see Fivush 1998. Such intrusions are not in themselves a bad thing, as this is how new, novel experiences are massaged into existing self-stories.

4. The mind-body link Pennebaker has spent years researching was brought to his attention through work with polygraphers. Through them, he became familiar with what he came to call the polygraph confession effect, or the physical changes that register on monitoring equipment once a confession is made. Revealing pent-up thoughts and feelings relaxes the body and is experienced as liberating.

5. Terri Orbuch (1992) advises that it is important to cultivate one's voice (i.e., perspective) *throughout* experiences of suffering and of loss—even, it appears, at the occasional risk of slipping into rumination.

6. "Labeling emotions correlates with decreased amygdala response and an increase in right prefrontal activation" (Cozolino 2010, 168).

7. These observations have largely been made in relation to individuals whose experiences of trauma are in the *past*, with writing exercises engaging their pain center around responses to *a particular event*. It may be that they become more detached through writing itself. George Herbert Mead (1934) argues that in this process, raw experiences are transformed into abstractions. Will similar findings and benefits hold for instances of bullying, which are ongoing and can seem relatively undifferentiated as temporal events (the unintegrated now)?

8. Victims of bullying are not always sympathetic characters. For example, they may be unable to interpret social cues, leading others to distance themselves from what is perceived to be inappropriate behaviors, ones that, perhaps, do not follow norms regarding appropriate topics of conversation, speaking volume, the give and take of a conversation, and so on.

9. Even if stories were available, the tendency to blame self remains a threat (self-scrutiny *is* the response to the mirroring of others). And self-judgments prevent "indi-

viduals from fully accessing the range of potential perspectives and emotional experiences that might otherwise be available to them, and thereby preventing reorganization and resolution of problematic emotional experience" (Gortner, Rude, and Pennebaker 2006, 300).

10. Experiments that replicate Pennebaker's work but control for variables other than rumination, such as gender (Nolen-Hoeksema and Jackson 2001), predispositions for neuroticism or depression (Gortner, Rude, and Pennebaker 2006), and the aspect of the experience that claims the attention of the victim (Lepore et al. 2002), have also added to our understanding of the benefits of expressive writing. Results of these protocols include the finding that formal expressive writing exercises are most beneficial to those who have a tendency to suppress their emotions (as opposed to girls who keep daily journals).

11. Coping strategies rely, in part, on individuals' expectation that they *will* help positively regulate the depressive affects related to the experience (see Catanzaro and Greenwood 1994; Catanzaro, Horaney, and Creasey 1995; Scheier, Carver, and Bridges 2001; Scheier and Carver 2003). Additional factors have a role in mediating the condition of expectancy (see, for example, Rusk, Tamir, and Rothbaum 2011).

12. This finding emerged in protocols that specifically studied the effects of expressive writing on rumination and depressive symptoms (see Gortner, Rude, and Pennebaker 2006). Chapter 4 notes the parallels and correlations between these findings and the paradoxical aspects of rumination.

13. Journals and diaries often reflect her attempts to do this, to sort and contain her unstoried, incomprehensible experiences through writing.

14. This difference translates into an inability, in chaotic states, to conceptualize a controllable future or even to construe the meaning of another individual's actions.

15. Gestures of social support are not necessarily *endorsements* of personal traits or behaviors. They are responses aimed at the nature and extent of social cruelties leveled at a victim, as opposed to a championing of her personal attributes or actions.

16. Whether language is seen as determining and colonizing human subjectivity, it sets the stage for a story, breaking the silence that surrounds chaos. Silence holds chaos.

17. Recall (from Chapter 4) that one of the benefits of moving beyond stage theories is that "no expert or well-meaning family member can tell the mourner what is 'normal' after, say, six months" (Walter 2007, 132).

18. C. Nathan DeWall offers concrete suggestions aimed at reducing the suffering of victims. Rooted in expressive writing exercises, they are intended to foster a sense of acceptance, thereby reducing negative effects of bullying, and include (1) instructing targets to call to mind a period of their life when they felt most accepted and in focusing on it mitigate the global assumptions that often follow repeated rejection; (2) encouraging victims to "consider their experience of being bullied at a high level of meaning, namely by thinking of how small of a part of their entire life their experience of being bullied really took up"; and (3) having all students engage in activities that promote mindfulness, or "intentionally attending to current experiences in a nonjudgmental and accepting manner" (2009, 219). These suggestions have the potential to prompt comprehensive cognitive change.

19. For specific exploration of expressive writing with children and adolescents, see Utley and Garza 2011 and DeGangi and Nemiroff 2010.

20. If something that can be described as 'factual reality' exists, we certainly have no way of accessing it. Even contemporary audio and video technology cannot provide information independent of our perceptions, interpretations, and memories, as these artifacts themselves are open to continual reappraisal, re-evaluation, and reinterpretation.

21. And if we are forging notions of ourselves, autobiographical memory must be "understood as a process of personal reconstruction [rather] than one of faithful reconstitution. Because this reconstruction is embedded within the broader developmental

context of the evolving self, processes of self-construction are inextricably linked to autobiographical memory recall" (Neimeyer and Metzler 1994, 105).

22. An additional dimension that must be factored into this process is that the creative configuration that comes to the fore as a memory is shaped by the very specific repositionings mandated by circumstance. *What* particulars we recall is a function of the intentionality underlying the act of bringing the past to mind. For example, when I discover, via a newspaper article, that Cecilia B. Bully has been arrested on assault charges, I remember all the deviant things she did in high school and am smugly not surprised. But when my daughter comes home devastated after a very public run-in with one of her classmates, I remember instead how crushed and humiliated I felt when Cecilia teased me in front of everyone. In retrieving information, individuals re-create it within the context of the situation in which it is recalled and along the lines of their current beliefs, interests, and overall perspective.

23. As Greg Neimeyer and April Metzler note, in this view "recollection is, ontologically speaking, wholly contingent upon comprehension, and developmental shifts in comprehension would therefore necessarily influence autobiographical recollection" (Neimeyer and Metzler 1994, 107).

24. Creating and manipulating tangential or other-centered written artifacts may help illustrate how easily one piece of information might change a person's perspective— even if she *is* culpable—loosening global indictments and the identities forming around them.

25. This is, admittedly, more difficult if the individual remains trapped in an unsafe, hostile, or even abusive environment. Small gestures by bystanders might go far toward creating the security and impetus necessary to exploring differing outcomes through expressive writing.

26. In this piece, Ada Calhoun deconstructs her own memories of being bullied in the face of evidence that she was, in fact, a pretty, popular girl. Is the passage of time, coupled with the "I was a victim of bullying" zeitgeist, responsible for this transformation, or did she actually feel like a victim at the time and has come to privilege that feeling?

27. Susan Brison, speaking from traumatic personal experience, writes that "to construct self-narratives we need not only the words with which to tell our stories, but also an audience able and willing to hear us and to understand our words as we intend them" (2002, 51; emphasis added).

28. I am indebted to Richard Holloway and his arguments in *Godless Morality: Keeping Religion Out of Ethics* (1999) for this metaphor.

CHAPTER 6

1. Note that *all* interviewees stated that intervention on the part of an adult—even a private, one-on-one acknowledgment of the pain and suffering being experienced— would have made a significant difference in their processing of torment. About half could point to a specific incident when an adult did come to their rescue; most could still, years later, recall even small gestures of support.

2. The concept of "emotional contagion" in Gustave Le Bon's ([1897] 1960) well-known treatise on crowds eradicates "conscious personality." Bullying may or may not call such contagion into play. Certainly scapegoating is indicative of such a dynamic, as behaviors aroused by shared sentiments often meld into a common mind-set, a highly suggestible herd mentality that may be integral to the mobbing of victims in cyberspace.

3. Erving Goffman contends that "the first set of sympathetic others is of course those who share his stigma" (1963, 20). The basis for sympathy—for investment in

other—is grounded in identification with them and familiarity with their social plight. But it seems clear that *identification need not lead to relationship*. Similarly deficient individuals may be the very last people willing to acknowledge identification with victims in a culture in which shame is hidden and its pain disenfranchised. They may, in fact, deny similarities and seek to differentiate themselves from victims.

4. John Eckenrode and Elaine Wethington also note that these contingencies include "position in the social structure: gender, age, life-cycle stage, ethnicity, and social status" (1990, 99).

5. On March 13, 1964, Kitty Genovese returned home to her apartment at 3:15 A.M. As she walked to her door, she was overtaken by an assailant and repeatedly stabbed, left for dead, and then attacked again. The *New York Times* article that ran, two weeks later, began, "For more than half an hour 38 respectable, law-abiding citizens in Queens watched a killer stalk and stab a woman in three separate attacks in Kew Gardens" (Gansberg 1964). While this account of the Genovese murder is misleading (it was a cold evening and windows were closed, muffling sounds—was it a struggle or a lover's quarrel?—and the initial attack is said to have punctured a lung, affecting Genovese's ability to scream), the perceived indifference of her neighbors received tremendous publicity and had an enormous national impact. Close on its heels was the 1965 knifing of seventeen-year-old Andrew Mormile on a New York subway. Here too, none of the onlookers (passengers on the train) intervened.

6. Kevin Cook's new book states of the bystanders in Genovese's murder that "in the most popular account there were thirty-eight of them. In another there were thirty-seven. In another there were only two or three" (2014, 3–4).

7. Decades before measurements of affect response through brain activity were possible, Goffman (1959) contended that situations causing public embarrassment to the individual make those who witness it uncomfortable, cueing their response. Goffman's claims might be linked, by extension, to Mead's (1934) well-known analysis of symbols. Mead argues that the symbol arouses in the individual making it the same kind of response that it elicits from those to whom it is addressed. These responses may be indicative of a link between emotional contagion and mirror neurons. Functional mechanisms in our brains allow us to unreflectively take the place of the other—in fact, to embody simulation. Observing someone else's plight recruits brain regions responsible for similar response, suggesting that bystanders are far from indifferent.

8. As it is unethical, if not impossible, to victimize subjects in any acute way, conclusive findings may be difficult to arrive at.

9. The recommendation of unsolicited support might take the form of advising a professional that an individual is in need of attention. Behavioral specialists are not precluded in support for victims (although their interventions, if not carefully couched, might further stigmatize victims). Professionals can work in tandem with bystanders and teachers, maintaining pride in the victim's ability to cope, yet perhaps sponsoring forums in which accounts might be exchanged, stories emerge, and support groups form.

10. Whether cyberbullying is an extension of traditional bullying or possesses unique characteristics and effects is still hotly debated. Dan Olweus (2012) sees great overlap, while other researchers, using differing definitions of cyberbullying (no single definition has been endorsed), have arrived at different conclusions. For an overview, see Bonanno and Hymel 2013 and Wingate, Minney, and Guadagno 2013.

11. The movie (and MTV-sponsored reality show) *Catfish* illustrates the extent to which online manipulations of data can confound the information (and cues) that face-to-face interaction supplies—especially if participants are unknown to each other.

12. "Uncertainty reduction through information seeking is virtually impossible in the cyberbullying context" (Pure 2009, 45).

13. Winnicott goes on to further claim that "there is a direct development from transitional phenomena to playing, and from playing to shared playing, and from this to cultural experiences" (1971, 51).

14. The transposition of MUD and MOO (multiuser dungeon, or dimension, and multiuser-dimension object-oriented) formats to chat rooms further muddles boundaries, creating heightened vulnerability in these arenas. Mimicking multiplayer accessibility and real-time actions, these unstructured forums all but *erase* fragments of correspondence between cyberworlds and reality. Moreover, in allowing for impersonation without an immediately identifiable digital footprint, they encourage social irresponsibility and may even facilitate a mob mentality. Although any accessible cybersite can become an arena for cruel spectator sport (the bystander effect in cyberspace, perhaps), chat rooms are particularly ripe for cyberabuse.

15. The right to be forgotten is considered by some a basic human right, and some courts in the European Union and Argentina have upheld this view. This right allows individuals to delete photos, information, and videos of themselves from Internet records, preventing them from being called up by a search engine in the future.

16. Ori Schwarz is prescient in noting that psychological definitions of intimacy "usually miss the fact that intimate interactions and relationships are always defined relative to the remainder of social interactions" (2011, 75).

17. This includes the role of secrecy, the sharing of which, Georg Simmel ([1908] 1955) notes, is an act that produces value, becoming a building block to intimacy.

APPENDIX B

1. Kotsko continues, "[This stands in stark opposition to] white theology [which] is dominated by abstraction, granting abstract authority to the Bible while missing its key message and reducing the Christian life to a matter of abstract internal dispositions with no relation to actual social conditions" (2010, 36).

2. According to Rise Jane Samra, "Whenever a person rejects the traditional hierarchy, he/she feels as if he/she fails and consequently acquires a feeling of guilt. [Kenneth] Burke compared rejection to original sin and he believed that guilt is inherent in society because people cannot accept all of the traditional hierarchy with all the demands it places on them. When conditions change, rejection of some of the tradition occurs. Each social institution—family, church, school, clubs, relationships, and political systems— has its own hierarchy. When the demands imposed by one hierarchy conflict with those of another, rejection is inevitable (Burke 1965)" (Samra 1998).

APPENDIX C

1. Is there a gendered component to the experiencing itself that facilitates hiving in men (resting on compartmentalization, which psychologists tell us men are better at)?

APPENDIX F

1. All teen magazines, from *Tiger Beat* to *YM* to *Teen*, have, for some time, included a most-embarrassing-moments column (for example, *YM*'s "It Happened to Me" and "Say Anything" features, *Teen*'s "Why Me?," or *Tiger Beat*'s "OMG Stories.")

REFERENCES

The works in this list that are not explicitly cited in the book were consulted for additional information and informed the author's analysis.

Ahmed, Eliza, Nathan Harris, John Braithwaite, and Valerie Braithwaite. 2001. *Shame Management through Reintegration*. New York: Cambridge University Press.

Allport, Gordon. 1954. *The Nature of Prejudice*. New York: Perseus Books.

Anderson, Benedict. (1983) 1991. *Imagined Communities*. London: Verso.

Asch, Solomon E. 1946. "Forming Impressions of Personalities." *Journal of Abnormal and Social Psychology* 41:258–290.

Atwood, Margaret. 1989. *Cat's Eye*. New York: Anchor Books.

Aulén, Gustav. 1931. *Christus Victor: An Historical Study of the Three Main Types of the Idea of the Atonement*. Translated by A. G. Herbert. London: Society for Promoting Christian Knowledge.

Averill, James R. 1982. *Anger and Aggression: An Essay on Emotion*. New York: Springer-Verlag.

Barclay, Craig R. 1986. "Schematization of Autobiographical Memory." In *Autobiographical Memory*, edited by David C. Rubin, 82–99. Cambridge: Cambridge University Press

———. 1994. "Composing Protoselves through Improvisation." In *The Remembering Self: Construction and Accuracy in the Self-Narrative*, edited by Ulrich Neisser and Robyn Fivush, 55–77. Cambridge: Cambridge University Press.

Barrett, Karen Caplovitz, and G. Christina Nelson-Goens. 1997. "Emotion Communication and the Development of the Social Emotions." *New Directions for Child and Adolescent Development*, no. 77: 69–88.

Bartky, Sandra L. 1990. *Femininity and Domination: Studies in the Phenomenology of Oppression*. New York: Routledge.

Bartlett, Frederic C. 1934. *Remembering: A Study in Experimental and Social Psychology*. Cambridge: Cambridge University Press.

Bateup, Helen S., Alan Booth, Elizabeth A. Shirtcliff, and Douglas A. Granger. 2002. "Testosterone, Cortisol, and Women's Competition." *Evolution and Human Behavior* 23 (3): 181–192.

Batson, C. Daniel. 1991. *The Altruism Question: Toward a Social-Psychological Answer.* Hillsdale, NJ: Erlbaum.

Baudrillard, Jean. 1983. *Simulations.* Translated by Phil Beitchman, Paul Foss, and Paul Patton. New York: Semiotext(e).

Baumeister, Roy. 1997. *Evil: Inside Human Violence and Cruelty.* New York: Holt.

Baumeister, Roy F., and C. Nathan DeWall. 2005. "The Inner Dimension of Social Exclusion: Intelligent Thought and Self-regulation among Rejected Persons." In *The Social Outcast: Ostracism, Social Exclusion, Rejection, and Bullying,* edited by Kipling D. Williams, Joseph P. Forgas, and William von Hippel, 53–74. New York: Psychology Press.

Baumeister, Roy F., and Mark R. Leary. 1995. "The Need to Belong: Desire for Interpersonal Attachments as a Fundamental Human Motivation." *Psychological Bulletin* 117 (3): 497–529.

Baumeister, Roy F., Arlene M. Stillwell, and Todd F. Heatherton. 1995. "Interpersonal Aspects of Guilt: Evidence from Narrative Studies." In *Self-conscious Emotions: The Psychology of Shame, Guilt, Embarrassment, and Pride,* edited by June Price Tangney and Kurt W. Fischer, 255–271. New York: Guilford Press.

Bazelon, Emily. 2013. *Sticks and Stones: Defeating the Culture of Bullying and Rediscovering the Power of Character and Empathy.* New York: Random House.

Bellah, Robert N., Richard Madsen, William M. Sullivan, Ann Swidler, and Steven M. Tipton. 1985. *Habits of the Heart: Individualism and Commitment in American Life.* Berkeley: University of California Press.

Berger, Peter L., and Thomas Luckmann. 1967. *The Social Construction of Reality: A Treatise in the Sociology of Knowledge.* New York: Anchor Books.

Berman, Matt. 2013. "The 7 Craziest Public-Shaming Sentences Given by U.S. Judges." *National Journal,* September 9. Available at http://www.nationaljournal.com/pictures-video/the-7-craziest-public-shaming-sentences-given-by-u-s-judges-2013 0909.

Berman, Morris. 2006. *The Twilight of American Culture.* New York: W. W. Norton.

Billig, Michael. 2001. "Humor and Embarrassment: Limits of 'Nice-Guy' Theories of Social Life." *Theory, Culture and Society* 18 (23): 23–43.

———. 2005. *Laughter and Ridicule: Toward a Social Critique of Humour.* London: Sage.

Blagg, Harry 1997. "A Just Measure of Shame: Aboriginal Youth and Conferencing in Australia." *British Journal of Criminology* 37:481–503.

Bobbitt, David A. 2007. *The Rhetoric of Redemption: Kenneth Burke's Redemption Drama and Martin Luther King, Jr.'s "I Have a Dream" Speech.* Lanham, MD: Rowman and Littlefield.

Bollmer, Julie M., Richard Milich, Monica J. Harris, and Melissa A. Maras. 2005. "A Friend in Need: The Role of Friendship Quality as a Protective Factor in Peer Victimization and Bullying." *Journal of Interpersonal Violence* 20 (6): 701–712.

Bonanno, Rina, and Shelley Hymel. 2013. "Cyber Bullying and Internalizing Difficulties: Above and Beyond the Impact of Traditional Forms of Bullying." *Journal of Youth and Adolescence* 42 (5): 685–697.

Bowen, Murray. 1978. *Family Therapy in Clinical Practice.* New York: Jason Aaronson.

Bowlby, John. 1969. *Attachment.* Vol. 1 of *Attachment and Loss.* London: Hogarth.

Boyd, Danah, and Alice Marwick. 2011. "Bullying as True Drama." *New York Times,* September 22. Available at http://www.nytimes.com/2011/09/23/opinion/why-cyber bullying-rhetoric-misses-the-mark.html?_r=0.

Braithwaite, John. 1989. *Crime, Shame and Reintegration.* Cambridge: Cambridge University Press.

Brison, Susan. 2002. *Aftermath: Violence and the Remaking of a Self.* Princeton, NJ: Princeton University Press.

Broucek, Francis. 1991. *Shame and the Self.* New York: Guilford Press.

Brown, Steven P., William L. Cron, and John W. Slocum Jr. 1998. "Effects of Trait Competitiveness and Perceived Intraorganizational Competition on Salesperson Goal Setting and Performance." *Journal of Marketing* 62 (4): 88–98.

Bruner, Jerome. 1994. "The 'Remembered' Self." In *The Remembering Self: Construction and Accuracy in the Self-narrative,* edited by Ulric Neisser and Robyn Fivush, 41–54. Cambridge: Cambridge University Press.

Buranelli, Vincent. 1975. *The Wizard from Vienna: Franz Anton Mesmer.* New York: Coward, McCann and Geoghegan.

Burke, Kenneth. 1965. *Permanence and Change.* Indianapolis, IN: Bobbs-Merrill.

Calhoun, Ada. 2011. "Geekdom Revisited." *New York Times,* July 29. Available at http://www.nytimes.com/2011/07/31/magazine/lives-geekdom-revisited.html?_r=0.

Calhoun, Lawrence G., and Richard G. Tedeschi. 2001. "Posttraumatic Growth: The Positive Lessons of Loss." In *Meaning Reconstruction and the Experience of Loss,* edited by Robert A. Neimeyer, 157–172. Washington, DC: American Psychological Association.

Carrette, Jeremy, and Richard King. 2005. *Selling Spirituality: The Silent Takeover of Religion.* New York: Routledge.

Catanzaro, Salvatore J., and Gregory Greenwood. 1994. "Expectancies for Negative Mood Regulation, Coping, and Dysphoria among College Students." *Journal of Counseling Psychology* 41 (1): 34–44.

Catanzaro, Salvatore J., Florence Horaney, and Gary Creasey. 1995. "Hassles, Coping, and Depressive Symptoms in an Elderly Community Sample: The Role of Mood Regulation Expectancies." *Journal of Counseling Psychology* 42 (3): 259–262.

Catfish. 2010. Directed by Henry Joost and Ariel Schulman. Supermarché, Hit the Ground Running Films.

Clark, Candace. 1987. "Sympathy Biography and Sympathy Margin." *American Journal of Sociology* 93 (2): 290–321.

A Clockwork Orange. 1971. Directed by Stanley Kubrick. Warner Bros.

Cohen, Anthony. 1985. *Symbolic Construction of Community.* London: Routledge.

Cohen, Dov. 2003. "The American National Conversation about (Everything but) Shame." *Social Research* 70 (4): 1075–1108.

Cook, Kevin. 2014. *Kitty Genovese: The Murder, the Bystanders, the Crime That Changed America.* New York: W. W. Norton.

Cooley, Charles Horton. (1902) 1922. *Human Nature and the Social Order.* New York: Scribners.

Cozolino, Louis. 2010. *The Neuroscience of Psychotherapy.* 2nd ed. New York: Norton.

Crescioni, A. William, and Roy F. Baumeister. 2009. "Alone and Aggressive: Social Exclusion Impairs Self-control and Empathy and Increases Hostile Cognition and Aggression." In *Bullying, Rejection and Peer Victimization: A Social Cognitive Neuroscience Perspective,* edited by Monica J. Harris, 251–278. New York: Springer.

Croson, Rachel, and Uri Gneezy. 2009. "Gender Differences in Preferences." *Journal of Economic Literature* 47 (2): 448–474.

Cullen, Dave. 2009. *Columbine.* New York: Twelve.

Cushman, Philip. 1995. *Constructing the Self, Constructing America: A Cultural History of Psychotherapy.* New York: Addison-Wesley.

Daiute, Collete, and Ellie Buteau. 2002. "Writing for Their Lives: Children's Narratives as Supports for Physical and Psychological Well-Being." In *The Writing Cure: How*

Expressive Writing Promotes Health and Emotional Well-Being, edited by Stephen J. Lepore and Joshua M. Smyth, 53–74. Washington DC: American Psychological Association.

Dangerous Liaisons. 1988. Directed by Stephen Frears. Warner Bros.

Darley, John M., and Bibb Latané. 1968. "Bystander Intervention in Emergencies: Diffusion of Responsibility." *Journal of Personality and Social Psychology* 8 (4): 377–383.

Davis, Christopher G., Camille B. Wortman, Darrin R. Lehman, and Roxane Cohen Silver. 2000. "Searching for Meaning in Loss: Are Clinical Assumptions Correct?" *Death Studies* 24:497–540.

Decety, Jean, and William Ickes, eds. 2009. *The Social Neuroscience of Empathy*. Cambridge, MA: MIT Press.

DeGangi, Georgia A., and Marc A. Nemiroff. 2010. *Kids' Club Letters: Narrative Tools for Stimulating Process and Dialogue in Therapy Groups for Children and Adolescents*. New York: Routledge.

Denzin, Norman K. 2007. *Symbolic Interaction and Cultural Studies: The Politics of Interpretation*. Oxford: Wiley-Blackwell.

Devine, Patricia. 1989. "Stereotypes and Prejudice: Their Automatic and Controlled Components." *Journal of Personality and Social Psychology* 56:5–18.

DeWall, C. Nathan. 2009. "The Pain of Exclusion: Using Insights from Neuroscience to Understand Emotional and Behavioral Responses to Social Exclusion." In *Bullying, Rejection, and Peer Victimization: A Social Cognitive Neuroscience Perspective*, edited by Monica J. Harris, 201–224. New York: Springer.

DeWall, C. Nathan, and Roy F. Baumeister. 2006. "Alone but Feeling No Pain: Effects of Social Exclusion on Physical Pain Tolerance and Pain Threshold, Affective Forecasting, and Interpersonal Empathy." *Journal of Personality and Social Psychology* 91 (1): 1–15.

DeWall, C. Nathan, Roy F. Baumeister, and E. J. Masicampo. 2009. "Rejection: Resolving the Paradox of Emotional Numbness after Exclusion." In *Feeling Hurt in Close Relationships*, edited by Anita L. Vangelisti, 123–142. New York: Cambridge University Press.

Dixon, Roz. 2007. "Scapegoating: Another Step towards Understanding the Processes Generating Bullying in Groups?" *Journal of School Violence* 6 (4): 81–103.

Doka, Kenneth J. 1989. *Disenfranchised Grief: Recognizing Hidden Sorrow*. Lexington, MA: Lexington Books.

———, ed. 2002. *Disenfranchised Grief: New Directions, Challenges, and Strategies for Practice*. Champaign, IL: Research Press.

Dolan, Kerry A., and Luisa Kroll. 2014. "Inside the 2014 Forbes Billionaires List: Facts and Figures." *Forbes*, March 3. Available at http://www.forbes.com/sites/luisa kroll/2014/03/03/inside-the-2014-forbes-billionaires-list-facts-and-figures.

Dolcos, Florin, and Gregory McCarthy. 2006. "Brain Systems Mediating Cognitive Interference by Emotional Distraction." *Journal of Neuroscience* 26:2072–2079.

Dunbar, Robin. 1992. "Why Gossip Is Good for You." *New Scientist* 21:28–31.

Durkheim, Émile. (1897) 1997. *Suicide*. New York: Free Press.

Eckenrode, John, and Elaine Wethington. 1990. "The Process and Outcome of Mobilizing Social Support." In *Personal Relationships and Social Support*, edited by Steve Duck and Roxane Cohen Silver, 83–103. London: Sage.

Eichenbaum, Luise, and Susie Orback. 1989. *Between Women: Love, Envy, and Competition in Women's Friendships*. New York: Penguin.

Elias, Norbert. 1978–1983. *The Civilizing Process*. 3 vols. New York: Vintage.

Emerson, Ralph Waldo. (1841) 1993. *Self-reliance and Other Essays.* New York: Dover.

Emler, Nicholas. 1994. "Gossip, Reputation and Social Adaptation." In *Good Gossip,* edited by Robert F. Goodman and Aaron Ben-Ze'ev, 117–138. Lawrence: University Press of Kansas.

Ewen, Stuart. 1988. *All Consuming Images: The Politics of Style in Contemporary Culture.* New York: Basic Books.

Fiske, John. 1989. *Understanding Popular Culture.* Boston: Unwin Hyman.

Fivush, Robyn. 1998. "Children's Recollections of Traumatic and Nontraumatic Events." *Development and Psychopathology* 10 (4): 699–716.

Forte, James A., Anne V. Barrett, and Mary H. Campbell. 1996. "Patterns of Social Connectedness and Shared Grief Work: A Symbolic Interactionist Perspective." *Social Work with Groups* 19 (1): 29–51.

Foucault, Michel. 1975. *Discipline and Punish.* New York: Vintage Books.

———. 1980. *Power/Knowledge: Selected Interviews and Other Writings, 1972–1977.* Edited by Colin Gordon. New York: Pantheon.

Frank, Arthur. 1995. *The Wounded Storyteller: Body, Illness, and Ethics.* Chicago: University of Chicago Press.

Franks, David D. 1989. "Alternatives to Collins' Use of Emotion in the Theory of Ritualistic Chains." *Symbolic Interaction* 12 (1): 97–101.

French, Sandra L., and Sonya C. Brown. 2011. "It's All Your Fault: Kenneth Burke, Symbolic Action, and the Assigning of Guilt and Blame to Women." *Southern Communication Journal* 76 (1): 1–16.

Freud, Sigmund. (1917) 1974. "Mourning and Melancholia." In *On the History of the Psycho-analytic Movement: Papers on Metapsychology and Other Works.* Vol. 14 of *The Standard Edition of the Complete Psychological Works of Sigmund Freud,* translated by James Strachey in collaboration with Anna Freud, 243–258. London: Hogarth Press.

———. (1926) 1959. *Inhibitions, Symptoms and Anxiety.* New York: W. W. Norton.

———. 1963. *The History of the Psychoanalytic Movement.* New York: Collier Books.

Gansberg, Martin. 1964. "Thirty-Eight Who Saw Murder Didn't Call Police." *New York Times,* March 27.

Garbarino, James. 2000. *Lost Boys: Why Our Sons Turn Violent and How We Can Save Them.* New York: Anchor.

"Gender Differences in Brain Response to Pain." 2003. *ScienceDaily,* November 5. Available at http://www.sciencedaily.com/releases/2003/11/031105064626.htm.

Gergen, Kenneth J. 1994. "Mind, Text and Society: Self-memory in Social Context." In *The Remembering Self: Construction and Accuracy in the Self-narrative,* edited by Ulric Neisser and Robyn Fivush, 78–104. Cambridge: Cambridge University Press.

Gergen, Kenneth J., and Mary M. Gergen. 1988. "Narrative and the Self as Relationship." In *Advances in Experimental Social Psychology,* vol. 21, edited by Leonard Berkowitz, 17–56. San Diego, CA: Academic Press.

Gilligan, Carol. 1982. *In a Different Voice: Psychological Theory and Women's Development.* Cambridge, MA: Harvard University Press.

Gilligan, James. 1997. *Violence: Reflections on a National Epidemic.* New York: Vintage Books.

———. 2003. "Shame, Guilt and Violence." *Social Research* 70 (4): 1149–1180.

Gluckman, Max. 1963. "Gossip and Scandal." *Current Anthropology* 4:307–316.

Goffman, Erving. 1959. *The Presentation of Self in Everyday Life.* New York: Doubleday Anchor.

———. 1963. *Stigma: Notes on the Management of Spoiled Identity*. Englewood Cliffs, NJ: Prentice-Hall.

Gold, Gregg J., and James R. Davis. 2005. "Psychological Determinants of Forgiveness: An Evolutionary Perspective." *Humboldt Journal of Social Relations* 29 (2): 111–134.

Gordon, Steven. 1981. "The Sociology of Sentiments and Emotion." In *Social Psychology: Sociological Perspectives*, edited by Morris Rosenberg and Ralph H. Turner, 562–592. New York: Basic Books.

Gortner, Eva-Maria, Stephanie S. Rude, and James W. Pennebaker. 2006. "Benefits of Expressive Writing in Lowering Rumination and Depressive Symptoms." *Behavior Therapy* 37 (3): 292–303.

Greenwald, Anthony G., and Mahzarin R. Banaji. 1989. "The Self as Memory System: Powerful but Ordinary." *Journal of Personality and Social Psychology* 57 (1): 41–54.

Gurstein, Rochelle. 2006. "'The Culture of Narcissism' Revisited." *Salmagundi*, Spring 2006, pp. 13–24.

Hammond, Leo Keith, and Morton Goldman. 1961. "Competition and Non-competition and Its Relationship to Individual and Group Productivity." *Sociometry* 24 (1): 46–60.

Haraway, Donna. 1999. *How Like a Leaf: An Interview with Thyrza Nichols Goodeve*. New York: Routledge.

Harris, Darcy. 2009–2010. "Oppression of the Bereaved: A Critical Analysis of Grief in Western Society." *Omega* 60 (3): 241–253.

Heath, Christian. 1988. "Embarrassment and Interactional Organization." In *Erving Goffman: Exploring the Interaction Order*, edited by P. Drew and A. Wooton, 136–160. Cambridge, UK: Polity Press.

Heller, Agnes. 2003. "Five Approaches to the Phenomenon of Shame." *Social Research* 70 (4): 1015–1030.

Herman, Barbara H., and Jaak Panksepp. 1978. "Effects of Morphine and Naloxone on Separation Distress and Approach Attachment: Evidence for Opiate Mediation of Social Affect." *Pharmacology, Biochemistry, and Behavior* 9:213–220.

Hewitt, John P. 1989. *Dilemmas of the American Self*. Philadelphia: Temple University Press.

Hochschild, Arlie. 1979. "Emotion Work, Feeling Rules, and Social Structure." *American Journal of Sociology* 85 (3): 551–575.

———. 1983. *The Managed Heart: Commercialization of Human Feeling*. Berkeley: University of California Press.

Holloway, Richard. 1999. *Godless Morality: Keeping Religion Out of Ethics*. Edinburgh, UK: Canongate Books.

Huyssen, Andreas. 2012. *Twilight Memories: Marking Time in a Culture of Amnesia*. New York: Routledge.

James, William. (1890) 1983. *Principles of Psychology*. Vols. 1 and 2. Cambridge, MA: Harvard University Press.

Janoff-Bulman, Ronnie. 1979. "Characterological versus Behavioral Self-blame: Inquiries into Depression and Rape." *Journal of Personality and Social Psychology* 37:1798–1809.

———. 1989. "Assumptive Worlds and the Stress of Traumatic Events: Applications of the Schema Construct." In "Stress, Coping, and Social Cognition." Special issue, *Social Cognition* 7:113–136.

———. 2002. *Shattered Assumptions*. New York: Free Press.

Janoff-Bulman, Ronnie, and Cynthia McPherson Frantz. 1997. "The Impact of Trauma on Meaning: From Meaningless World to Meaningful Life." In *The Transformation of Meaning in Psychological Therapies*, edited by Mick Power and Chris R. Brewin, 91–106. New York: Wiley.

Janson, Gregory R., and Richard J. Hazler. 2004. "Trauma Reactions of Bystanders and Victims to Repetitive Abuse Experiences." *Violence and Victims* 19 (2): 239–255.

Jaworski, Adam, and Justine Coupland. 2005. "Othering in Gossip: 'You Go Out You Have a Laugh and You Can Pull Yeah Okay but Like. . . .'" *Language in Society* 34 (5): 667–694.

Julian, James W., and Franklyn A. Perry. 1967. "Cooperation Contrasted with Intra-group and Inter-group Competition." *Sociometry* 30 (1): 79–90.

Juvonen, Jaana, and Elisheva F. Gross. 2005. "The Rejected and the Bullied: Lessons about Social Misfits from Developmental Psychology." In *The Social Outcast: Ostracism, Social Exclusion, Rejection, and Bullying*, edited by Kipling D. Williams, Joseph P. Forgas, and William von Hippel, 155–170. New York: Psychology Press.

Katz, Jack. 1988. *The Seductions of Crime*. New York: Basic Books.

Kauffman, Jeffrey. 2002. "The Psychology of Disenfranchised Grief: Liberation, Shame, and Self-Disenfranchisement." In *Disenfranchised Grief: New Directions, Challenges, and Strategies for Practice*, edited by Kenneth Doka, 61–78. Champaign, IL: Research Press.

Kilduff, Gavin J., Hillary A. Elfenbein, and Barry M. Staw. 2010. "The Psychology of Rivalry: A Relationally Dependent Analysis of Competition." *Academy of Management Journal* 53 (5): 943–969.

Kilminster, Richard. 2008. "Narcissism or Informalization? Christopher Lasch, Norbert Elias and Social Diagnosis." *Theory, Culture and Society* 25 (3): 131–151.

Kimmel, Michael. 2005. "Men, Masculinity, and the Rape Culture." In *Transforming a Rape Culture*, edited by Emilie Buchwald, Pamela Fletcher, and Martha Roth, 139–158. Minneapolis, MN: Milkweed Editions.

King, Laura. 2002. "Gain without Pain? Expressive Writing and Self-regulation." In *The Writing Cure: How Expressive Writing Promotes Health and Emotional Well-Being*, edited by Stephen J. Lepore and Joshua M. Smyth, 119–134. Washington, DC: American Psychological Association.

Klass, Dennis, Phyllis R. Silverman, and Steven L. Nickman. 1996. *Continuing Bonds: New Understandings of Grief*. Philadelphia: Taylor and Francis.

Klein, Kitty. 2002. "Stress, Expressive Writing, and Working Memory." In *The Writing Cure: How Expressive Writing Promotes Health and Emotional Well-Being*, edited by Stephen J. Lepore and Joshua M. Smyth, 135–156. Washington, DC: American Psychological Association.

Kotsko, Adam. 2010. *The Politics of Redemption: The Social Logic of Salvation*. London: T&T Clark International.

Kowalski, Robin M., and Susan P. Limber. 2013. "Psychological, Physical, and Academic Correlates of Cyberbullying and Traditional Bullying." *Journal of Adolescent Health* 53:S13–S20.

Kübler-Ross, Elisabeth. 1969. *On Death and Dying*. New York: Scribner.

Langens, Thomas A., and Julia Schüler. 2005. "Written Emotional Expression and Emotional Well-Being: The Moderating Role of Fear of Rejection." *Personality and Social Psychology Bulletin* 31:818–830.

———. 2007. "Effects of Written Emotional Expression: The Role of Positive Expectancies." *Health Psychology* 26 (2): 174–182.

Langman, Peter. 2009. *Why Kids Kill: Inside the Minds of School Shooters*. New York: Palgrave Macmillan.

Larkin, Ralph. 2007. *Comprehending Columbine*. Philadelphia: Temple University Press.

Lasch, Christopher. 1979. *The Culture of Narcissism*. New York: W. W. Norton.

Latané, Bibb, and John M. Darley. 1970. *The Unresponsive Bystander: Why Doesn't He Help?* Englewood Cliffs, NJ: Prentice-Hall.

Lears, T. J. Jackson. 1981. *No Place of Grace*. Chicago: University of Chicago Press.

Leary, Mark R., Robin M. Kowalski, Laura Smith, Stephen Phillips. 2003. "Teasing, Rejection, and Violence: Case Studies of the School Shootings." *Aggressive Behavior* 29:202–214.

Leary, Mark R., Jean M. Twenge, and Erin Quinlivan. 2006. "Interpersonal Rejection as a Determinant of Anger and Aggression." *Personality and Social Psychology Review* 10 (2): 111–132.

Le Bon, Gustave. (1897) 1960. *The Crowd*. New York: Viking Press.

Lehtinen, Ullalina. 1998. "How Does One Know What Shame Is?" *Hypatia* 13 (1): 56–77.

Lepore, Stephen J. 1997. "Expressive Writing Moderates the Relation between Intrusive Thoughts and Depressive Symptoms." *Journal of Personality and Social Psychology* 73 (5): 1030–1037.

Lepore, Stephen J., and Melanie A. Greenberg. 2002. "Mending Broken Hearts: Effects of Expressive Writing on Mood, Cognitive Processing, Social Adjustment and Health following a Relationship Breakup." *Psychology and Health* 17 (5): 547–560.

Lepore, Stephen J., Melanie A. Greenberg, Michelle Bruno, M. and Joshua M. Smyth. 2002. "Expressive Writing and Health: Self-regulation of Emotion-Related Experience, Physiology, and Behavior." In *The Writing Cure: How Expressive Writing Promotes Health and Emotional Well-Being*, edited by Stephen J. Lepore and Joshua M. Smyth, 99–117. Washington, DC: American Psychological Association.

Lepore, Stephen J., Jennifer D. Ragan, and Scott Jones. 2000. "Talking Facilitates Cognitive-Emotional Processes of Adaptation to an Acute Stressor." *Journal of Personality and Social Psychology* 78 (3): 499–508.

Lewis, Cynthia, and Bettina Fabos. 2005. "Instant Messaging, Literacies, and Social Identities." *Reading Research Quarterly* 40 (4): 470–501.

Lewis, Helen. 1971. *Shame and Guilt in Neurosis*. New York: International Universities Press.

Lewis, Michael. 1992. *Shame: The Exposed Self*. New York: Free Press.

———. 2000. "Self-Conscious Emotions: Embarrassment, Pride, Shame, and Guilt." In *Handbook of Emotions*, edited by Michael Lewis and Jeannette M. Haviland-Jones, 623–636. New York: Guilford.

———. 2003. "The Role of the Self in Shame." *Social Research* 70 (4): 1181–1204.

Linton, Marigold. 1986. "Ways of Searching and the Contents of Memory." In *Autobiographical Memory*, edited by David C. Rubin, 50–68. Cambridge: Cambridge University Press.

Linville, Patricia W., and Edward E. Jones. 1980. "Polarized Appraisals of Out-Group Members." *Journal of Personality and Social Psychology* 38 (5): 689–703.

Lofland, Lyn H. 1982. "Loss and Human Connection: An Exploration into the Nature of the Social Bond." In *Personality, Roles, and Social Behavior*, edited by William Ickes and Eric S. Knowles, 219–242. New York: Springer-Verlag.

———. 1985. "The Social Shaping of Emotion: The Case of Grief." *Symbolic Interaction* 8 (2): 171–190.

Lorenz, Konrad. 1963. *On Aggression*. New York: Bantam Books.

Lutgendorf, Susan K., and Philip Ullrich. 2002. "Cognitive Processing, Disclosure, and Health: Psychological and Physiological Mechanisms." In *The Writing Cure: How*

Expressive Writing Promotes Health and Emotional Well-Being, edited by Stephen J. Lepore and Joshua M. Smyth, 177–196. Washington, DC: American Psychological Association.

Lynd, Helen Merrell. 1958. *On Shame and the Search for Identity*. New York: Science Editions, 1961.

MacDonald, G., and M. Leary. 2005. "Why Does Social Exclusion Hurt? The Relationship between Social and Physical Pain." *Psychological Bulletin* 131 (2): 202–223.

Mackie, Diane M., David L. Hamilton, Joshua Susskind, and Francine Rosselli. 1996. "Social Psychological Foundations of Stereotype Formation." In *Stereotypes and Stereotyping*, edited by C. Neil Macrae, Charles Stangor, and Miles Hewstone, 41–78. New York: Guilford.

Manovich, Lev. 2001. *The Language of New Media*. Cambridge, MA: MIT Press.

Marques, José M., Vincent Y. Yzerbyt, and Jacques-Philippe Leyens. 1988. "The 'Black Sheep Effect': Extremity of Judgments towards Ingroup Members as a Function of Group Identification." *European Journal of Social Psychology* 18 (1): 1–16.

Martocci, Laura. 2013. "Girl World and Bullying: Intersubjective Shame in Margaret Atwood's *Cat's Eye*." In *The Female Face of Shame*, edited by Erica L. Johnson and Patricia Moran, 149–165. Bloomington: Indiana University Press.

Matousek, Mark. 2011. *When You're Falling, Dive: Lessons in the Art of Living*. New York: Bloomsbury.

McCall, Michael. 1990. "The Significance of Storytelling." *Studies in Symbolic Interaction* 11:145–161.

McMurtry, John. 1991. "How Competition Goes Wrong." *Journal of Applied Philosophy* 8 (2): 201–209.

Mead, George Herbert. 1934. *Mind, Self, and Society: From the Standpoint of a Social Behaviorist*. Edited by Charles W. Morris. Chicago: University of Chicago Press.

Mean Girls. 2004. Directed by Mark Waters. Paramount Pictures.

Mesoudi, Alex, Andrew Whiten, and Robin Dunbar. 2006. "A Bias for Social Information in Human Cultural Transmission." *British Journal of Psychology* 97 (3): 405–423.

Metts, Sandra. 1992. "The Language of Disengagement: A Face-Management Perspective." In *Close Relationship Loss*, edited by Terri L. Orbuch, 111–127. New York: Springer-Verlag.

Miller, Rowland. 1996. *Embarrassment: Poise and Peril in Everyday Life*. New York: Guilford Press.

Moffett, James, and Kenneth R. McElheny. 1966. *Points of View: An Anthology of Short Stories*. New York: Signet.

Moore, Carley. 2011. "Invasion of the Everygirl: *Seventeen* Magazine, 'Traumarama!' and the Girl Writer." *Journal of Popular Culture* 44 (6): 1248–1267.

Morris, David 2003. "The Meanings of Pain." In *Social Construction: A Reader*, edited by Mary Gergen and Kenneth J. Gergen, 43–47. London: Sage.

Moss, Sydney Z., and Miriam S. Moss. 2002. "Nursing Home Staff Reactions to Resident Deaths." In *Disenfranchised Grief: New Directions, Challenges, and Strategies for Practice*, edited by Kenneth Doka, 197–216. Champaign, IL: Research Press.

Mulvey, Paul W., and Barbara A. Ribbens. 1999. "The Effects of Intergroup Competition and Assigned Group Goals on Group Efficacy and Group Effectiveness." *Small Group Research* 30 (6): 651–677.

Navaro, Leyla. 2007. "Snow Whites, Stepmothers, and Hunters: Gender Dynamics in Envy and Competition in the Family." In *Envy, Competition and Gender: Theory,*

Clinical Applications and Group Work, edited by Leyla Navaro and Sharan L. Schwartzberg, 68–82. New York: Routledge.

Neimeyer, Greg J., and April E. Metzler. 1994. "Personal Identity and Autobiographical Recall." In *The Remembering Self: Construction and Accuracy in the Self-narrative*, edited by Ulric Neisser and Robyn Fivush, 105–135. Cambridge: Cambridge University Press.

Neimeyer, Robert A. 2000a. "The Language of Loss: Grief Therapy as a Process of Meaning Reconstruction." In *Meaning Reconstruction and the Experience of Loss*, edited by Robert Neimeyer, 261–292. Washington, DC: American Psychological Association.

———. 2000b. "Narrative Disruptions in the Construction of the Self." In *Constructions of Disorder: Meaning-Making Frameworks for Psychotherapy*, edited by Robert A. Neimeyer and Jonathan D. Raskin, 207–242. Washington, DC: American Psychological Association.

———. 2000c. "Searching for the Meaning of Meaning: Grief Therapy and the Process of Reconstruction." *Death Studies* 24:541–558.

———, ed. 2001. *Meaning Reconstruction and the Experience of Loss*. Washington, DC: American Psychological Association.

Neisser, Ulrich. 1981. "John Dean's Memory: A Case Study." *Cognition* 9:1–22.

Nelson, Eric E., and Jaak Panksepp. 1998. "Brain Substrates of Infant-Mother Attachment: Contributions of Opioids, Oxytocin, and Norepinephrine." *Neuroscience and Biobehavioral Reviews* 22 (3): 437–452.

Newman, Katherine S., Cybelle Fox, David J. Harding, Jal Mehta, and Wendy Roth. 2004. *Rampage: The Social Roots of School Shootings*. New York: Basic Books.

Niederle, Muriel, and Lise Vesterlund. 2008. "Gender Differences in Competition." *Negotiation Journal* 24 (4): 447–463.

Nolen-Hoeksema, Susan. 1991. "Responses to Depression and Their Effects on the Duration of Depressive Episodes." *Journal of Abnormal Psychology* 100:569–582.

———. 2001. "Ruminative Coping and Adjustment to Bereavement." In *Handbook of Bereavement Research*, edited by Margaret S. Stroebe, Robert O. Hansson, Wolfgang Stroebe, and Henk Schut, 545–562. Washington, DC: American Psychological Association.

Nolen-Hoeksema, Susan, and Benita Jackson. 2001. "Mediators of the Gender Difference in Rumination." *Psychology of Women Quarterly* 25 (1): 37–47.

Nolen-Hoeksema, Susan, Judith Larson, and Carla Grayson. 1999. "Explaining the Gender Difference in Depressive Symptoms." *Journal of Personality and Social Psychology* 77 (5): 1061–1072.

Nolen-Hoeksema, Susan, Louise E. Parker, and Judith Larson. 1994. "Ruminative Coping with Depressed Mood following Loss." *Journal of Personality and Social Psychology* 67 (1): 92–104.

Olweus, Dan. 2012. "Cyberbullying: An Overrated Phenomenon?" *European Journal of Developmental Psychology* 9:520–538.

Orbuch, Terri L. 1992. "A Symbolic Interactionist Approach to the Study of Relationship Loss." In *Close Relationship Loss*, edited by Terri L. Orbuch, 192–206. New York: Springer-Verlag.

Parsons, Talcott. 1975. "The Sick Role and the Role of the Physician Reconsidered." *Milbank Memorial Fund Quarterly: Health and Society* 53 (3): 257–278.

Pederson, William C., Thomas F. Denson, R. Justin Goss, Eduardo A. Vasquez, Nicholas J. Kelley, and Norman Miller. 2011. "The Impact of Rumination on Aggressive

Thoughts, Feelings, Arousal and Behaviour." *British Journal of Social Psychology*, no. 50: 281–301.

Pennebaker, James W. 1986. "Confronting a Traumatic Event: Toward an Understanding of Inhibition and Disease." *Journal of Abnormal Psychology* 95:274–281.

———. 1991. "Self-expressive Writing: Implications for Health, Education, and Welfare." In *Nothing Begins with N: New Investigations of Freewriting*, edited by Pat Belanoff, Peter Elbow, and Sheryl I. Fontaine, 157–172. Carbondale: Southern Illinois University Press.

———. 1992. "Overcoming Traumatic Memories." In *The Handbook of Emotion and Memory*, edited by Sven-Ake Christianson, 359–388. Hillsdale, NJ: Erlbaum.

———. 1997. *Opening Up: The Healing Power of Expressing Emotion*. Rev. ed. New York: Guilford.

Pickering, Michael. 2001. *Stereotyping: The Politics of Representation*. New York: Palgrave Macmillan.

Plaford, Gary. 2006. *Bullying and the Brain: Using Cognitive and Emotional Intelligence to Help Kids Cope*. Lanham, MD: Rowman and Littlefield Education.

Post, Robert. 1994. "The Legal Regulation of Gossip: Backyard Chatter and the Mass Media." In *Good Gossip*, edited by Robert F. Goodman and Aaron Ben-Ze'ev, 65–71. Lawrence: University Press of Kansas.

Probyn, Elspeth. 2005. *Blush: Faces of Shame*. Minneapolis: University of Minnesota Press.

Pure, Rebekah A. 2009. "Uncertainty and Psychological Consequences Due to Cyberbullying." In *Anti and Pro-social Communication: Theories, Methods, and Applications*, edited by Terry A. Kinney and Maili Pörhölä, 39–48. New York: Peter Lang.

Putnam, Robert B. 2000. *Bowling Alone: The Collapse and Revival of American Community*. New York: Simon and Schuster.

Reincke, Nancy. 1991. "Antidote to Dominance: Women's Laughter as Counteraction." *Journal of Popular Culture* 24 (4): 27–37.

Retzinger, Suzanne. 1987. "Resentment and Laughter: Video Studies of the Shame-Rage Spiral." In *The Role of Shame in Symptom Formation*, edited by Helen Block Lewis, 151–181. Hillsdale, NJ: Erlbaum.

Ribbens McCarthy, Jane. 2006. *Young People's Experiences of Loss and Bereavement: Towards an Interdisciplinary Approach*. Berkshire, UK: Open University Press.

Rieff, Philip. 1966. *The Triumph of the Therapeutic: Uses of Faith after Freud*. New York: Harper and Row.

Riesman, David. 1950. *The Lonely Crowd*. New Haven, CT: Yale University Press.

———. 1961. "The Lonely Crowd: A Reconsideration in 1960." In *Culture and Social Character: The Work of David Riesman Reviewed*, edited by Seymour Martin Lipset and Leo Lowenthal, 419–458. New York: Free Press.

Rivers, Ian. 2004. "Recollections of Bullying at School and Their Long-Term Implications for Lesbians, Gay Men, and Bisexuals." *Crisis: The Journal of Crisis Intervention and Suicide Prevention* 25 (4): 169–175.

Rosenblatt, Paul. 1988. "Grief: The Social Context of Private Feelings." *Journal of Social Issues* 44 (3): 67–78.

Roy, Arundhati. 1998. *The God of Small Things*. New York: Harper.

Rude, Stephanie S., Kacey Little Maestas, and Kristin Neff. 2007. "Paying Attention to Distress: What's Wrong with Rumination?" *Cognition and Emotion* 21 (4): 843–864.

Rusk, Natalie, Maya Tamir, and Fred Rothbaum. 2011. "Performance and Learning Goals for Emotion Regulation." *Motivation and Emotion* 35 (4): 444–460.

Russell, Steven. 1998. "Reintegrative Shaming and the 'Frozen Antithesis': Braithwaite and Elias." *Journal of Sociology* 34 (3): 303-313.

Ryan, Francis J. 1997. "Narcissism and the Moral Sense: Moral Education in the Secondary Sociology Classroom." *Social Studies* 88 (5): 233-237.

Ryan, Francis, Maryanne Bednar, and John Sweeder. 1999. "Technology, Narcissism, and the Moral Sense: Implications for Instruction." *British Journal of Educational Technology* 30 (2): 115-128.

Sabini, John, Brian Garvey, and Amanda L. Hall. 2001. "Shame and Embarrassment Revisited." *Society for Personality and Social Psychology* 27 (1): 104-117.

Samarel, Nelda. 1995. "The Dying Process." In *Dying: Facing the Facts*, 3rd ed., edited by Hannelore Wass and Robert A. Neimeyer, 89-116. Washington, DC: Taylor and Francis.

Samra, Rise Jane. 1998. "Guilt, Purification, and Redemption." *American Communication Journal* 1 (3). Available at http://ac-journal.org/journal/vol1/iss3/burke/samra.html.

Sandel, Michael J. 2009. *Justice. What's the Right Thing to Do?* New York: Farrar, Straus, and Giroux.

Sandstrom, Kent L., Daniel D. Martin, and Gary Alan Fine. 2009. *Symbols, Selves, and Social Reality*. New York: Oxford University Press.

Scheff, Thomas J. 1990. *Microsociology: Discourse, Emotion, and Social Structure*. Chicago: University of Chicago Press.

———. 2000. "Shame and the Social Bond: A Sociological Theory." *Sociological Theory* 18 (1): 84-99.

———. 2001. "Shame and Community: Social Components in Depression." *Psychiatry* 64 (3): 212-224.

———. 2003. "Shame in Self and Society." *Symbolic Interaction* 26 (2): 239-262.

———. 2005. "Looking Glass Self: Goffman as Symbolic Interactionist." *Symbolic Interaction* 28 (2): 147-166.

———. 2011. "Social-Emotional Origins of Violence: A Theory of Multiple Killing." *Aggression and Violent Behavior* 16 (6): 453-460.

Scheff, Thomas J., and Suzanne M. Retzinger. 1991. *Emotions and Violence: Shame and Rage in Destructive Conflicts*. Lexington, MA: Lexington Books.

Scheier, Michael F., and Charles S. Carver. 2003. "Goals and Confidence as Self-regulatory Elements Underlying Health and Illness Behavior." *The Self-regulation of Health and Illness Behaviour*, edited by Linda D. Cameron and Howard Leventhal, 17-41. London: Routledge.

Scheier, Michael F., Charles S. Carver, and Michael W. Bridges. 2001. "Optimism, Pessimism, and Psychological Well-Being." In *Optimism and Pessimism: Implications for Theory, Research, and Practice*, edited by Edward C. Chang, 189-216. Washington, DC: American Psychological Association.

Schutz, Alfred. 1967. *Phenomenology of the Social World*. Evanston, IL: Northwestern University Press.

Schwarz, Ori. 2011. "Who Moved My Conversation? Instant Messaging, Intertextuality and New Regimes of Intimacy and Truth." In *Media, Culture and Society* 33 (1): 71-87.

Schweder, Richard. 2003. "Toward a Deep Cultural Psychology of Shame." *Social Research* 70 (4): 1109-1130.

Seale, Clive. 1998. *Constructing Death: The Sociology of Dying and Bereavement*. Cambridge: Cambridge University Press.

Sedikides, Constantine, Nils Olsen, and Harry T. Reis. 1993. "Relationships as Natural Categories." *Journal of Personality and Social Psychology* 64 (1): 71-82.

Serpe, Nick. 2013. "Reality Pawns: The New Money TV." *Dissent*, Summer. Available at http://www.dissentmagazine.org/article/reality-pawns-the-new-money-tv.

Sherif, Muzafer, O. J. Harvey, B. Jack White, William R. Hood, and Carolyn W. Sherif. (1954) 1961. *Intergroup Conflict and Cooperation: The Robbers Cave Experiment.* Norman, OK: University Book Exchange.

Simmel, Georg. (1908) 1955. *Conflict.* Translated by Kurt Wolff. New York: Free Press.

Simmons, Rachel. 2002. *Odd Girl Out: The Hidden Culture of Aggression in Girls.* New York: Harcourt.

Singer, Jefferson A., and Peter Salovey. 1993. *The Remembered Self: Emotion and Memory in Personality.* New York: Free Press.

Slonje, Robert, and Peter K. Smith. 2008. "Cyberbullying: Another Main Type of Bullying?" *Scandinavian Journal of Psychology* 49:147–154.

Small, Neil. 2001. "Theories of Grief: A Critical Review." In *Grief, Mourning and Death Ritual,* edited by Jenny Hockey, Jeanne Katz, and Neil Small, 19–48. Philadelphia: Open University Press.

Steiner, John. 1996. "The Aim of Psychoanalysis in Theory and Practice." *International Journal of Psychoanalysis* 77:1073–1083.

Stroebe, Margaret S., and Henk Schut. 1999. "The Dual Process Model of Coping with Bereavement: Rationale and Description." *Death Studies* 23 (3): 197–224.

———. 2001. "Meaning Making in the Dual Process Model of Coping with Bereavement." In *Meaning Reconstruction and the Experience of Loss,* edited by Robert A. Neimeyer, 55–76. Washington, DC: American Psychological Association.

Tajfel, Henri. 1963. "Stereotypes." *Race* 5 (2): 3–14.

Tangney, June P., and Rhonda Dearing. 2002. *Shame and Guilt.* New York: Guilford.

Tauer, John M., and Judith M. Harackiewicz. 1999. "Winning Isn't Everything: Competition, Achievement Orientation, and Intrinsic Motivation." *Journal of Experimental Social Psychology* 35 (3): 209–238.

———. 2004. "The Effects of Cooperation and Competition on Intrinsic Motivation and Performance." *Journal of Personality and Social Psychology* 86 (6): 849–861.

Taylor, Gabriele. 1994. "Gossip as Moral Talk." In *Good Gossip,* edited by Robert F. Goodman and Aaron Ben-Ze'ev, 34–46. Lawrence: University Press of Kansas.

Taylor, Lou. 1983. *Mourning Dress: A Costume and Social History.* New York: Routledge.

Terrell, JoAnne Marie. 2005. *Power in the Blood? The Cross in African American Experience.* Eugene, OR: Wipf and Stock.

Thomas, Laurence. 1994. "The Logic of Gossip." In *Good Gossip,* edited by Robert F. Goodman and Aaron Ben-Ze'ev, 47–55. Lawrence: University Press of Kansas.

Thomas, William I., and Dorothy Swaine Thomas. 1928. *The Child in America: Behavior Problems and Programs.* New York: Knopf.

Thomson, Irene Taviss. 1985. "From Other-Direction to the Me Decade: The Development of Fluid Identities and Personal Role Definitions." *Sociological Inquiry* 55 (3): 274–290.

Thoreau, Henry David. (1849) 2013. *Civil Disobedience.* Empire Books.

Tomkins, Silvan S. 1962–1992. *Affect, Imagery, Consciousness.* 4 vols. New York: Springer.

Treynor, Wendy, Richard Gonzalez, and Susan Nolen-Hoeksema. 2003. "Rumination Reconsidered: A Psychometric Analysis." *Cognitive Therapy and Research* 27 (3): 247–259.

Triplett, Norman. 1898. "The Dynamogenic Factors in Pacemaking and Competition." *American Journal of Psychology* 9 (4): 507–533.

Tucker, Abigail. 2013. "Are Babies Born Good?" *Smithsonian,* January. Available at http://www.smithsonianmag.com/science-nature/are-babies-born-good-165443013.

Twenge, Jean M., Roy F. Baumeister, C. Nathan DeWall, Natalie J. Ciarocco, J. Michael Bartels. 2007. "Social Exclusion Decreases Prosocial Behavior." *Journal of Personality and Social Psychology* 92 (1): 56–66.

Twenge, Jean M., Roy F. Baumeister, Dianne M. Tice, and Tanja S. Stucke. 2001. "If You Can't Join Them, Beat Them: Effects of Social Exclusion on Aggressive Behavior." *Journal of Personality and Social Psychology* 81 (6): 1058–1069.

Twenge, Jean M., and W. Keith Campbell. 2003. "'Isn't It Fun to Get the Respect That We're Going to Deserve?' Narcissism, Social Rejection, and Aggression." *Personality and Social Psychology Bulletin* 29 (2): 261–272.

Twenge, Jean M., Kathleen R. Catanese, and Roy F. Baumeister. 2003. "Social Exclusion and the Deconstructed State: Time Perception, Meaninglessness, Lethargy, Lack of Emotion, and Self-awareness." *Journal of Personality and Social Psychology* 85 (3): 409–423.

Ullrich, Philip M., and Susan K. Lutgendorf. 2002. "Journaling about Stressful Events: Effects of Cognitive Processing and Emotional Expression." *Annals of Behavioral Medicine* 24 (3): 244–250.

Urbina, Ian. 2009. "It's a Fork, It's a Spoon, It's a . . . Weapon?" *New York Times*, October 11. Available at http://www.nytimes.com/2009/10/12/education/12discipline.html?_r=1&.

U.S. Department of Health and Human Services. 2001. *Youth Violence: A Report of the Surgeon General*. Rockville, MD: Office of the Surgeon General.

Utley, Allison, and Yvonne Garza. 2011. "The Therapeutic Use of Journaling with Adolescents." *Journal of Creativity in Mental Health* 6:29–41.

Van Vugt, Mark, David De Cremer, and Dirk P. Janssen. 2007. "Gender Differences in Cooperation and Competition: The Male-Warrior Hypothesis." *Psychological Science* 18 (1): 19–23.

Walter, Tony. 2007. "Modern Grief, Postmodern Grief." *International Review of Sociology* 17 (1): 123–134.

Weber, Ann L. 1992. "The Account-Making Process: A Phenomenological Approach." In *Close Relationship Loss*, edited by Terri L. Orbuch, 174–191. New York: Springer-Verlag.

Wegner, David. 1994. *White Bears and Other Unwanted Thoughts*. New York: Guilford.

Weiss, Robert S. 2001. "Grief, Bonds, and Relationships." In *Handbook of Bereavement Research*, edited by Margaret S. Stroebe, Robert O. Hansson, Wolfgang Stroebe, and Henk Schut, 47–62. Washington, DC: American Psychological Association.

Wenzlaff, Richard M., and David D. Luxton. 2003. "The Role of Thought Suppression in Depressive Rumination." *Cognitive Therapy and Research* 27 (3): 293–308.

Whellis, Allen. 1958. *The Quest for Identity*. New York: Norton.

White, Michael. 2003. "Narrative Therapy and Externalizing the Problem." In *Social Construction: A Reader*, edited by Mary Gergen and Kenneth J. Gergen, 163–168. London: Sage.

Whitman, Walt. (1855) 2001. *Song of Myself*. Dover.

Wilkinson, Rupert. 2010. "'The Lonely Crowd,' at 60, Is Still Timely." *Chronicle of Higher Education*, September 12. Available at https://chronicle.com/article/The-Lonely-Crowd-at-60-Is/124334/.

Willard, Nancy. 2007. "Educator's Guide to Cyberbullying and Cyberthreats." Available at http://www.franklin.k12.nh.us/SAU/Ed%20Guide%20to%20Cyberbullying.pdf.

Williams, Kipling D., and Steve A. Nida. 2009. "Is Ostracism Worse than Bullying?" In *Bullying, Rejection and Peer Victimization: A Social Cognitive Neuroscience Perspective*, edited by Monica J. Harris, 279–296. New York: Springer.

Wingate, V. Skye, Jessy A. Minney, and Rosanna E. Guadagno. 2013. "Sticks and Stones May Break Your Bones, but Words Will Always Hurt You: A Review of Cyberbullying." *Social Influence* 8 (2–3): 87–106.

Winnicott, D. W. 1971. *Playing and Reality*. London: Tavistock.

Wiseman, Rosalind. 2002. *Queen Bees and Wannabes: Helping Your Daughter Survive Cliques, Gossip, Boyfriends and the New Realities of Girl World*. New York: Crown.

Wittgenstein, Ludwig. (1953) 2009. *Philosophical Investigations*. 4th ed. Edited by P.M.S. Hacker and Joachim Schulte. Malden, MA: Wiley-Blackwell.

Young, Katherine. 2002. "The Memory of the Flesh: The Family Body in Somatic Psychology." *Body and Society* 8 (3): 25–47.

Zijderveld, Anton. 1983. "Introduction: The Sociology of Humor and Laughter—an Outstanding Debt." *Current Sociology* 31 (1): 1–6.

INDEX

analgesic response, 121, 136, 146; and numbness, 73–76, 90, 92, 105, 107–108, 110–112, 127–128, 130–131, 180–181n36, 186n1

anger: and aggression, 67, 70–72, 75, 179n29; and expressive writing, 141; and lack of affect/flatness, 73–74; and management of shame, 5–6, 64–70, 160–161, 178n17; psychosomatic consequences of, 122; as related to guilt versus shame, 79–80; at social disapproval, 21; and stage theories, 96. *See also* rage

Asch, Solomon, 40–41

atonement: disgrace as a condition of, 15, 86; and group dynamics, 16, 103; and guilt versus shame, 77, 80, 83; and inadequacy, 21, 113; loss of possibility of, 4–5, 8–9, 19, 77, 82; possibility for, 77, 80, 82–88, 91, 113, 141, 147, 161; and social bonds, 84–85; and socialization of children, 20; in traditional culture/Christian narratives, 15–17, 87, 158–159, 168n4. *See also* hope: of social redemption

autobiography: and developing self, 13–14, 21; and unique self, 157; as woven with memory in construction of self, 134–137, 187–188n21, 188n23

Averill, James, 71

Baumeister, Roy, 27, 63, 65, 81, 147, 181n37, 181n39

belonging: belief in or hope for possibility of, 5, 69, 130; competition and, 50; experiments on, 50, 72–73; feeling of, 4, 12; femininity

and, 48; need for, 63–64, 82, 87, 107, 115, 171n26, 178n13; orchestration and facilitation of, 31, 47; redemption and, 19, 53; rejection and, 5, 42, 91–92; signaling of, 5, 13, 131, 152; sympathy rules and, 95; victim category and, 140

bereavement. *See* grief

bonds: and atonement, 20–21, 78, 80, 141; and evolution, 30, 44, 118–119; and gendered competition, 47–50, 175n26; and gossip, 29, 31–34; and laughter, 35–40, 174n10; Scheff and Retzinger on, 82–84, 160–161; severance of, through shame, 62–63, 68–70, 82, 88–89, 92–93, 115, 147, 161, 186n1; significance of, 61–62, 88, 98–100, 178n13; social functions of, 5, 25, 85, 97, 103, 165, 186n1; and tethering of self, 6, 12, 93, 99, 165 (*see also* other-directedness); threats to, 73, 82; types of, 162, 183n1

Boyd, Danah, 104

Brison, Susan, 131, 188n27

Broucek, Francis, 152, 171n25, 182–183n51

bullying narratives. *See* narratives of bullying

bystander effect, 146, 190n14

bystanders: acknowledgment of shame to, 182n49; as audience, 25, 138, 145; bystander effect, 146, 190n14; as caricatures, 138–139; differentiation of, 144–145, 148; felt witnessing by, 147, 149, 189n7; gestures of intervention by, 34, 39–40, 76, 95–97, 99, 130, 141, 145, 148, 154–155, 188n25; guilt and, 147; importance of, 6–7, 161; investment in victim by, 139, 141, 146; power and authority of,

bystanders (*continued*)
53, 77, 85, 87; role of, 15–16, 24, 35, 53–54,
55, 61, 78, 85, 87–88, 100, 124–125, 139, 141;
support of bystanders by, 145–147; tacit support by, 38, 52–53, 86, 97, 108, 110

Carneal, Michael, 1–2, 68–69
chaos, 5, 63, 101, 105, 120–121, 126–131, 187n16
childhood socialization: acquisition of stereotypes, 174n18; and child-centeredness,
171–172n30; development of feminine identity, 48–49; development of interpersonal
relationships, 19–21, 30–31, 174n13; development of masculine identity, 48; development
of social emotions, 171n29; development of
story-brain complexity, 117–120; and languaging emotions, 118; and play, 129–130
Christie, Zachary, 141
Clark, Candace, 94–95, 145
cognitive functioning, 40–42, 73–76, 101, 118n,
123, 135, 145, 177n4, 185n24; destruction
of, 66, 76, 106–110, 119, 128–129; high-level
versus low-level, 113, 125–126, 128–131, 137,
180n31; restructuring/reorganization of,
19, 71, 110–111, 120–121, 125, 137, 153, 163,
185n25, 187n18
Columbine shooting, 1–2, 23, 27, 69, 167n5,
178n20
communication: computer-mediated, 149, 152;
inadequate, 165; nonverbal, 31, 76, 173n1; and
ready intelligibilities, 40, 139, 186n1; respectful and reintegrative, 160–161; social, 30, 151;
uncommunicable experiences, 114, 121
competition, 45–54, 175n30, 176n32; economic, 47, 52; and gender, 47–50, 175n26,
175n28, 176nn34–35; and loss, 53–54, 90,
176nn36–37; and Robbers Cave experiment,
49–50, 175n31; as social dynamic, 5, 8, 28,
45–48, 49–50, 52–54, 94, 160
Cooley, Charles Horton, 58–60, 177n6
Cozolino, Louis, 117–119
Cullen, Dave, 167n5
culpability: admitting, 83, 88, 103–104, 112,
125, 132–133, 135, 182n49; bystander awareness of, 24, 77, 95, 132–133; determinations
of, 78; hiding, 16
cyberbullying, 148–150, 156, 168n7, 188n2,
189n10, 190n14

Darley, John, 146
depression, 67, 90, 96–97, 102, 109–112, 180–
181n36, 185n23
DeWall, C. Nathan, 64, 181n37, 187n18
diffusion of responsibility, 146

drama, 23–24, 104, 127
dual process model (DPM), 101, 110, 184n14

evolution, 6–7, 29, 44, 50–51, 64, 72, 117,
176n35, 180n32
executive brain, 118. *See also* cognitive functioning: high-level versus low-level
expressive writing: and bullying, 187n18,
188n25; and chaos, 127; with children,
187n19; control for variables in research on,
187n10; and creative potential, 141, 151; and
depression, 187n12; as emotion-regulation
strategy, 120; enhancement of cognitive
functioning and, 110–111, 125–126; and
judgments, 112; languaging shame through,
112, 120–121; and memory, 133, 136–137;
and positioning of self and asserting of
control, 121, 124, 137, 141, 184n17; positive
expectancy and, 125; prompts for, 112, 114,
136; as a safe holding environment, 130–131;
why it works, 125, 163

Fiske, John, 21n
forgiveness. *See* atonement
Foucault, Michel, 4n, 29, 173n2
Frank, Arthur, 116, 120, 131, 133
Freud, Sigmund, 47, 96, 123, 168n2, 171n25,
183n7, 184n11

gaze: authority and power of, 15–16, 19; becoming the gazer, 20, 62, 146; as connection, 57,
76, 130, 154; Foucault on, 4n; and humiliation, 57, 77; and identity construction, 12,
13–14, 117; investment in others', 4, 98–99,
146; and judgment, 61, 100, 182n49; negotiating others', 63; and other-directedness, 12,
13–14, 15–16, 99; virtual reality as removed
from, 148–149
Genovese, Kitty, 146, 189nn5–6
gestures: as connection, 35, 54, 83, 95, 145; as
embodiments of shame, 114, 176–177n3;
as giving hope, 33–35, 38, 76, 78, 91, 130,
138–141, 145, 151, 154, 187n15, 188n25;
Mead and, 146, 189n7; of resistance, 37;
unsolicited, 147
Gilligan, Carol, 48, 175n23, 175n26
Gilligan, James, 65–67, 178n18, 179n22
Goffman, Erving, 59–64, 103, 149, 176–177n3,
177n9, 182n44, 188–189n3, 189n7
Gortner, Eva-Maria, 111–112
gossip, 28–35, 173–174n8; as bonding, 31–32;
and competition, 47–48; and creation of
significance, 32, 34, 135, 173n7; as cruelty,
25, 33, 78, 85, 108–109, 148; dual nature of,

6, 31–34, 53; in evolutionary scheme, 29–30; and laughter, 36, 39; as play, 30–31, 173n3; refusing to participate in, 34, 54, 154; as social force, 3, 5, 8, 28, 51, 173n6, 174n20; and stereotypes, 40, 42, 46–47, 174n20; as trivial, 29–30

grief: allowances for, 6; and belongingness needs, 63; and Columbine tragedy, 23; disenfranchised, 91–92, 93–94, 103, 143, 147, 186n27; and DPM, 101–102, 184n14; etiquette and, 93–94, 130; expressive writing and, 124, 151; grief narratives, 90, 93–94, 100–101, 120, 125, 138, 141, 184n14; grieving and grief work, 93–96, 99–102, 121, 153, 183n4; as joint story, 115; and language, 121; in processing of social pain/shame, 6, 106; and rumination and depression, 93, 106–107, 131, 147; social space for, 116, 129–130, 184n9; and stage theories, 95–99, 183n7; and types of bond, 183n1

guilt, 79–83; and Braithwaite's theories of social justice, 82; and culpability, 57, 104, 181n40, 182n49, 190n2; derogation as minimizing, 147; as hiving, 81, 87–88, 113, 138, 165, 190n1 (appendix C); and inhibition of violence, 66; in Old Testament versus New Testament, 82; and psychologistic culture, 87, 119; versus shame, 79–81, 83, 177n5, 181n42, 182nn43–45

Harris, Eric, 1, 69, 167n2, 178n20, 179n25

Hewitt, John, 169n11, 171n26

hiving, 81, 87–88, 113, 138, 165, 190n1 (appendix C)

hope: embodiment of, 125; and expressive writing, 125; gatekeepers of, 138, 161; of interrupting shame-rage cycle, 72, 108; liberation theology and, 158–159; of otherworldly salvation, 15, 18; and resolution of shame, 5, 54, 80, 91, 93, 153, 161; of social redemption, 5, 15, 33, 54, 76–77, 80, 84–85, 91, 93, 95, 103–104, 108, 130, 140, 147; and space for grief, 116; of winning, 173n40

hopelessness, 22, 69, 105, 107, 125, 150–151, 183n3

identity construction: in adolescence, 14, 21, 130; in cyberspace, 149, 151–152; and experiential writing, 124; and gender, 47–48; as joint project, 32, 98–99, 173n5; and language, 121; after loss, 90, 93, 102; and memory, 133, 135, 137, 187–188n21; other-oriented, 12–14, 61; and personality, 10; and the social brain, 117–119; and social norms,

171n28; surrender of, 105, 129. See also presentation of self

in-group social dynamics, 41, 83–84, 102

inner-directedness, 11–12, 16, 169n8

intent: of gossip, 33, 173–174n8; of grief work, 98; in in-group classifications, 41; of laughter, 37–39; and memory, 134, 188n22; in narrative writing, 111, 123, 141; of repentance, 78; to shame, 84, 88, 161; slippery slope of determining, 24, 87

internal psychic reality, 118, 129–130, 150

Janoff-Bulman, Ronnie, 80, 98

Jesus, 15, 40, 41, 158–159, 168n4, 170n20

judgment: authority to judge, 19, 22, 25, 53, 173–174n8; challenges to, 44–45, 136, 138; and cognitive functioning, 123; and culpability, 24, 43; and gaze of others, 11, 13, 57–58, 61, 169n12; in gossip, 31; and guilt, 80; of in- and out-group members, 40–41, 144, 174n17; and power of public opinion, 4, 15–16; and psychoanalytic culture, 17; and reality TV, 86, 183n52; refusal to judge, 39, 45, 139, 155, 185n24; and rumination, 111–114; self-judgment, 57, 62, 66, 100, 104–105, 112–114, 126, 163, 185n24, 186–187n9; and shame, 25, 38, 57–58, 66, 177n6; tacit, 35, 38, 86

Katz, Jack, 65

Klebold, Dylan, 1–2, 69, 179n25

Kotsko, Adam, 158, 190n1 (appendix B)

labeling: as an aspect of languaging, 96, 118, 186n6; of interactions as bullying, 104, 168n6, 172n35; as social categorizing, 22, 40–41, 61, 114; of social problems, 23

language and languaging, 22, 85–87, 97, 104, 112, 114, 117–123, 144, 164, 186n1, 187n16; body language, 31, 48, 76, 154 (see also gestures); language games, 28, 53, 86, 165, 182–183n51

Lasch, Christopher, 169n10

Latané, Bibb, 146

laughter, 35–40; bystanders and, 38–40, 54; construction of bonds and, 35–36, 39–40, 174n10; destructive consequence of, 35, 39, 105, 108–109; dual nature of, 35, 38–40, 53, 155; and humiliation, 36, 38, 52, 55, 144; inclusive and reintegrative, 21, 36–37, 54; nature of, 28, 35, 51; nuances of, 27, 37, 86; and positioning of self, 36–37; as a social dynamic, 5, 28, 35–36, 38–40, 42, 51, 77; socialization and, 36–37

Leary, Mark, 63, 65, 178n19
letting go: challenge to possibility of, 98–100; of self in play, 129, 159; of suffering, 9; and traditional grief theories, 96, 184n10
Lewis, Helen, 63–65, 67, 79, 82, 178n11, 179n23, 181n41
Lewis, Michael, 14, 65, 179n29
Lewis-Braithwaite hypothesis, 83–84
liberation theology: 18, 22, 158
Lynd, Helen, 62, 79, 170n18

Marwick, Alice, 104
Mean Girls, 2, 174n15
memory, 133–138; and autobiography, 134–135, 187–188n21; and CMCs, 151; embodied, 80; expressive writing and, 136; fragments of, 121; as joint project, 134, 139; relativity of, 135, 139, 188n22; re-remembering, 113, 136–137, 143, 151–153
mirroring: inability to reflect, 127–128, 185–186n26; reflection of self, 88, 104–106, 109–114, 123–124, 132, 136–137, 165, 177n8, 185nn23–24; reflections of others, 13, 39, 58–59, 81, 117, 153, 186–187n9; and response of bystanders, 146, 149, 189n7, 189n9

narcissistic culture, 14, 17, 80, 83–84, 152, 157
narcissists: and aggression, 67, 75, 150; and empathy, 81, 171–172n30; and guilt, 81; narcissistic injury, 92; and neediness, 13–14, 77; and other-directedness, 13, 170n17; personality traits of, 12–13, 69, 80, 178n20; and rage, 81
narratives of bullying: absence of, 25, 102, 111, 114, 136; emerging, 81–82, 84, 89, 115, 143; as joint narratives, 115, 152; narcissist in, 12; and responsibility for violence, 2; transformation in, 6; and victim caricature, 168n6
narratives of culture: limitations of, 53, 140–141; master narratives, 42–43; religious, 9, 18, 32, 37, 171n27; secular, 9, 18, 47, 49, 61, 67–68, 104, 114, 117–119, 125, 137, 165 (*see also* grief; inner-directedness; narcissistic culture)
narratives of self: audience assessment of, 61, 188n27; and chaos, 127–131; and coherence, 99, 101–102, 104–106, 117, 123–125, 130–133, 137–138; in cyber age, 151–153; elements of, 120–121, 124–125, 132, 138; and gossip, 30, 32; inadequacy in, 66; and laughter, 37; and memory, 134–137; transformation in, 6; and uniqueness, 157. *See also* autobiography
neurophysiology: and belongingness needs, 63–64, 115; and laughter, 35; and nature versus nurture debate, 48–49; neurocogni-

tive functioning, 137, 172n36; and the social brain, 116–121; and social pain/numbness, 70, 72–74, 108, 180n32, 181n37; and stereotyping, 41–42, 144
Nolen-Hoeksema, Susan, 106, 109
nonjudgmental activities, 111–113, 139, 155, 187n18
numbness. *See* analgesic response

oppression: Burke on, 171n28, 172n33; collusion in one's own, 18–19, 127; resistance to, 22, 158–159
other-directedness, 12–20
Othering, 3, 34, 38, 40, 42–44, 103
others' opinions: and aggression or rage, 75, 180n31; and competition, 50–51; cultivation and management of, 11, 37, 60–61; in cyberspace, 148–149, 152–153; and expressive writing, 127–131, 165–166; and loss, 93–94, 97, 99; and self-judgment, 186–187n9; and shame, 58–59, 77, 79, 182n49; as shaping identity, 4–5, 99, 105, 119, 135, 157, 169n12, 177n10; as shifting, 13–14; and trust, 31

pain: acknowledgment of, by bystanders, 53, 90, 99, 103–104, 139, 188n1; acknowledgment of, by victims, 91, 110, 112–114, 120, 131; denial of, 107–108, 163, 172n37, 188–189n3; displays of, 48; legitimation of, 53, 92, 93–95, 97, 115, 147; negotiation of, 89, 94, 116, 121, 123–124, 130–131, 141, 185n21, 186n1; of others, 75, 107; physical, 64–66, 72–73, 180nn31–34, 180–181n36, 181n37; responsibility for, 9–10, 27; social-psychological, 5–6, 64–66, 68, 72–73, 76–78, 80, 87–88, 165–166, 170–171n21, 183n7
parents, 2, 17, 19–21, 69–70, 83–84, 118, 126, 139, 172n35, 176n35
Pennebaker, James, 110, 120, 122–124, 186n4, 187n10
Pickering, Michael, 44–45
play: as boundarylessness, 30–31, 128–129, 132, 139, 150, 173n3; and social roles, 12, 125; and virtual reality, 148, 150; Winnicott on, 128–129, 150, 173n3, 190n13
presentation of self: as caught up in dramas, 104; in cyberspace, 149; through expressive writing, 132–133; historically, 10; and impression management, 60–62, 66, 161, 182n44; and management of shame, 179n22; and narcissism, 12–13
Probyn, Elspeth, 66, 88, 186n27
psychologistic culture, 3, 9–11, 17, 27, 59, 87, 168n2

psychology: adaptation, 10–11; and affect labeling, 118, 121; and benefits of expressive writing, 120, 123, 163; and child development,
19–20, 129, 171n24, 174n18; of competition,
47–48, 50–51; of cruelty and abuse, 3, 21,
27, 53, 89, 91, 107–108, 150; of denial, 5–6,
67–69, 119, 121–122, 182n46, 182–183n51;
depression and rumination, 63, 67, 69, 90,
106–109; of ennui and meaninglessness, 4,
97, 102, 105, 108, 113, 168n2; evolutionary,
176n35; grief, 90; of healthy response, 37,
80, 109; intolerable psychological states, 65;
of investment in others, 20, 58, 99; need to
belong, 5–6, 63, 82; and physical effects, 58,
64, 70–71, 119, 181n37; of shame, 80, 91, 107,
119, 178n15, 180n34; of soliciting help, 147;
of violence, 167n4
public opinion, 4, 12, 19, 51, 72

rage: contrasted with anger and aggression,
70–71, 73, 179n29; and disruptions to cognitive functioning, 74–75 (see also shame:
unacknowledged); and narcissism, 75, 81, 92;
and pain, 72–74, 131; and shame, 5–6, 68,
178n15, 180n31, 186n1; and shame-rage cycle, 65, 70–72, 74, 147, 179n23, 180–181n36;
and storying blame, 125; on television,
183n52
reality television, 25, 53, 86, 148, 183n52
redemption: bystanders and, 145, 161, 165;
Christianity and, 15–19, 158–159, 168n4;
conditions for, 36, 45, 113, 173n40; and guilt,
80, 82–87; lack of strategy for, 18, 22, 54;
loss of possibility of, 4–5, 8, 19, 34, 54, 95,
105, 119; self-redemption, 105, 113, 153; and
shame, 56, 66
reintegration into society, 20, 36, 69, 82–84,
86–87, 105, 161
reintegrative shaming, 21, 82–84, 160–161, 165
rejection: and anger, 67, 180n30; in bullying,
104–106; and cognitive abilities, 107–108,
126; and denial, 67; and gender, 68; invalidation of, 91; neurological implications of, 6,
73–76, 119, 181n39; ontological implications
of, 64, 84, 93, 132, 157, 178n14; recursive
loop of, 108, 179n23; and self-blame, 68;
tacit endorsement of, 38
relational aggression, 4, 90, 98, 102, 148,
170n14
religion: and liberation theology, 158–159; traditional, 4–5, 8–9, 15–19
remembering and re-remembering, 113,
133–137, 139, 188n22; and cyberspace, 151.
See also memory

Retzinger, Suzanne, 59, 65, 67, 82–85, 112,
160–161, 179n29, 182n46, 182nn49–50
Riesman, David, 4, 11–12, 170n15
Robbers Cave experiment, 49–50, 175n31
Rude, Stephanie, 111–112, 163
rumination, 93, 106–111, 114, 120, 147, 162,
180–181n36, 185nn23–24; and women,
184–185n18, 187n10
Ruminative Response Scale (RRS), 111–112
rumors, 48, 68, 148, 150

salvation. See redemption
scapegoating, 27, 33–34, 159, 174n9, 188n2
Scheff, Thomas, 59, 61, 65, 67, 82–85, 103,
108, 112, 160–161, 177n9, 178n11, 179n23,
179n25, 182n46, 182nn49–50
Schut, Henk, 101–102
self-reflection. See mirroring
shame, 55–79, 176n2, 181n41; broken bonds
and, 38, 43, 62–64; cognitive functioning
and, 72–76, 119; collusion in, 18, 86, 107,
127, 158 (see also guilt); embarrassment
and, 60–61, 165, 178n11; embodied, 57–58,
114–115, 121, 147; and grief, 89, 91–92, 95,
103–104; versus guilt, 79–81, 177n5, 181n42,
182nn43–44; and losing, 53–54; and narcissism, 13, 67, 75, 80; religion, secularization,
and, 15–17, 158–159; re-visioning of, 81–88,
160–161; shame-rage cycle, 64–75, 147,
172n33, 178nn15–18, 179n23, 179n29, 180–
181n36; significance of, 1, 5–6, 14–15, 57–64,
89; socialization of children and, 19–21, 25;
unacknowledged, 6, 54, 67, 82–83, 112, 119,
133, 137, 179n23, 182n46, 188–189n3 (see
also pain: denial of; psychology: of denial).
See also judgment; "Traumarama!"
silence: of bystanders, 108, 110, 147; cultural,
14–15, 53–54, 66, 86–87, 141, 161
social brain, 29, 44, 118–119
social pain. See pain
social problems, construction of, 3, 7, 22–24,
29, 142, 156, 172n35
stage theories of grief, 95–102, 184n10, 186n2
stereotypes, 2, 5, 28, 40–48, 51–54, 55, 139,
174n14, 174nn18–21
storying self: and the brain, 116–120; after loss,
99–100; and restorying self, 110, 120, 133,
138, 141, 151, 153, 138, 164–166; and writing
chaos, 123–125, 126–128, 130–132, 135. See
also narratives of self
Stroebe, Margaret, 101–102, 184n14
sympathy: claims to, 91, 94–95, 97, 104, 117,
129–130, 188–189n3; sympathy etiquette/
rules, 6, 90, 93–94, 144

Tangney, June, 65, 66, 74, 181n42, 182n43, 183n3

Tomkins, Silvan, 59, 178n11

"Traumarama!," 140, 164–166

Twenge, Jean, 75, 178n19

"unresponsive bystander" hypothesis, 146–147

voice: and bystanders, 39–40, 99–100, 141; ceding of, 36, 39, 110, 127; discovery of, 20–21, 110, 138; reclaiming of, 6, 116, 120–121, 130, 132, 153, 184n17, 186n5; and shame, 164–166

Walter, Tony, 184n14

Winnicott, D. W., 128–129, 150, 173n3, 190n13

Laura Martocci is a sociologist and the Founder and Director of the S.A.R.A. Project® (Students Against Relational Aggression). Most recently, she was a faculty member and an Associate Dean at Wagner College.